Tender Is the Night

ESSAYS IN CRITICISM

Tender Is the Night

ESSAYS IN CRITICISM

EDITED BY

Marvin J. LaHood

Indiana University Press
Bloomington & London

Published in Canada by Fitzhenry & Whiteside Limited, Don Mills, Ontario

Library of Congress catalog card number: 77–85091

Standard Book Number: 253–35846–9 [CL]
253–20131–4 [PA]

Manufactured in the United States of America

For my Parents

Salem and Anna Mahfoud LaHood

I shall not look upon their like again

Contents

Contents

Introduction

After thirty-five years *Tender Is the Night* has achieved critical acclaim as one of the finest American novels of the century. Published when those hungover from the Twenties did not wish to be reminded of that lost decade, shadowed by *The Great Gatsby* and Fitzgerald's own life, it never achieved in its author's lifetime anything like the wide reading and praise it now enjoys. The anguish of the nine years between the publication of *The Great Gatsby* (1925) and *Tender Is the Night* (1934) must have seemed in vain to Fitzgerald by the time he died in 1941. He had put all that he knew into this novel, and it had failed. His vision and his technique were called into doubt by readers who looked at the book through several subjective prisms, seeking in it things that were not there: the superb structure of *The Great Gatsby*, a message for the message-thirsty Thirties, the great American novel, and various other attributes that Fitzgerald never intended but upon which, nonetheless, the novel was judged.

What is there is the carefully wrought story of a man of great ability who does not fulfill his promise. This man is not Fitzgerald—that he did fulfill his promise must by now be clear to even the blindest of skeptics. Nor is he Gerald Murphy or any other real person. The novel needs no extra-fictional context or dimension to make it the poignant and beautifully modulated tale of a human being's decline and fall that it is.

Dick Diver's life lacks the sharply etched tragic climax of Gatsby's, but his world contains more things than Gatsby's philosophy ever dreamed of. Gatsby's past consists of a dream of youthful love on the veranda of a Louisville mansion, Diver's past consists of all that we cherish in Western Civilization. His defeat signifies more than the impossibility of repeating the past, it stands for the defeat of much that was valuable in the cultural legacy of twenty-five centuries. Fitzgerald's eloquent description of a World War I battle as "a love battle—there was a century of middle-class love spent here. This was the last love battle," also describes Dick's struggle with the forces that defeat him.

Fitzgerald knew well what he was doing when he described Dick's mind as "sometimes exercised without power but always with substrata of truth under truth." He knew that Dick's mind could not be fashioned on Dan Cody's yacht, that it needed the ritual and spiritual-intellectual legacy available at Johns Hopkins, Oxford, and Vienna. If that mind can crack, if Dick can be defeated, all men of mind should take notice. And Dick is defeated by more than the Warren money, Nicole's illness, and his own obvious weaknesses; he is also defeated by the modern, materialistic, anarchic world. In 1934 such a prophetic vision was unusual; by 1969 the daily demise of honor and integrity hardly raises an eyebrow. The fumbling in the greasy till and mere anarchy of modern life were as real to Fitzgerald as to Yeats. Both realized that the Armageddon between materialism and all that they cherished was going on, and both realized that we had come to a point in history when we had finally a great deal to lose. Yeats has often been given credit for this kind of vision; Fitzgerald seldom has.

It is not surprising that Fitzgerald makes his knight gallant; what is surprising is the bent of that gallantry. Dick's social graces clearly indicate not just the good manners so attractive to Baby Warren's sensibilities, but a form of love. His heightened sensitivity to the feelings of others transcends mere affability and reaches the level of charity. Interestingly, Gatsby shares this quality; his smile "understood you just as far as you wished to be understood, believed in you as you would like to believe in yourself, and assured you that it had precisely the impression of you that, at your best, you hoped to convey."

Dick alone possesses this quality in *Tender Is the Night.* When his integrity is intact he uses it to the benefit of all—from making thoughtful introductions to understanding Nicole to the point of healing her. When he begins to decline, this empathy begins to disappear. By the end it is gone; Dick is no longer "charming." Mary North, Baby, and even Nicole cannot understand the real significance of the loss. The forces inimical to those cherished attributes of humanity which constitute man's dignity are triumphant. Two decades earlier Yeats had expressed well the hopelessness of the battle:

> For how can you compete,
> Being honour bred, with one
> Who, were it proved he lies,
> Were neither shamed in his own
> Nor in his neighbours' eyes?

This ideological struggle is only one of several aspects of the novel. Because it was Fitzgerald's most ambitious and most profound work, it cannot be elucidated by any single method or from any single perspective. The several essays presented here represent various attempts to help the reader understand the novel. Each seems momentarily to violate the book's integrity, but only for clarification, and with full cognizance of the ultimate inviolability of a work of art. It is our hope that the reader of these essays will return to the novel able to respond to it more fully.

MARVIN J. LAHOOD

State University College
Buffalo, New York

Tender Is the Night

ESSAYS IN CRITICISM

1. Scott Fitzgerald: Romantic and Realist

by JOHN KUEHL

Scott Fitzgerald's themes are derived from two large areas of subject matter, which, for the lack of more precise terms, I shall call romanticism and social realism. In his finest work, he combines the elements of the novel of manners and those of the romance. Richard Chase defines the two:

> The novel renders reality closely and in comprehensive detail. It takes a group of people and sets them going about the business of life. We come to see these people in their real complexity of temperament and motive. They are in explicable relation to nature, to each other, to their social class, to their own past.
>
> By contrast the romance, following distantly the medieval example, feels free to render reality in less volume and detail. It tends to prefer action to character . . . Character itself becomes, then, somewhat abstract and ideal, so much so in some romances that it seems to be merely a function of plot. The plot we may expect to be highly colored. Astonishing events may occur, and these are likely to have a symbolic or ideological, rather than a realistic, plausibility. Being less committed to the immediate rendition of reality than the novel, the romance will more freely veer toward mythic, allegorical and symbolistic forms.[1]

Social realism came to Fitzgerald from two literary sources: the English tradition of the novel as exemplified particularly by

From *Texas Studies in Literature and Language*, 1 (Autumn 1959).

Butler and Thackeray, and American realists and naturalists. Some of his romanticism is in the American tradition, but, for the most part, he reached back to the early nineteenth-century English Romantic poets and their successors, the latter-day romanticists of the Victorian period. With various modifications, additions, and changes of emphases, he took over much of the aesthetic of the Romantic poets: the use of the artist's personal experience as subject matter; the stress on the individual and his private world; the importance of the hero and heroism; the conflict between the world as it is and as it might be (the real and the ideal); the importance of the moment; the importance of wonder (man's capacity to respond to the infinite possibilities of his existence).

Although Scott Fitzgerald was influenced very little by Henry James, a statement of James's in his Preface to *The American* may well be used to describe his method:

> The balloon of experience is in fact of course tied to the earth and, under that necessity we swing, thanks to a rope of remarkable length, in the more or less commodious car of the imagination; but it is by the rope we know where we are, and from the moment that cable is cut we are at large and unrelated: we only swing apart from the globe–though remaining as exhilarated, naturally, as we like, especially when all goes well. The art of the romancer is, "for the fun of it," insidiously to cut the cable, to cut it without our detecting him.[2]

That Fitzgerald is connected firmly to experience and reality and is also skillful at cutting James's cable should be made clear by the ensuing examination of his three major novels, one early, one written in his middle period, and the other his last work. In a way they constitute his trilogy, since, different though they are in many ways, they are the ultimate expression of themes and attitudes that dominated the life of a man who was both a romantic and a realist.[3]

I

Of Fitzgerald's three major novels *The Great Gatsby* (1925) most successfully combines the elements of the romance and those of the novel of manners; it blends the abstract, the ideal, and the mythical, and a realistic treatment of our culture with uniform excellence of craftsmanship.

Gatsby is not a hero simply in the conventional sense of being the main character in the novel. Fitzgerald thought of him as a hero in the older sense of demigods and knights of myth, romance, and fairy tale. As was appropriate in the treatment of a legendary figure, his author deliberately concealed many details of his life under a blanket of secrecy.[4] The result is that Gatsby inspires "romantic speculation" in the reader as he does among the people who surround him; neither they nor we ever learn so much about him that this "sense of mystery" vanishes. Both in the story "Absolution," a sort of prologue to the novel, and in the novel itself Fitzgerald used, consciously or subconsciously, elements from the age-old "hero myth." In "Absolution" Rudolph, who feels superior to his father, a freight agent and immigrant, refuses to believe that he is his son and retreats from his environment into a world of fantasy where he becomes the noble and romantic Blatchford Sarnemington. In the novel Gatsby has never accepted his parents, "shiftless and unsuccessful farm people." He has sprung "from his Platonic conception of himself" and is "a son of God."(pp. 74–75) He too rejects his real name, James Gatz, and invents a new, more glamorous one, Jay Gatsby. He invents a fictitious background also: like his aristocratic ancestors, he has been educated at Oxford. The imagery in "Absolution" and *The Great Gatsby* is a modernized version of that of the romance or fairy tale. Blatchford Sarnemington is a character from whom "a suave nobility flowed," a character who "lived in great sweeping triumphs." His fantasy world is full of military images: "flag," "silver pennon," the "crunch of leather," "silver spurs," "a troop of horsemen." Gatsby's pursuit of Daisy is "the following of a grail," and Daisy herself is "the king's daughter, the golden girl" who lives "high in a white palace."(p. 91) As a true knight Gatsby is faithful to his lady. He spends five years in constant devotion, poring over the Chicago papers on the slight chance of seeing her name. Observing the rules of chivalry, he has dedicated himself to his lady's welfare. After the automobile accident, he insists that he, not she, was driving. His night-watch outside the Buchanan house is a sacred vigil undertaken to protect Daisy from her husband. Gatsby, the demigod, the knight, is a hero of war as Scott Fitzgerald was never able to be. We learn that "he did extraordinarily well in the war." When Wolfsheim first meets him, Gatsby is "covered over with medals." The memories of legend and fairy tale that permeate the book lift *The Great Gatsby* out of time and place as if the novel were a story celebrated for ages in song, folklore, and literature, a story deeply rooted in the psyche of the western world.

Jay Gatsby is a hero because he is a romantic who has ideals, dreams, and illusions, who answers a call to something beyond life, who has the capacity to respond to the infinite possibilities of existence, who sees the world not as it is but as it might be. He has a "heightened sensitivity to the promises of life . . . an extraordinary gift for hope, a romantic readiness."(p. 4) His reveries give him "a satisfactory hint of the unreality of reality, a promise that the rock of the world was founded securely on a fairy's wing." (p. 75) He is convinced that one can repeat the past, can "fix everything just the way it was before." (p. 84) As a romantic he pursues the ideal, the illusion of something beautiful and wonderful, something akin to the eternal in transcending the drab facts of life. Because he is a romantic, he realizes that illusion itself, not its materialization, is important. When reality cuts across dreams and Daisy visits him for the first time, the green light, which has symbolized his quest for her, loses its "colossal significance" and Gatsby's "count of enchanted objects" is "diminished by one." Yet this is not her fault. If she falls short of his dreams, it is because Gatsby's illusion "had gone beyond her, beyond everything." (p. 73)

But *The Great Gatsby* is not only romance. It is also a realistic study of a nation's values and their effect on an individual. Both Rudolph and young James Gatz are thoroughly immersed in the American tradition of "success." Rudolph sleeps among Alger books and lives with a father who has a "mystical worship of the Empire Builder, James J. Hill," with the result that, like many middle-class American boys, he creates a world of fantasy in which he is both successful and superior. Gatsby's father, who is also an admirer of Hill, shows Nick the ragged old copy of

Hopalong Cassidy in which his son has set down fantasies drawn from Alger and Franklin. The boy's self-imposed "SCHEDULE" calls for activities that will improve him both physically and mentally. Among the "GENERAL RESOLVES" that accompany the "SCHEDULE" are: "no more smokeing or chewing," "bath every other day," and "read one improving book or magazine per week." Mr. Gatz observes: "Jimmy was bound to get ahead." All this has prepared him for his meeting with Cody, whose yacht represents "all the beauty and glamour in the world" to the "quick and extravagantly ambitious" young man.

Because of his experiences with Cody—experiences that convince him of the importance of wealth and reinforce the early influence of Franklin, Alger, and Hill—Gatsby is ready to love Daisy, the girl with the voice "full of money." Inevitably, he makes the tragic mistake of allowing his abstract ideals, dreams, and illusions to become incarnated in her:

> One autumn night, five years before, they had been walking down the street . . . Out of the corner of his eye Gatsby saw that the blocks of the sidewalk really formed a ladder and mounted to a secret place above the trees—he could climb to it, if he climbed alone, and once there he could suck on the pap of life, gulp down the incomparable milk of wonder.
>
> His heart beat faster and faster as Daisy's white face came up to his own. He knew that when he kissed this girl, and forever wed his unutterable visions to her perishable breath, his mind would never romp again like the mind of God. So he waited, listening for a moment longer to the tuning-fork that had been struck upon a star. Then he kissed her. At his lips' touch she blossomed for him like a flower and the incarnation was complete.(p.84)

His immediate reaction to the life of wealth combines realism and romance. It is less the material possessions per se that interest him than the kind of life money might buy, a life which would fulfill the dreams of his romantic quest. He is "overwhelmingly aware of the youth and mystery that wealth imprisons and preserves." Daisy's house, as well as the girl herself, symbolizes this.

In his efforts to win Daisy Buchanan, "gleaming like silver, safe and proud above the hot struggles of the poor,"(p.114)

Gatsby becomes another Trimalchio,[5] with a modern idiom and setting. He engages in bootlegging and other "shady" activities, earning enough money in three years to buy an imitation French villa, an elaborate road-house. As "proprietor" of this establishment, he endeavors to acquire the right kind of speech and manner. But there is a deep gulf between West Egg, the colony of the *nouveau riche*, and East Egg, the world of the real aristocracy of inherited wealth. Gatsby is not capable of making the transition. He cannot copy, far less acquire, the qualities, particularly the grace of the people across the bay. His ostentatious house, his cream-coloured car, and his pink suit are vulgar. His attempts at formality are ridiculous. The pursuit of Daisy has cost him his ideal inner nature:

> He talked a lot about the past, and I gathered that he wanted to recover something, some idea of himself perhaps, that had gone into loving Daisy. His life had been confused and disordered since then, but if he could once return to a certain starting place and go over it all slowly, he could find out what that thing was. (p.84)

Like *Huckleberry Finn*, *The Great Gatsby* is an American myth. As Gatsby rises from "rags to riches," an ascent theoretically at least open to all Americans, he is a culture hero. Insofar as the concepts of American civilization deceive him, convince him that money can buy the ideal life of his dreams and illusions, divert him from his quest for the transcendental, and force him into the position of Trimalchio, his is the tragedy of a romanticist in a materialistic society. To the extent that American concepts deceive Gatsby by making him believe that he can really buy his way into a higher class and that this class, the rich, is superior to ordinary humanity, the novel is the tragedy of the middle-class American under the democratic-capitalistic system.

A good example of Fitzgerald's combination of romance and social realism in *The Great Gatsby* is his interweaving of pastoral nostalgia and cultural history. In the novel we feel the author's idealization of a lost America. At the end Nick says:

> And as the moon rose higher the inessential houses began to melt away until gradually I became aware of the old island here that

> flowered once for Dutch sailors' eyes—a fresh, green breast of the new world. Its vanished trees, the trees that had made way for Gatsby's house, had once pandered in whispers to the last and greatest of all human dreams; for a transitory enchanted moment man must have held his breath in the presence of this continent, compelled into an aesthetic contemplation he neither understood nor desired, face to face for the last time in history with something commensurate to his capacity for wonder. (p.137)

This passage is filled with pastoral nostalgia, a longing for an older civilization when America was "a fresh, green breast of the new world." Now the virgin forests have been cut down to make houses for Gatsby and his neighbors. The real symbol of change, however, is that valley of ashes between West Egg and New York, that "wasteland," that "dumping ground," "a fantastic farm where ashes grow like wheat into ridges and hills and grotesque gardens." The natural—"farm," "wheat," and "gardens"—has become unnatural—"fantastic," "ashes," and "grotesque." The valley is bordered by mechanization and urbanization: a highway, a railroad, and Wilson's dingy garage. In front of this garage where Wilson repairs cars, Myrtle, his wife, is killed by an automobile—Fitzgerald's symbol of violent death in the machine age.

From Nature that awed the Dutch sailors, early Americans drew their feeling for the spiritual, for the transcendental. Like the first settlers, Gatsby too has a feeling for the spiritual, for the transcendental. Because of the bootlegger's "incorruptible dream," Nick comes to describe him as superior to those with whom he has associated: " 'They're a rotten crowd,' I shouted across the lawn. 'You're worth the whole damn bunch put together.' " (p.117) Essentially a man of the spirit, Gatsby is engulfed by modern American materialists like Cody, Tom, and Daisy, who, creating God in their own image, have made even Him materialistic! Jay Gatsby, who ironically enough becomes His son, finds "he must be about His Father's business, the service of a vast, vulgar, and meretricious beauty," the service, in other words, of American materialism. God is reduced to Dr. T. J. Eckleburg in much the same way that Gatsby is reduced to Trimalchio. As Eckleburg He advertises eyeglasses at the same time he broods over the valley of ashes.

Nick says that *The Great Gatsby* is a "story of the West," and that all the leading characters are Westerners who "possessed some deficiency in common which made us subtly unadaptable to Eastern life."(p.134) The East, then, destroys the older American qualities with which these Midwesterners have grown up, qualities that only Gatsby and Nick manage to retain. Gatsby believes that he can realize his dreams, ideals, and illusions here, but that it is impossible is clear from Nick's comment:

> He had come a long way to this blue lawn, and his dream must have seemed so close that he could hardly fail to grasp it. He did not know that it was already behind him, somewhere back in that vast obscurity beyond the city, where the dark fields of the republic rolled on under the night.(p.137)

For Gatsby and for America the transcendental, the spiritual, can be found only in "towns beyond the Ohio," which, because they are still located in a pastoral setting, are morally superior to the materialistic East.

By showing that the early ideals of the country–ideals inspired by Nature and by an agrarian economy–have almost entirely disappeared in the new urban, industrial society, Fitzgerald warns us that democracy and capitalism are, perhaps, not compatible. By giving Jay Gatsby the qualities of that earlier America and placing him among post-Civil War materialists, by paralleling his pursuit of the green light to the Dutch sailors' quest for the "fresh, green breast of the new world," the author succeeds in making the novel a sort of cultural-historical allegory.

II

Tender is the Night (1934), a fine novel but not comparable to *The Great Gatsby*, is in a sense misnamed, for although its final title was derived from that prototype of romantic poems, Keats's "Ode to a Nightingale," it has practically no romance. Its orientation, partly to be attributed to the influence Hemingway exerted on Fitzgerald during its composition and partly to the circumstance that it was published during the thirties when almost every American writer was concerning himself with man's relation to his environment, is realistic, psycho-sociological.

In this most autobiographical of the three major novels, the hero is descended from a Southern family. His great-grandfather had been governor of North Carolina, he numbers Mad Anthony Wayne among his ancestors, and his father, who told him about Mosby, came North immediately after the Civil War. Dick Diver still has cousins in Virginia. Upon returning to the United States for his father's funeral, he begins to feel at home only when he enters Westmoreland County:

> Next day at the churchyard his father was laid among a hundred Divers, Dorseys, and Hunters. It was very friendly leaving him there with all his relations around him. Flowers were scattered on the brown unsettled earth. Dick had no more ties here now and did not believe he would come back. He knelt on the hard soil. These dead, he knew them all, their weather-beaten faces with blue flashing eyes, the spare violent bodies, the souls made of new earth in the forest-heavy darkness of the seventeenth century.

"Good-bye, my fathers–good-bye, all my fathers."(p.222) From his father, who in turn inherited them from his ancestors, Dick learns the manners and code of morality Scott Fitzgerald always associated with the pre-Civil War South:

> Dick loved his father–again and again he referred judgments to what his father would probably have thought or done . . . He told Dick all he knew about life, not much but most of it true, simple things, matters of behavior that came within his clergyman's range . . . his father had been sure of what he was, with a deep pride of the two proud widows who had raised him to believe that nothing could be superior to "good instincts," honor, courtesy, and courage.(pp.220–21)

Dick Diver, then, has been brought up on older American values –"honor, courtesy, and courage"–values that as an adult he finds manifested only occasionally as, for example, in the "gold-star muzzers" (mothers) and in Mrs. Speers. These are the values that make him "a natural idealist," "a spoiled priest," "a moralist in revolt."[6] They are responsible for his "layer of hardness . . . self-control and . . . self-discipline," the reasons "he wanted to be good . . . kind . . . brave and wise."

Fitzgerald said in 1932 that although Dick Diver is "a superman in possibilities," he lacks "tensile strength."[7] His weaknesses—a hidden respect for money, and a great need to be admired, accepted, and loved—like his good qualities—"honor, courtesy, and courage"—are results of his childhood. We learn that Dick's father sent him to college on his mother's small fortune and that he, the father, was "very much the gentleman, but not much get-up-and-go about him." We learn also that watching the older man's struggles "wedded a desire for money to an essentially unacquisitive nature." But more important than the fear of poverty is Dick's need to be accepted, a need explained by the fact that his family had "sunk from haute burgeoisie to petit burgeoisie."[8] As "the last hope of a decaying clan," he tries to recapture a lost heritage, to regain a lost status. In his "social climbing"[9] he capitalizes on the attribute that often destroys its possessor—charm:

> He got up and, as he absorbed the situation, his self-knowledge assured him that he would undertake to deal with it—the old fatal pleasingness, the old forceful charm, swept back with its cry of "Use me!" He would have to go fix this thing that he didn't care a damn about, because it had early become a habit to be loved, perhaps from the moment when he had realized that he was the last hope of a decaying clan. On an almost parallel occasion, back in Dohmler's clinic on the Zurichsee, realizing this power, he had made his choice, chosen Ophelia, chosen the sweet poison and drunk it. Wanting above all to be brave and kind, he had wanted, even more than that, to be loved. So it had been. So it would ever be.(p.321)

Although himself a noncombatant, Dick Diver is more deeply conscious of the war than anyone else in the novel. On one occasion, he has a long dream in which there are "fire engines, symbols of disaster, and a ghastly uprising of the mutilated"; on another, he is deeply distressed to see "veterans going to lay wreaths on the tombs of the dead," their faces "only formally sad." But it is not only the war's butchery and the indifference of the public that trouble Dick. Even more disturbing is the fact that, when his "beautiful lovely safe world blew itself up," the old values—economic, political, religious, and sexual—disappeared. He feels himself in "the broken universe of the war's ending," in a society that has forsaken its former traditions and been unable to replace them.

The European aristocracy, having lost in the war what remained of its power and prestige, has become degenerate. There is Lady Caroline Sibley-Biers, a "fragile" and "tubercular" Englishwoman, bearing aloft "the pennon of decadence, the last ensign of the fading empire." There is Tommy Barban, half-French and "utterly aristocratic," who, as "the end product of an archaic world," has served the cause of the nobility almost everywhere, his business killing people like Russian communists. Barban's efforts notwithstanding, the cause of the European aristocracy is futile. Displaced and financially insolvent, it develops a penchant for wealthy Americans, a group only too glad for an opportunity to mingle with it, a group typified by the Anglophile Baby Warren. McKisco's experiences with the American rich, with people like the Warrens—a "ducal family without a title"—is that they have taken from the English "their uncertain and fumbling snobbery, their delight in ignorance, and their deliberate rudeness." Both the wealthy Americans and their idols of the European aristocracy are paying for their corruption and perversion by wasting away in hotels, sanitariums, tuberculosis resorts and psychiatric clinics.

As a concrete symbol for this postwar sickness of the upper classes, Fitzgerald created Nicole Warren, a schizophrenic described as a "prototype of that obscure yielding up of swords that was going on in the world about her." Nicole, "the product of much ingenuity and toil," the American rich girl for whom the entire capitalistic system "swayed and thundered onward," like the powerful of the world everywhere, contains within herself her "own doom."

In part as "a spoiled priest" and in part as a social climber Dick Diver functions in this corrupt society. The "priest role" is clear from various phrases: Diver looks at the floor "like a priest in the confessional";(p.322) he is like "another man . . . in front of a church in Ferrara, in sackcloth and ashes . . . paying some tribute to things unforgotten, unshriven, unexpurgated";(p.153) as he leaves Europe, he raises his hand and "with a papal cross" blesses the beach.(p.333) As priest and as gentleman Dick has a code of morality, the code he has learned from his father, the minister and Southerner, the representative of older American values. When Rosemary indicates her willingness to have an affair with him, he refuses on the grounds that "old-fashioned" as the idea might be, he wants her to meet her first love "all intact." Nicole tells us that aside from the times when children were born, "Dick had not spent a night apart from her since their marriage." When he discovers what Mary North and Lady Caroline have done, his tendency is "to order fifty stripes of the cat and a fortnight of bread and water." A priest-doctor, he serves the upper classes as consoler and moralist. As consoler, he reassures them that things are not so bad as they seem and even creates for them a haven on the French Riviera to which they can retreat from the turmoil of the outside world. As moralist, he tries to instill in them a system of ethics; when he fails, he says: "I've wasted nine years teaching the rich the A B C's of human decency."[10]

Yet although Dick is genuinely interested in the welfare of the people around him, his interest is not entirely selfless. He needs the approval of society as much as society requires his reassurances and guidance. When he is the center of activity, the person upon whom all eyes are admiringly focused, he feels accepted and loved, and it is this feeling of acceptance and love that appeases his desire to regain that lost "haute burgeoisie" status which his family has previously occupied.

Dick's relation to Nicole, that symbol of postwar sickness, is as ambivalent as is his relation to the upper classes in general. On the one hand, as priest-doctor he is interested in an objective way in Nicole's spiritual and mental well-being. Bringing her "back to the world she had forfeited" is, to a great extent, a selfless endeavor. Nicole admits at the height of her rebellion from him that Dick has probably planned this, has probably willed it. On the other hand, because Dick is a social climber, his marriage to Nicole is not completely altruistic. How better could he fulfill his need to be accepted, his compulsion to regain the lost heritage of his "clan" than to marry into an American "ducal family"?

Fitzgerald tells us that between the time Dick discovers Nicole "flowering under a stone on the Zurichsee" and the time he first meets Rosemary "the spear had been blunted."(p.218) Dick's emotional bankruptcy, "a lesion of enthusiasm" and "a process of deterioration," is manifested in many ways. There is a general physical decline, as he loses his once superb strength and energy. There is a moral decline too. He becomes sexually promiscuous, falling in love "with every pretty woman" he sees. An argument with a taxicab driver results in a brawl which lands him in jail. He drinks heavily and develops prejudices: "He would suddenly unroll a long scroll of contempt for some person, race, class, way of life, way of thinking." Doctor Diver degenerates from the serious, brilliant professional whose learned articles have been standard in their line, whose ambition was "to be a good psychologist—maybe to be the greatest one that ever lived," to an absolute failure. He returns to America "to be a quack . . . only a shell to which nothing matters but survival as long as possible with the old order."[11]

Emotional bankruptcy to Scott Fitzgerald was caused primarily by personal relationships, whether with an individual or with a group. Dick loses his vitality in part through his efforts as a priest-doctor to console and instruct both his friends and Nicole. When Mary North says that people only "want . . . to have a good time" and that if you deny them this "you cut yourself off from nourishment," Dick replies, "Have I been nourished?" He has lost his vitality helping people who have given him nothing in return. Nicole, whose "transference" to her husband has saved her,[12] is even more of a "vampire" than the friends and acquaintances.[13]

As Dick loses his energy as a priest-doctor, he also loses it in the role of social climber. Desiring status, he has allowed the Warrens to buy him for their daughter: "He had been swallowed up like a gigolo and had somehow permitted his arsenal to be locked up in the Warren safety-deposit vaults."(pp.218–19) Although he manages to maintain "a qualified financial independence"—he wants position rather than money—his subsequent life of ease and daily association with the rich have an effect on him, as Fitzgerald's "Notes" suggest:

> The novel should do this. Show a man who is a natural idealist, a spoiled priest, giving in for various causes to the ideas of the haute Burgeoisie, and in his rise to the top of the social world, losing his idealism, his talent and turning to drink and dissipation.[14]

Insofar as Dick becomes an emotional bankrupt in his efforts to reassure and guide the upper classes and their representative, Nicole, corrupt postwar society and not he is at fault. As this degeneration results from an inner necessity to acquire status, he has only himself to blame.

Tender is the Night, a realistic study of "the broken universe of the war's ending," is the tragedy of both an individual and a society. It is the tragedy of an individual by virtue of its placing a basically good man, Dick Diver, with one serious flaw—social climbing—in a situation where the flaw destroys him. It is the tragedy of a society, and particularly of that society's upper classes, by virtue of its showing us a group of people, sick because they have lost former traditions and moralities, misuse and cast aside the priest-doctor who has a cure—the older American values of "honor, courtesy, and courage."

III

Unfinished and published posthumously (1941), *The Last Tycoon* was the last of Scott Fitzgerald's works. He wrote in his "Notes": "If one book could ever be 'like' another, I should say it is more 'like' *The Great Gatsby* than any other of my books. But I hope it will be entirely different."(p.141)

The Last Tycoon is more like *The Great Gatsby* than any other of the author's novels because Monroe Stahr is more like James Gatz than any other of the author's characters. Like Gatsby, Stahr is a hero not only in the sense that he is the person around whom the action revolves, but in the larger sense of the legendary figure and culture ideal. As a legendary figure, his early life is as obscure as Gatsby's. Of Stahr's youth, we learn no more than that "he was one of a gang of kids in the Bronx," that he took "a night-school course in stenography," that as a boy of fifteen looking through a window of a restaurant in Erie, Pennsylvania, he was impressed with "the terribly strange brooding mystery of people and violin music,"(p.114) and that shortly after this he went to New York. Like Gatsby, he is described in images of grandeur. He is likened to Napoleon and Lincoln. At times he seems to be almost godlike:

> He had flown up very high to see, on strong wings, when he was young. And while he was up there he had looked on all the kingdoms, with the kind of eyes that can stare straight into the sun . . . You could say that this was where an accidental wind blew him, but I don't think so. I would rather think that in a "long shot" he saw a new way of measuring our jerky hopes and graceful rogueries and awkward sorrows, and that he came here from choice to be with us to the end.(p.20)

A culture-hero, Stahr, by the age of twenty-two, has risen from "rags to riches," from a lower-middle-class background to a position of power and fortune. These legendary and symbolic overtones are in sharp contrast to the psycho-sociological orientation of *Tender is the Night*. In this respect, *The Last Tycoon* is a return to romance.

At the same time, Fitzgerald realized his hope that the new novel would be "entirely different" from *The Great Gatsby*. Jay Gatsby is a hero because he is a romantic, one who believes that illusion itself and not its materialization is important. Monroe Stahr's heroic stature results from his losing illusions, from confronting and dealing with reality:

> Beginning at about twelve, probably, with the total rejection common to those of extraordinary mental powers, the "See here: this is all wrong–a mess–all a lie–and a sham–," he swept it all away, everything, as men of his type do; and then instead of being a son-of-a-bitch, as most of them are, he looked around at the barrenness that was left and said to himself, "*This* will never do." And so he had learned tolerance, kindness, forbearance, and even affection like lessons.(p.97)

Stahr and Gatsby possess "goodness" in common. But because Stahr learns to live in the world of actuality, he is able to develop qualities practically nonexistent in Gatsby—perception, the ability to lead men, and artistic integrity. Stahr, a "rationalist" with "an intense respect for learning," has "run ahead through trackless wastes of perception" and can see "below the surface into reality." ("Notes," p.154) He is an obvious leader: as a rather frail boy, he walked at "the head of his gang . . . occasionally throwing a command backward out of the corner of his mouth"; as a man, almost single-handed, he carries on "a long war on many fronts" to improve motion pictures. Although Stahr is an artist only "as Mr. Lincoln was a general, perforce and as a layman," the fact that he has guided "movies" "way up past the range and power of the theatre" makes him "a marker in industry like Edison and Lumiere and Griffith and Chaplin."(p.28) He is so concerned about the caliber of his productions and their effect on the audience that when a Negro he meets on the beach tells him that he never allows his children to go to moving pictures because there is "no profit" in it, Stahr immediately plans improvements. Facing death with few illusions left, it was inevitable that Scott Fitzgerald create as his new hero a man of action functioning in the present rather than another dreamer pursuing the transcendental and the timeless.

The Last Tycoon, like *The Great Gatsby* and *Tender is the Night*, is the story of a superior man in a corrupt society. The Eastern materialists who surround Gatsby and the degenerate upper classes among whom Dick Diver moves have been replaced by the equally materialistic and equally degenerate Hollywood group. In numerous letters and short stories Fitzgerald emphasized the suspicion, insecurity, and hypocrisy which he found in the motion picture industry. But what affected him even more than Hollywood's general corruption was the character of the people in power. Cecilia's description of her father, the symbol of these people, indicates that he knows nothing about the medium that has treated him so well:

> Most of what he accomplished boiled down to shrewd. He had acquired with luck and shrewdness a quarter interest in a booming circus—together with young Stahr . . . Father didn't know

> the ABC's of dubbing or even cutting. Nor had he learned much about the feel of America as a bar boy in Ballyhegan, nor did he have any more than a drummer's sense of a story.(p.28)

On other occasions, we are told that Brady is interested in producing moving pictures only as they will "benefit his bank account" ("Notes," p.140) and that he is in the business "as another man might be in cotton or steel." To this society's degeneracy, Stahr opposes the older American values of "honor, courtesy, and courage." To the ignorance and materialism of its powerful figures, he opposes his own knowledge and artistic conscience.

Judging from the text, Edmund Wilson's synopsis of the unfinished part of the book, and Fitzgerald's "Notes," one gathers that Stahr's conflict with society has a political as well as a moral significance. As "an old-fashioned paternalistic employer" wanting his employees to be "contented" and "on friendly terms," he struggles against Brady, who, like "the four great railroad kings of the coast," is "the monopolist at his worst." At the same time, as an individualist, he is opposed to collectivism—to the unions and to the Communists—"believing that any enterprising office-boy can make his way to the top." That Stahr will lose on both fronts is indicated:

> Stahr is now being pushed into the past by Brady and by the unions alike. The split between the controllers of the movie industry, on the one hand, and the various groups of employees, on the other, is widening and leaving no place for real individualists of business like Stahr, whose successes are personal achievements and whose career has always been invested with a certain personal glamor. He has held himself directly responsible to everyone with whom he has worked; he has even wanted to beat up his enemies himself. In Hollywood he is "the last tycoon."(p.131)

By indicating the defeat of Stahr at the hands of the monopolists and collectivists, Fitzgerald tells us that it is impossible—albeit desirable, perhaps even the solution to contemporary political problems—to combine individualism and social responsibility in modern America.

In his "Notes" the author says that *The Last Tycoon* "unlike

Tender is the Night" is not a "story of deterioration."(p.141) Although the novel is not dominated by emotional bankruptcy, this theme does play a part in it. At thirty-four, Stahr is desperately ill, on the verge of death. That he has experienced a "lesion of vitality" is evident from his telling Cecilia that he would marry her if he were not "too old and tired to undertake anything" and from Fitzgerald's informing us that his procrastination with Kathleen indicates that "his balanced judgment" which "thousands of people depended on" has been blunted. Stahr's emotional bankruptcy is manifested in the usual ways: he begins to drink and he expresses the desire "to beat up Brimmer." If the condition has been caused by a general life-weariness and by his marriage to Minna, it has also been caused by his efforts to instil older American values into corrupt contemporary society. He is destroyed in part by degenerate, materialistic, post-Civil War civilization. In this way, as in many others, he is a counterpart of the man who created him. So too are the heroes of Scott Fitzgerald's other two major novels, one of which at least, *The Great Gatsby*, will remain his permanent memorial, a masterpiece of American literature.

Notes

1. *The American Novel and its Tradition* (Garden City, New York, 1957), pp.12–13.

2. *The Future of the Novel*, ed. Leon Edel (New York, 1956), pp. 46–47.

3. I have used as text *Three Novels of F. Scott Fitzgerald: The Great Gatsby; Tender is the Night; The Last Tycoon* (New York, 1953).

4. In a letter to John Jamieson of 1934, Fitzgerald wrote that the story "Absolution" (*All the Sad Young Men*, New York, 1926, pp. 109–132), which was intended to be a picture of Gatsby's early life, was cut from the book in order to "preserve the sense of mystery."

5. The vulgar and ostentatious multi-millionaire of Petronius Arbiter's *Satyricon*, who is the subject of literary allusion because of an extravagant banquet he gave. Fitzgerald once thought of calling the novel *Trimalchio*.

6. Arthur Mizener, "Notes" to *Tender is the Night, The Far Side of Paradise* (Boston, 1951), pp.307–308.

7. Ibid., p.310.

8. Ibid., p.308.

9. Ibid., p.310.

10. P.219. There are political undertones to all of this. In 1932 Fitzgerald said that Dick was a "communist," a "liberal," as well as an "idealist, a moralist in revolt," and went on to state that he sent his son to the Soviet Union for an education ("Notes" to *Tender is the Night*, Mizener, p.308). Originally, then, his author conceived of Dick Diver as a man with political as well as moral convictions.

11. "Notes" to *Tender is the Night*, Mizener, p.309.

12. Ibid., p.312.

13. Fitzgerald indicated in his "Notes" what a terrible toll curing Nicole exacted from Dick: "Medically Nicole is nearly cured but Dick has given out and is sinking toward alcoholism and discouragement. It seems as if the completion of his ruination will be the fact that cures her—almost mystically. However this is merely hinted at." (Mizener, p.314).

14. Ibid., pp.307–308.

2. F. Scott Fitzgerald: *The Great Gatsby, Tender is the Night, The Last Tycoon*

by G. C. MILLARD

The quality that permeates the novels of Fitzgerald is one of a disenchantment; the word in itself, 'disenchantment,' has delicacy and gentleness, both in the recognition of the failure of a previous experience, and in the enduring state of mind. The sense of failure and disillusionment in the novels never becomes, for any main character, bitterness, violence or resolution, because of the writer's acute, personal, obsessive sympathy with the experience of intense hope, the non-realization of which cannot invalidate the experience. One notices, in *The Great Gatsby*, how badly those characters finally come off who have not known the particular kind of yearning which Gatsby experiences; it is the centre of his life and the energy behind his affability comes from the simplicity of his devotion to this yearning. Nothing can invalidate the actual experience of devotion, no matter how deluding it is.

In his youth Gatsby went through an adolescent phase of an obvious kind of hope. He wanted to be rich and to enter the realms of the seemingly glamorous. When, as a young officer in the army, he meets Daisy, a rich, beautiful and spoiled person, she comes to embody everything he wants. But she marries while

From English Studies in Africa, 8 (March 1965). Reprinted by permission of the Witwatersrand University Press.

he is at the front in Europe. He returns to America not so much with the intention of getting rich fast and unscrupulously, which he does do, but to recapture the experience of past perfection with Daisy; he builds his great house in sight of Daisy's home and settles back to enjoy dreaming about meeting with the Daisy he once knew. He lives in the past and in the future; the here and now is something to which he is not committed; he is suspended between memory and dreams so that he transcends his personality, his immediate egoism, and he appears to have the capacity for a kind of reverence. The following passage describes this:

> He smiled understandingly—much more than understandingly. It was one of those rare smiles with a quality of eternal reassurance in it, that you may come across four or five times in your life. It faced—or seemed to face—the whole eternal world for an instant, and then concentrated on *you* with an irresistible prejudice in your favour. . . . Precisely at that point it vanished.[1]

The two words placed together, "irresistible prejudice", in themselves generate a quality that is to be found in many passages throughout the book. "Prejudice" comes from Fitzgerald's intelligent awareness and partial judgment, while the "irresistible" is from that part of him that cannot transcend the limits of his vision. The writer sees Gatsby as transcending commonplace conventionality, with its dullness but also with its common sense which prescribes formal acquaintanceship and slow evaluation, rather than optimistic over-estimation beforehand, in any relationship. In this unusual combination, the word "prejudice", with all its unpleasant associations, is reinstated by the possible benefit from this quality, to the person smiled at, just as an habitual moral code can be distorted when an action promises unexpected rewards. We are persuaded in this book to continue to like Gatsby in spite of his vulgarity and criminal associations, because, in knowing him, we have felt the "irresistible" quality of any obsession; we sense Gatsby's universality just as we respond to the "whole eternal world" which here suffuses convention, for we have an instinctive response waiting for the suggestion of the possible attainment of some timeless love and security. The question is therefore: to what extent is this universality of Gatsby to be found to dominate the book, as a personal obsession of Fitzgerald?

The narrator of the story, Carraway, is similar to Gatsby; he says at the beginning of the book:

> In my younger and more vulnerable years my father gave me some advice that I've been turning over in my mind ever since. "Whenever you feel like criticising anyone" he told me, "just remember that all the people in this world haven't had the advantages that you've had."[2]

This leads Carraway to believe that "reserving judgements is a matter of infinite hope."[2a] The very idea of infinite hope suggests not only the absence of facile villainizing but also the absence of philosophical detachment or firm moral judgement in the characterization, suggesting too that Carraway will be, towards new people, at first, intensely sympathetic but then proportionately disillusioned.

Disenchantment is a state of mind, a mood, that implies a degree of petulant regret for lost ideals, a mood which tends to be harsh on those who did not live up to the "infinite hope." The frank criticism by the writer, Carraway or Fitzgerald, of those weaknesses which create the naivete in the "infinite hope," would lead to a firmer attitude to himself. In this way, purged of the strong, personal quality of the "infinite hope," by an understanding of the degree to which he wants people to live up to his exaggerated expectations, compensating for those weaknesses, he would not leave us with such careless distaste for lesser characters when they are no longer sensed with poignancy, or when they are not shown as being people in themselves deluded by the lingering glory of past achievement.

Tom and Daisy Buchanan, who emerge from the story in an unfavourable light, are, at the beginning of the story, touched with a kind of lingering sympathy:

> . . . but I felt that Tom would drift on for ever seeking, a little wistfully, for the dramatic turbulence of some irrecoverable football game.[3]

When Carraway meets Daisy at the beginning of the book, we have the following:

> She laughed again, as if she said something very witty, and held my hand for a moment, looking up into my face, promising that there was no one in the world she so much wanted to see. . . It was the kind of voice that the ear follows up and down, as if each speech is an arrangement of notes that will never be played again.[4]

We are constantly reminded of the beauty of Daisy's voice; it is as though Fitzgerald can never forget the absolute quality of beauty—like the absolute nature of any obsession—no matter what the human and moral situation might be; and one is made aware of the effect of Daisy's voice on the observing, evaluating Carraway. By comparing the following passages one can see how Carraway's judgement is in constant conflict with his own nostalgia, or perhaps, how Fitzgerald's judgement, compared to his sympathy, becomes strangely harsh, in a rather superficial dismissal of those who can no longer serve as reflections of this personal longing:

> Daisy began to sing with the music in a husky, rhythmic whisper, bringing out a meaning in each word, that it had never had before and would never have again.[5]

> They were careless people, Tom and Daisy—they smashed up things and creatures and then retreated back into their money or their vast carelessness. . .[6]

There is a degree of judgement throughout the book, sometimes direct, but mostly implied. That Carraway himself is a romantic is suggested, not only by the gentle quality of his observation even in the most sordid situations, but by the mood that sometimes comes to him involuntarily when he is alone. He says:

> I liked to walk up Fifth Avenue and pick out romantic women from the crowd and imagine that in a few minutes I was going to enter into their lives, and no one would ever know or disapprove . . . At the enchanted metropolitan twilight I felt a haunting loneliness sometimes, and felt it in other . . . young

> clerks in the dusk, wasting the most poignant moments of night and life.[7]

It is like this that Fitzgerald approaches his characters, and seldom does he do anything but let them show us, with vivid immediacy, how unfulfilled, shallow and pointless their lives are. He manages to leave an effect of poignancy even after describing, in Chapter Two, such basically unlikeable people as Tom and the McKees and Myrtle Wilson, all thrown together with Carraway in a small flat high over New York on a hot day. The interrelationship between them is evoked with deadly accuracy, showing them as being out of touch, trivial, vulgar, yet each with his or her own vitality and sense of self-worth. Somehow they are to be neither despised nor loved, and our feelings are guided towards a kindliness for these rootless, shapeless personalities, by three things:

First, the chapter starts with a description of the approach to New York:

> About halfway between West Egg and New York the motor road hastily joins the railroad and runs beside it for a quarter of a mile, so as to shrink away from a certain desolate area of land. This is a valley of ashes—a fantastic farm where ashes grow like wheat into ridges and hills . . .[8]

One feels that people living in a civilization which makes such a place possible, must necessarily be victims at least as much as they are perpetrators; each one, like McKee who must survive somehow in competition with other photographers, must create his or her own sense of dignity:

> He informed me that he was in the "artistic game" and I gathered later that he was a photographer . . .[9]

In the middle of this rather sordid chapter, we are told:

> The late afternoon sky bloomed in the window for a moment like the blue honey of the Mediterranean.[10]

Fertility and regeneration are suddenly there, in contrast to the people and to the description of the approach to the city;

but it is a contrast in which the adjacent objects are, to some extent, kept together by a generosity and nostalgia that seems beyond the faults and vulgarity.

The second thing that removes us from any facile condemnation of these people, is the suggestion of an omniscient God in the advertisement sign above the "valley of ashes":

> The eyes of Doctor T. J. Eckleburg are blue and gigantic—their retinas are one yard high . . . Evidently some wild wag of an oculist set them there to fatten his practice in the borough of Queens, and then sank down himself into eternal blindness, or forgot them and moved away. But his eyes, dimmed a little by many paintless days, under sun and rain, brood on over the solemn dumping ground.[11]

Later in the book Wilson gives to these eyes the quality of that divine power and justice in which, to preserve his sanity, he must be able to believe after the violent, pointless death of his wife. But in this quotation we sense how ironical it is that advertising and competitive vulgarity should have created the only thing, for miles around, which could possibly satisfy the instinct in people for wanting to recognize their common humanity and greater destiny. This advertisement is really a graven image, an idol that has betrayed its creator who, as it were, prayed to it for success and attempted to convert people to his faith. Faded, and no longer of use, obviously to be despised in a world that worships success, the eyes of Dr. Eckleburg are deprived of associations with business, and become whatever passers-by happen to make them, project on to them; they become absolute eyes, watching and recording; for Wilson they become the eyes of an omniscient and personal God.

The third thing that persuades us to become kindly within our criticism of these people, is the way in which Carraway, whom we have learned to regard as being a quiet, intelligent and 'decent' person, is never superior and detached from humanity, from the feeling that these people are members of the same human race to which he belongs. We sense his disgust and boredom, but we also sense his involvement:

> Yet high over the city our line of yellow windows must have contributed their share of human secrecy to the casual watcher in the darkening streets, and I saw him too, looking up and wondering. I was within and without, simultaneously enchanted and repelled by the inexhaustible variety of life.[12]

The sense of Carraway's involvement is strong in the descriptions of Gatsby's parties. We are made clearly aware of the fact that a great deal of money is the real basis for the occasions, that Gatsby hardly knows the people he invites, that many people come only for free drinks or for snobbish reasons. But once this is conceded, we sense with sympathy the contrasting poverty of these people as far as purposeful living is concerned; we sense the loneliness within their callousness; somehow we feel them to be, in part, victims of a way of life. Although the atmosphere is impersonal, bought, with the unnatural vitality of drink and the excitement of Gatsby's associations with notoriety, we cannot but sense, through Daisy, in the following quotation, the nameless yearning underlying it all. Daisy's feelings seem spread over all the guests:

> Her glance left me and sought the lighted top of the steps, where "Three O'Clock in the Morning", a neat, sad little waltz of that year, was drifting out the open door. After all, in the very casualness of Gatsby's party there were romantic possibilities totally absent from her world. What was it up there in the song that seemed to be calling her back inside? What would happen now in the dim, incalculable hours?[13]

The formality of the phrase "romantic possibilities" suggests the writer's awareness of what he is doing; the phrase "dim, incalculable hours" shows the writer's full sympathy and understanding of the nature of romantic yearning.

The following passage lends to the party, to everyone there no matter why they are there or how they behave, a timeless quality; the absolute quality of belonging or being lonely, makes us forget the questionable motives for each person's presence at the party:

> The lights grow brighter as the earth lurches away from the sun, and now the orchestra is playing yellow cocktail music, the

> opera of voices pitches a key higher. Laughter is easier minute by minute, spilled with prodigality, tipped out at a cheerful word. The groups change more swiftly, swell with new arrivals, dissolve and form in the same breath: already there are wanderers, confident girls who weave here and there among the stouter and more stable, become for a sharp, joyous moment the centre of a group, and then, excited with triumph, glide on through the sea-change of faces and voices and colour under the constantly changing light.[14]

It is the phrase "the earth lurches away from the sun" that provides a framework for the paragraph. Absolute nature, the unchangeable cycle of night and day, is inversely established by the word "lurches," which suggests a deliberate, rash tearing away from established truth or practice; there is nevertheless a strong suggestion of eternal forces which people cannot, no matter what they believe, ever disturb. The hyphen-word "sea-change" seems to contain perfectly the two qualities of permanence and change. It suggests, half-consciously, that these people, so very much of their age, the jazzy twenties, are a link in an unbroken chain of life and time.

The following quotations from the party scenes reveal again how conscious the writer is of the empty, wasteful way of life, while remaining aware of the deeper, temporarily eclipsed worth and fineness of people:

> There was dancing now on the canvas in the garden; old men pushing young girls backwards in eternal graceless circles, superior couples holding each other tortuously, fashionably . . . vacuous bursts of laughter rose toward the summer sky . . . The moon had risen higher, and floating in the Sound was a triangle of silver scales, trembling a little to the stiff, tinny drip of the banjoes on the lawn.[15]

These descriptions place together the old traditional symbols and association with aspects of the contemporary way of life; there is regret for the passing of the formal ballroom; for the summer evenings no longer associated with rest and the cycle of the seasons; for the sickening use made of the old associations in new forms, so that the geometrical pattern is forced on the moonlight by the arid, repetitive music. But the poignancy of the scene is the lasting impression; we are held suspended between criticism and tenderness.

So far I have tried to show that Fitzgerald's personal obsession, while being pervasive, is artistically balanced in *The Great Gatsby* by good sense and implied criticism and by a frequent suggestion of an impersonal scheme of things within which his characters exist, a scheme that comprises a sense of the past, a sense of nature, and a sense of absolute beauty. Gatsby's obsession and an identification with his yearning, does certainly pervade the book, but there is sufficient in the writing which contains the three qualities named above, to keep Gatsby dramatically vivid, existing in himself, as well as in a framework of transcendental motifs, and not just a self-projection of Fitzgerald.

Like most creative writers, Fitzgerald restricts himself to one kind of society, one kind of person; it is only in certain kinds of people, the rich, the brilliant, the "beautiful and the damned," that he can look for something that obsesses him, something he has lost. It is, perhaps, that wealth and beauty seemed once to have been the final end, achievement or possession, and all his writing is an attempt to understand his disillusionment. The unhappiness of the rich, talented and beautiful seems in a way like the unhappiness of the children of the gods. They are favoured, they have a tantalizing chance of finding real, inner happiness, for there is nothing obvious and extraneous to aim for; yet they are most likely to be blind to inner values.

What happens in Fitzgerald's stories and novels before *The Crack-Up*, is that the characters can only wear themselves out by repeating certain things that are possible for them to do and be: to yearn, to entertain, to have pleasure, to be admired. Only one who, like Fitzgerald, has been less rich and who has known the feeling of yearning for their way of life, is conscious of the shallowness and feels the disenchantment. But his fascination and yearning were so strong that he could not abandon the idols of his false worship. Instead he half-stagnated with the rich and famed, being both fascinated and appalled.

Where he had expected to find a paradise, he found only ordinariness; and his expectations of the people were so high that their actual natures were perhaps more disillusioning to him than they would have been to others who had not yearned to be among them and who had therefore not expected the people to match the creatures of his imagination. It is not so much the disenchantment that more consciously obsesses Fitzgerald in his novels, as the universal quality of longing, the hoping for a state of intense happiness that each person instinctively believes in, or believes is possible to find through or among other people, or by means of wealth or other earthly achievement. The imagining beforehand will itself be a kind of reality whose end human nature is somehow never prepared for, an end, which, when reached, makes happiness the remembered energy and devotion, towards the end.

Gatsby took five years to amass his fortune, build his house and prepare to entice Daisy to join him in a re-creation of the past. The intensity of the experience which he wanted to recapture is felt in the following description of his early love for Daisy:

> Her porch was bright with the bought luxury of star-shine; the wicker of the settee squeaked fashionably as she turned towards him and he kissed her curious and lovely mouth . . . and Gatsby was overwhelmingly aware of the youth and mystery that wealth imprisons and preserves, of the freshness of many clothes, and of Daisy, gleaming like silver, safe and proud above the hot struggles of the poor.[16]

Critical awareness and fascination exist side by side in the phrase "imprisons and preserves"; these qualities give to the handling of the theme of wealth a subtlety which reveals the poverty of any purely moral condemnation of "material ambition." There is, for Fitzgerald, a quality of fineness and infinite possibility, in the possession of wealth; there is a liberation from the thing that preoccupies the mass of mankind who have to work hard and stick to a routine in order to survive; those qualities in human beings which a sensitive nature would associate with transcendental awareness, are freed. The "youth and mystery" become separate from the normal cares of human beings, but what Fitzgerald notices, is that these qualities can so easily become useless and evil. The person is "imprisoned" from his or her fellow-beings by the selfishness and indulgence which the liberation of these qualities induces. But, of course, the imagination of anyone who aspires to the "youth and mystery" will not see the imprisonment until he approaches near.

The unnatural, unhealthy intensity of the feelings from the days when Gatsby was courting Daisy, is powerfully conveyed in the following quotation. Gatsby walks Daisy home:

> Out of the corner of his eye Gatsby saw that the blocks of the sidewalks really formed a ladder and mounted to a secret place above the trees—he could climb to it, if he climbed alone, and once there he could suck on the pap of life, gulp down the incomparable milk of wonder . . . He knew that when he kissed this girl and forever wed his unutterable visions to her perishable breath, his mind would never romp again like the mind of God.[17]

The imagery clearly suggests elemental physical nourishment of a man whose godless ego is hungry for peace and perfection as extensions of the idea of Mother, with its safety and timelessness. Gatsby, the orphan and dreamer, has no roots in any life other than that which he imagines and dreams; there is nothing to control the intensity of his yearning.

When Gatsby finally meets Daisy, it is confusing for him. For five years he has "waited with his teeth set, so to speak, at an inconceivable pitch of intensity."[18]

> Suddenly the day comes; he shows Daisy his mansion: Sometimes, too, he stared around at his possessions in a dazed way, as though in her actual and astounding presence none of it was any longer real. Once he nearly toppled down a flight of stairs.[19]

The five years were the meaningful ones for Gatsby, because he had created a goal for himself; he had devoted himself to the unattainable, to an imagined communion of the future. Then finally he meets Daisy and is caught up in the mundane complexity of human relationships. The security and quiet strength that his 'delusion,' his dream and devotions, gave, disintegrate as soon as he tries to win Daisy away from her husband. One sees Gatsby lose his dreamy, amiable dignity, and become no more than selfish and grasping, hating to have his wishes thwarted, egotistical as either Tom or Daisy:

> "Your wife doesn't love you," said Gatsby. "She's never loved you. She loves me."
> "You must be crazy!" exclaimed Tom automatically.
> Gatsby sprang to his feet, vivid with excitement.
> "She never loved you, do you hear?", he cried . . .[20]

Gatsby remains universally human, free from any suggestion of being the favoured child or more facile self-projection of Fitzgerald's obsession.

Soon Gatsby sees, without admitting it, that Daisy has been amused, flattered and entertained by the recalling of a past love; but she has no intention of becoming embroiled in the practical business of divorce and new adjustment. She is by no means the exceptional girl, the supreme love of Gatsby's dreams. The heat and dreariness of this Sunday, when the argument occurs, is wonderfully evoked; at the time Gatsby is facing a great challenge, Carraway, a few feet away in the same room, is more aware of his own bodily irritation:

> The prolonged and tumultuous argument that ended by herding us into that room eludes me, though I have a sharp physical memory that, in the course of it, my underwear kept climbing like a damp snake around my legs . . .[21]

The absence of any deep sympathy between the five people, the weariness and triviality which arises from this lack, when money and atmosphere cannot help, is vividly suggested. Each character is kept human, each is artistically authentic. The shallowness of their relationship is universal.

The episode soon after, when Daisy, driving back with Gatsby, runs over Myrtle Wilson and does not stop, follows on quite naturally from the general feeling of chaos and carelessness about other people. Wilson's misunderstanding, which leads him to shoot Gatsby, is an inevitable working out, or self-exhaustion, of the chaotic energy that has been released through Gatsby's argument with Tom; Wilson, whose garage is near the valley of ashes and the eyes of Dr. Eckleburg, sees in the latter the presence and omniscience of God who seems to offer Wilson personal and equally chaotic justification for revenge:

> Standing behind him, Michaelis saw with a shock that he [Wilson] was looking at the eyes of Doctor T. J. Eckleburg . . . "God sees everything," repeated Wilson.[22]

The book ends by repeating, in a wider context, the theme of wonder and disenchantment, dream and attainment:

> . . . for a transitory enchanted moment man must have held his breath in the presence of this continent, compelled into an aesthetic contemplation he neither understood nor desired, face to face for the last time in history with something commensurate to his capacity for wonder . . . Gatsby believed in the green light, the orgiastic future that year by year recedes before us . . .[23]

The "capacity for wonder" can achieve great things. But it seems to Fitzgerald that something inherent in human nature directs that capacity at definite objects. The capacity for wonder continues endlessly in all people, but it goes through continuous disillusionment in that the focus of wonder, an object or a person, fails to satisfy once it or the person has been possessed or attained. The reason is that, as Daisy was to Gatsby, the object of devotion is unconsciously expected to have inherent qualities "commensurate to his capacity for wonder." The "valley of ashes" in Chapter Two suggests what has happened to the wonder of the first people who saw America and "felt the presence of this continent."

The book leaves one wondering where this capacity for wonder might profitably, in the deepest sense of the word, be directed; that it is inherently wonderful and dangerous, Fitzgerald has vividly shown. The artistic control of the pervading theme creates a sense of balance and universality.

Before going on to discuss Fitzgerald's next major novel, *Tender is the Night*, published 1934, I should like to discuss his essay *The Crack-up*, written in 1936; in this essay he attempts to analyse his previous adult life, a life which he could no longer bear. He says:

> One harrassed and despairing night I packed a brief-case and went off a thousand miles to think it over . . . I only wanted absolute quiet to think out why I had developed a sad attitude towards sadness, a melancholy attitude towards melancholy and tragic attitude towards tragedy—*why I had become identified with the objects of my horror or compassion.* Does this seem a fine distinction? It isn't: identification such as this spells the death of accomplishment . . .[24]

This seems to be an accurate appraisal of the duality in Fitzgerald's novels up to this time; Carraway embodies the critical and moral attitude as well as the romantic involvement. His disenchantment is not bitter. The persistent self-delusion is more deeply felt in *Tender is the Night*. But from the essay *The Crack-up*, one can see how similar Fitzgerald is to Gatsby in the intensity of identification. The essay goes on to reveal the unpleasant revulsion and deliberate rejection of "compassion" after Fitzgerald had experienced his disillusionment; when he had gained the wealth and fame that he had longed for, he discovered as Gatsby did in Daisy, the unchanged reality of ordinary relationships. Carraway, and Dick Diver in *Tender is the Night*, are perpetually willing to believe well of others; they are romantically sympathetic to others; but, of course, and as the essay reveals, they are living their own lives through others, seeing their own longings in everybody, experiencing a kind of self-love, or "identification", through the imagined quality of others. This search outside of himself by Fitzgerald, to find love, a sense of belonging and wonder, exhausts itself; he reconsiders his whole life in *The Crack-up*; but the final conclusions reflect an unpleasant self-preservation, a hardness, partly belied by the continuing 'tenderness' in *The Last Tycoon.* This novel was written five years after the essay, and it was not complete when Fitzgerald died in 1941.

The new self that Fitzgerald proclaims in *The Crack-up*, is, underneath the humor and sensitivity, a direct result of disappointment; but we see strongly that he rejects much as though a belief or a person is more to blame for his unhappiness, than his own creation of that belief or person through "identification":

> So what? This is what I think now: that the natural state of the sentient adult is a qualified unhappiness. I think also that in an adult the desire to be finer in grain than you are, "a constant striving" (as those people say who gain their bread by saying it) only adds to this unhappiness in the end—that end that comes to our youth and hope . . . and I think that my happiness, or talent for self-delusion or what you will, was an exception. It was not the natural thing but the unnatural—unnatural as the Boom: . . . I do not any longer like the postman, nor the grocer, nor the editor, nor the cousin's husband, and he in turn will come to dislike me, so that life will never be very pleasant again, and the sign *Cave Canem* is hung permanently just above my door. I will try to be a correct animal though, and if you throw me a bone with enough meat on it I may even lick your hand.[25]

Clearly then, the rejection and resignation are as extreme as the earlier romantic longing and compassion. In *Tender is the Night*, as I should now like briefly to show, there is the same quality of "romantic possibility" and lingering sadness, until a certain point in the story. The second half of the book shows the ugliness and sordidness of disenchantment, and, just as *The Great Gatsby* ends without real bitterness, this book completed in 1934, runs to unresolved exhaustion just as Fitzgerald was to do two years afterwards.

The theme of the book is simple to state. Dick Diver, a young American psychologist, studying in Switzerland after the First World War, falls in love with a psychiatric patient, Nicole, who is both rich and beautiful, and utterly self-absorbed. They marry and live on the Riviera. Slowly Dick loses his capacity for work and clear thinking; he succumbs to the temptation to indulge his weakness for wanting to be the admired one, the all-knowing entertainer with a genius for organizing people in an intimate way. He slowly comes to see that everything he does, after marrying Nicole, has nurtured the vanity of a boy who has not grown up emotionally, in whose adulthood, as measured by years, the facile accomplishments outstripped the capacity for evaluation.

For five years after his marriage he believes in the image of himself that is reflected by his friends and which he unconsciously encourages, an image of himself as something very fine. When he and Rosemary, a young actress, meet on the beach at the Riviera, we have this as Rosemary's first impression (like Carraway's impression of Gatsby's "eternal reassurance"):

> He seemed kind and charming—his voice promised that he would take care of her, and that a little later he would open up whole new worlds for her, unroll an endless succession of magnificent possibilities.[26]

For some months Dick can convince himself that his life is still under control and that his love for Rosemary is a comfortable interlude in this life. His parties are an unconscious attempt to isolate his gathered friends and himself from conscience and clear realization:

> There were fireflies riding on the dark air and a dog baying on some low and far-away ledge of the cliff. The table seemed to have risen a little toward the sky like a mechanical dancing platform, giving the people around it a sense of being alone with each other in the dark universe, nourished by its only food, warmed by its only lights . . . And for a moment the faces turned up toward them [the Divers] were like the faces of poor children at a Christmas tree.[27]

This passage beautifully suggests that these people, not very likeable, who do not very easily rouse our sympathy, can be pitied, even loved, when they are stripped, as they are here, of their pretensions, when they have their lazy egoism taken from them; here they are shown as simply being spiritually undernourished and baffled by their own unhappiness; unconsciously they yearn for simplicity and cannot understand a transcendent experience which is not artificially created, or which simply arrives without their having bought or arranged it. Fitzgerald's deepest sensibility is revealed here, controlling his obsession.

Soon afterwards the group of which the Divers are the centre, go to Paris to see Abe North off at the Gare Saint Lazare:

> They stood in an uncomfortable little group weighted down by Abe's gigantic presence: he lay athwart them like the wreck of a galleon, dominating with his presence his own weakness and self-indulgence, his narrowness and bitterness. All of them were conscious of the solemn dignity that flowed from him, of his achievement, fragmentary, suggestive, and surpassed. But they were frightened at his survivant will, once a will to live, now become a will to die.[28]

This is judgment without harshness, pity without sentimentality. Fitzgerald manages to create with quiet, intelligent, sensitive sympathy, the unspoken bonds between people who know one another only fitfully, only in association with shared pleasures and boredom; suddenly the most ordinary, familiar person is transformed, and those for whom he is transformed, are themselves transformed. There is warm but helpless comradeship, a sense of deeper common humanity that comes, somehow, too late. In this passage, simultaneous with the new, unexpected respect for Abe, is a sharp, final perception and revaluation of his failure. He is stripped by his imminent departure, of the depersonalizing, flabby tolerance of holiday friendships, and becomes a man caught in his own, but also some other, inescapable reality. Through the others' intuitive perception of this, they see for themselves their own realities; their fear of his "survivant will" is the unexpected moment of insight into their own guilt. While the Diver group to which Abe had belonged, was intact, was kept together and amused, Abe's faults were less obvious and so was his "dignity", both of which qualities required, in order to be clearly sensed, this moment of isolation and perspective on the station, before his leaving the group; in the same way the hot afternoon when Carraway and Tom are at the McKees in *The Great Gatsby*, has suggestions of another perspective, another and deeper sense of humanity, so that as with Abe's "self-indulgence" and "narrowness", the severe judgment is not a dismissal nor is it moralizing in tone, but rather, it is made to refer us to the deeper sympathy in us which can only come from a suggestion of the universal, the divine or mysterious in all people. In this way Fitzgerald's obsession with success and failure is perfectly balanced by intelligence and artistry.

Dick realizes within a short time that, just as Abe had been able to pretend and indulge because of Dick's group, so Dick himself has not allowed himself to be clear-thinking and so, vulnerable. Quite suddenly, after Abe's departure, which coincides with a shooting on the station involving a lover's quarrel— Dick needs Rosemary; he is no longer sure of himself because he can no longer admire himself or believe in the admiration of his group. We have the following passage, a distinct 'movement' that marks the middle of the book:

> He knew that what he was doing marked a turning point in his life–it was out of line with everything that had preceded it, even out of line with what effect he might hope to produce upon Rosemary. Rosemary saw him always as a model of correctness–his presence walking around this block (to see her) was an intrusion. But Dick's necessity of behaving as he did was a projection of some submerged reality; he was compelled to walk there . . . his red hair cut exactly, his hand holding his small brief-case like a dandy–just as another man once found it necessary to stand in front of a church in Ferrara, in sackcloth and ashes. Dick was paying some tribute to things unforgotten, unshriven, unexpurgated.[29]

One is reminded of the allegory at the end of *The Great Gatsby*. Tribute is made there not only to Gatsby but to the universal passion or longing in all people, to their capacity for wonder and devotion. The early settlement of America or Gatsby's plans to relive the past, provide for this passion. In the above extract Dick's act of watching for Rosemary is the admission by him of his need to serve, to adhere to, of his need to need, to devote himself to, to long for and search for; it is an admission of his failure to sustain the idea of himself; he is not in the same circumstances as those "in front of a church in Ferrara", who matched their outward appearance with inner humility or abasement; but he is aware of how inappropriate his appearance is to his behaviour.

That he hungers for the "orgiastic future" as Gatsby did, a physical intensity that he fears is going to elude him is suggested by the following: Dick overhears a talk in which Rosemary is mentioned as having had a previous lover:

> The vividly pictured hand on Rosemary's cheek, the quicker breath, the white excitement of the event viewed from outside, the inviolable secret warmth within.[30]

So Dick breaks with the past, which had been really no more than a sterile orderliness, comfort and self-gratification; nothing had really disturbed his good opinion of himself; the immature longing for admiration had been perpetually satisfied.

From now on the story shows the continuous muddle in Dick's life; relations with Nicole and his friends become strained; he uses Nicole's money to start a sanatorium, but he is perpetually tipsy and has to give up the partnership; he tries to emulate the physical performances of his youth and, in view of everyone, fails to do (on a surfboard) what he once had managed with ease. He becomes involved in a sordid street fight; Nicole finds a lover and she and Dick separate; Dick returns to America and obscurity as a small-town doctor, still looking for the triumphs and admiration without which he cannot survive.

There is something relentless in the way Fitzgerald allows Dick to fail to come to terms with himself; he can only grow older and less distinguished although his charm, intelligence and sensitivity seem unchanged. When Gatsby senses the way in which he has been deluded, he is baffled and unsure of himself; soon afterwards he is dead and the theme of dream and devotion is left as something almost impersonal in the ending of the book. But *Tender is the Night* ends with the horror of dramatic irony; we see Dick and perceive his faults, yet we have a last glimpse of him going on and on in pursuit of an idea of himself. In the following passage, almost at the end of the book, Dick is with a new acquaintance. He is about to leave the Riviera, Nicole, the children, Rosemary. Yet he is completely absorbed by yet another involuntary urge to assert the unchanged idea of himself, a self that can only exist in such a moment as this:

> His eyes, for the moment clear as a child's, asked her sympathy and stealing over him he felt the old necessity of convincing her that he was the last man in the world and she was the last woman.[31]

On the last page of the book we still have Dick doing the same thing; in spite of our awareness of how far he has fallen, we are shown him as a being almost unconscious of this, or uncaring; whatever experience he survives, whether in his early years of courting Nicole, or in his later years back in America, the delusion persists and he cannot come to any new assessment of himself. This experience came, I think, in *The Crack-up*. Fitzgerald could not let himself drift on as he leaves Dick doing. Fitzgerald's personal life is not, taking the book as a whole, artistically transformed in *Tender is the Night*. Without some form of struggle, dramatic or internal, a character cannot really be given a satisfying dimension in literature.

I have not touched on other aspects of *Tender is the Night*. There is, for example, the theme of money, sapping the initiative of the characters; there is the suggestion of these people being uprooted from America; I have not mentioned the way in which Nicole's complete self-absorption and dependence on Dick, helps to prevent their love from developing further. But the basic thing in the book is Dick's self-delusion, his devotion to an idea of himself, an idea which was a compensation for unsatisfied needs. I should like now to compare Dick and Gatsby.

Gatsby, when he first met Daisy, had found the experience unforgettable, for Daisy embodied all the things he had longed for, all dependent on money and status. The brief courtship was a powerful, almost life-giving experience (sucking on the pap of life). To resurrect that experience became his single intention. He found that the experience could never be repeated, not only because he had exaggerated it in his memory and in his anticipation of its resurrection, but because he now possessed the money and status that had made Daisy seem to be a creature close to the gods; possession of Daisy was possession of all that Jay Gatz had wanted. We are left, therefore, with the emotion and concept of devotion and future attainment, as something in itself, no matter what the end is.

By comparison, Dick's delusion is more difficult to trace, for we are not shown him as ever having had actual burning ambitions to compensate for weakness or failure or poverty. There is one passage early in the book, during his courtship of Nicole, where we can sense the similarity to and the difference from Gatsby's courtship of Daisy:

> Dick wished she had no background, that she was just a girl lost with no address save the night from which she had come. They went to the cache where she had left the phonograph, turned a corner by the workshop, climbed a rock, and sat down behind a low wall, facing miles and miles of rolling night . . . The thin tunes, holding lost times and future hopes in liaison, twisted upon the Valais night. In the lulls of the phonograph a cricket held the scene together with a single note.[32]

One senses here that for Dick and for Fitzgerald this moment is charged with a mixture of the things that make a mood as close to happiness as is possible to achieve; the remoteness from the hum-drum world, the timelessness suggested by the "miles and miles"; the memory of the past merged into the suggestion of future ecstasy in the growing, present love of a man and a woman. Both future and past are here in a specially enriching way, so that their connection with a wider present, suggested by the cricket, is mechanical, an accidental reminder of a wider, self-diminishing relationship of things. For Dick the moment is magical and tantalizing, as Daisy and the intense present of being with her, was for Gatsby. A difference is, of course, the relative absence in Dick's case, of the dual interest that Daisy gave to Gatsby—her beauty and her way of life created by wealth. The intensity of Dick's experience in the above quotation comes from the same kind of longing; it is not the approaching fulfillment of a life's ambition—to be rich, as in Gatsby's case—but, instead, a longing to belong to a moment of preconceived romanticism, involving something that Nicole represents and helps to create. Neither Nicole nor Daisy are given any depth of personality by Fitzgerald; they appear to be subservient to the mood of intense peace of which Gatsby and Dick make them no more than essential parts. They emerge, somehow, as creatures who are expected to serve the romantic dreams of their lovers, and are therefore not quite full-blooded. In this consideration Fitzgerald's obsession, the limits of his personality, prevent him from creating a wider universality of characters who have depth and who are different from the main character, the successful artistic projection of Fitzgerald himself.

In a way Dick is like the Americans he watches arrive in Paris:

> So the well-to-do Americans poured through the station on to the platforms with frank new faces, intelligent, considerate, thoughtless, thought-for.[33]

We are told also:

> A part of Dick's mind was made up of the tawdry souvenirs of his boyhood . . .[34] the cloudy waters of unfamiliar ports, the lost girl on shore, the moon of popular songs.[35]

He was brought up:

> amid the starchy must of Sunday clothes. He listened to the wisdom of the Near East, was Crucified, Died, and was Buried in the cheerful church . . .[36]

He is still a child in many ways, and we sense how he himself feels about being away from America and home, and how his mind, in which he always "managed to keep alive the low painful fire of intelligence,"[37] perceives its home in a way that chills his feelings. Dick is in a cablecar in Switzerland, above Geneva:

> On the centre of the lake, cooled by the piercing current of the Rhone, lay the true centre of the Western world. Upon it floated swans like boats and boats like swans, both lost in the nothingness of the heartless beauty.[38]

Neither Dick Diver nor Gatsby came to terms with the imbalance in their respective natures; Gatsby is killed before he can try, and Dick does not try. *The Great Gatsby* is rounded off effectively as far as the plot is concerned; *Tender is the Night*, a much longer book, seems to run dry, to exhaust itself as Dick loses his hold on things, the feeling of dissatisfaction from the book is perhaps because the writer seems unaware of the spinelessness of Dick's character and the monotony of his slow decline. He is completely identified with Dick, with "the object . . . of his compassion" (*The Crack-up*).

In both books the tenderness and judgment run side by side; the tenderness is Fitzgerald's personal obsession with the quality of wonder and longing; the judgment is his common sense, his artistic distance. That the balance between the two qualities could not indefinitely continue in Fitzgerald's own life, is shown in *The Crack-up*. The artistic result of the struggle with himself, is revealed in *The Last Tycoon*, fragmentary as it is.

The scenes of *The Great Gatsby* and *Tender is the Night* are usually permeated with bought glamour and a kind of immunity from both the dreariness and virtues of humdrum, average-income living. *The Last Tycoon* is set in the glamour of Hollywood, and concerns those whose lives are intimately connected with film-making; but there is no suggestion that Fitzgerald has any delusions or even romanticism about the industry. Stahr, the main character, is not a dreamer:

> Like many brilliant men, he had grown up dead cold. Beginning at about twelve, probably, with the total rejection common to those of extraordinary mental powers, the "See here: this is all wrong—a mess—all a lie—and a sham—", he swept it all away, everything, as men of his type do; and then instead of being a son-of-a-bitch as most of them are, he looked around at the barrenness that was left and said to himself, "*This* will never do." And so he had learned tolerance, kindness, forbearance, and even affection like lessons.[39]

The phrase "like lessons" suggests the difficulty in maintaining these qualities; it suggests, I feel, the further stage in Fitzgerald's development since his 'crack-up'—his realization that he had reacted too far. The "tolerance" and "kindness" suggests his effort to go out to people again. But Stahr, who seems to embody these qualities in a passive way, is immensely weary and dying of overwork; the overwork appears to be a desperate effort to keep a hold on and an interest in life, which in turn, suggests great disillusionment. We know that Stahr, like Fitzgerald, has lost his wife and that it hurts him to remember her; we know that his kind of work entails unremitting alertness to people and that, to a considerable extent, he believes in his work, likes it, likes his authority and the kind of creativity he is able to express. But he does not have the gentle disenchantment or the romantic hopefulness of Gatsby and Dick Diver. He is harder, yet kinder, more constructive, more sensible.

His love for Kathleen is a weary reliving of things done and valued before. His disappointment in her is subdued by the great amount of experience, working, loving and suffering, that he has had; little can really disturb him or make him enthusiastic.

So we are faced with another Fitzgerald character who, while he is creative and hard-working, is unable and unwilling to change from one way of feeling, thinking, to another, to balance his compulsion to die from exhaustion:

> Fatigue was a drug as well as a poison, and Stahr apparently derived some rare almost physical pleasure from working light-headed with weariness.[40]

There is no suggestion in the love of Stahr and Kathleen of that extreme intensity of feeling which Gatsby and Dick Diver felt when near to the possession of a woman. Kathleen does not embody wealth or status; (although the notes tell us, Stahr could not have married Kathleen because she was without "the grandeur Stahr demands of life"). But essentially one has no clear idea of what Stahr wants in life—of what could possibly bring him peace of mind and relaxation. One passage in the book suggests that Stahr could not communicate in any deep and lasting way with anyone or anything. He and Kathleen have recently met, and after a friendly day together they interrupt the drive back to have a meal in a roadside drugstore. There has been no gesture or word of love: the situation is as in the quotations from *The Great Gatsby* and *Tender is the Night*, when Gatsby and Dick Diver respectively have an intense sense of the past and future before they come to possess their respective loves. But for Stahr there is already a sense of the inability of either himself or Kathleen to maintain for very long the sense of peace that the day has given them:

> They sat on high stools and had tomato broth and hot sandwiches. It was more intimate than anything they had done, and they both felt a dangerous sort of loneliness, and felt it in each other. They shared in various scents of the drug-store, bitter and sweet and sour, and the mystery of the waitress, with only the outer part of her hair dyed and black beneath, and when it was over, the still life of their empty plates—a sliver of potato, a sliced pickle, and an olive stone.[41]

This, to me, is one of the best paragraphs Fitzgerald wrote. It suggests the essence of Fitzgerald after his 'crack-up'. There is the intensely vivid sense of the world around him, the concrete world of smell and colour. There is the sensitive but unsentimental awareness of people in the way in which even the brief appearance of one person modifies, in some way, one's mood or belief; the smells of the drug-store are the smells of life, "bitter and sweet and sour"; the waitress's dyed hair is the more conspicuous aspect of the human struggle to survive; it is a crude disguise of a deep urge that is part of her and everyone's "mystery", and Stahr senses vaguely that his own forms of disguise are, though less obvious, just as desperate, and his very act of being with Kathleen is in itself a disguise of his deepest being, proclaiming his unwillingness to come to terms wth that being. The "loneliness" is "dangerous" because Stahr and Kathleen seem to expect so much of each other—they are using each other as a temporary shield, which, they both sense, will crumble if they get any more intimate, any more dependent, any more demanding, and so, any more burdensome to each other. After the shared experience of a meal, they become intensely aware of external objects; these objects are clearly separate from Stahr and Kathleen, either as single individuals or as a partnership against the world of loneliness. The deliberate way in which the potato and pickle are in themselves fragmented ("sliver", "sliced"), emphasizes the degree to which the external world is as we care to make or unmake it, to use or abuse it; the last sentence ends emphatically with "stone", the hard core of an eaten olive. The three objects are faintly mocking; they are the relics of the expression of an easy form of human power and action, and seem to suggest that the humans who have so finished with them, are themselves fragmented, cut off, and unable to find the hard core of their more vulnerable forms of life.

The book's further development has been suggested by the notes which Fitzgerald left. The cinema-industry is posed as Stahr's real enemy, since it demands more debased films than he is prepared to make; but, during the struggle, Stahr realizes that he is his own enemy; he resorts to the same kind of methods as his opponents–murder and gangsterism, but just before a murder, which he arranges, is to take place, "he realises that he has let himself be degraded to the same plane of brutality as Brady."[42]

But though Stahr intends to prevent the murder, his plane crashes and he is killed. Once again therefore, Fitzgerald does not permit his central character to struggle for very long–Gatsby dies with his delusion, Dick Diver does not struggle–Stahr, who, we have been told, had gone through moral crises, is not permitted to feel the consequences of the phrase "*has left himself*"; i.e. that he is really his own enemy. The funeral was to have been described as something scarcely connected with him at all; it is a publicity stunt. In the rootless, heartless film-world, Stahr, no longer alive and useful or active as an opponent, is no more than the olive stone he laid bare; but he is really the victim of himself; from the little that was written and from the notes, one can see that Stahr was not going to dominate the book as the Fitzgerald projection does in other books. A great deal of concrete authenticity is provided and we see the inner workings of the film-industry; there is greater variety of characters, each more fully treated than lesser figures in the earlier novels. Although Stahr reflects Fitzgerald's world-weariness, his excess of experience, his essential creativity, this book has a quality of universality that is superior to the partial universality in the earlier books. Disenchantment and judgment, side by side, so wonderfully controlled in the earlier books, changes to detachment, a wider sense of the 'world', a sense of variety in character and situation. The notes and one's imagination lead to the feeling that, if it had been completed, the story, the overall structure, the array of characters and relationships, the authentic handling of the inner workings of the film-industry, would have given us a book in which Stahr is more in contrast to, or given more significant links with, the entire book, than the main characters of the earlier novels.

In his recent book on Fitzgerald, Turnbull writes:

> But *The Crack-up* was also the work of a lapsed Catholic, for whom confession was a rhythm of the soul. The Church had a stronger hold on Fitzgerald than he perhaps realised or would have admitted.[43]

This religious element gives to Fitzgerald's works their vividness, intensity and immediacy; by 'religious' I mean an acceptance of the basic impulses that give life both its beauty and its horror. By evoking with equal force these two qualities Fitzgerald allows us to participate in certain absolute states of being, in adoration, yearning, regret, or in the futile ugliness of self-seeking. In all Fitzgerald's writing we sense the characters as being part of something more powerful than themselves whether this be an idea of themselves (Dick), an obsessional striving (Gatsby), or a creative integrity (Stahr); the sense of the characters being tragic victims as well as fools, romantics or defeatists, is enhanced and made significant by a continual reference in the stories to absolute, enduring facts, namely physical beauty, youth and decay, the transient moods of cities, gardens, mountains, and, perhaps above all, the sensitive intelligence that modifies as it evokes situations, giving an unobtrusive moral value with an overall grace and humility.

Notes

1. *The Bodley Head Scott Fitzgerald*, Vol. I, 'The Great Gatsby' (London, Bodley Head, 1960), p.162.

2. Ibid., p.125.

2.a. Ibid., p.125.

3. Ibid., p.129.

4. Ibid., pp.131–2.

5. Ibid., p.210.

6. Ibid., p.267.

7. Ibid., pp.170–1.

8. Ibid., p.142.

9. Ibid., p.148.

Great Gatsby, Tender is the Night, Last Tycoon

10. Ibid., p.151.
11. Ibid., p.142.
12. Ibid., p.152.
13. Ibid., p.211.
14. Ibid., p.156.
15. Ibid., p.161.
16. Ibid., p.243.
17. Ibid., pp.212–3.
18. Ibid., p.197.
19. Ibid., p.197.
20. Ibid., p.228.
21. Ibid., p.224.
22. Ibid., p.252.
23. Ibid., pp.268–9.
24. Ibid., 'The Crack-up', p.285.
25. Ibid., pp.288–9.
26. *Tender is the Night* (London, Penguin, 1960), p.83.
27. Ibid., p.101.
28. Ibid., p.151.
29. Ibid., p.160.
30. Ibid., p.157.
31. Ibid., p.333.
32. Ibid., p.41.
33. Ibid., p.152.
34. Ibid., p.216.
35. Ibid., pp.215–6.
36. Ibid., p.215.
37. Ibid., p.216.
38. Ibid., p.53.
39. *The Last Tycoon* (London, Penguin, 1962), p.117.
40. Ibid., p.131.
41. Ibid., p.103.
42. Ibid., pp.158–9.
43. Andrew Turnbull, *Scott Fitzgerald* (London, Bodley Head, 1962).

3. The Moralism of the Later Fitzgerald

by KENT & GRETCHEN KREUTER

When F. Scott Fitzgerald died in 1940, he left among his papers some notes for the novel he had not yet finished, *The Last Tycoon.* One scene that he had roughed out concerned the effect upon three young people of their discovery of jewels, fine leather, and other evidences of wealth in the wreckage of a crashed airplane. "Give the impression," Fitzgerald wrote to himself, "that Jim is all right,—that Frances is faintly corrupted . . . and that Dan has been completely corrupted and will spend the rest of his life looking for a chance to get something for nothing. I cannot be too careful not to rub this in or to give it the substance or feeling of a moral tale."[1]

No critical discussion of Fitzgerald's work can long ignore his attitudes toward wealth and its effect upon different people. A deep concern with money and the things a great deal of it can buy is clearly evident in the lines above. Yet there is another and more important implication in them—the fear Fitzgerald had that he should seem to be moralizing. This was not the only occasion on which he recognized such a tendency in himself. In a letter to his daughter he once confessed that he had turned away from a career as a writer of musical comedy because, "I am too much of a moralist at heart, and really want to preach at people in some accceptable form rather than to entertain them."[2] And in an essay written in 1933 he alluded briefly to his "New England conscience developed in Minnesota."[3]

The New England conscience did not dominate the work Fitzgerald produced in the twenties. Although his characters were frequently confronted with moral issues, the author was more interested in chronicling the delights and the decadence of the twenties than in coming to grips with the moral problems they raised.

By the early thirties, however, a series of personal misfortunes brought moral issues to the center of his thought and made it necessary for him to develop ways of dealing with them. His misfortunes have been frequently related: his wife was mentally ill and was at length confined permanently to a sanitarium. He himself was plagued with alcoholism—the party was over but the hangover seemed permanent. He was disappointed with his writing. None of it brought him the financial rewards he had anticipated and he was constantly in debt. He seemed in the thirties to be suffering the consequences of a misspent youth, and he experienced a growing sense of guilt and a need to pass some sort of moral judgment upon himself and the decade that had come to such an abrupt climax in 1929.

In the writing he did during the last ten years of his life, three elements connected with this need constantly recur. First there is the idea of failure and non-fulfillment that appears conspicuously in most of his short stories, in *Tender is the Night*, and in "The Crack-Up." Second, there is the concern with the morality of wealth, most evident in *Tender is the Night*. Finally, and most important, there is the problem of individual moral responsibility. Though this last is the landscape for nearly all of Fitzgerald's later work, it is most succinctly revealed in the climax he had outlined for *The Last Tycoon*.

An examination of these three ideas in the fictional contexts in which they appeared reveals a great deal not only about the quality of Fitzgerald's moral perceptions, but about his effectiveness as a literary artist as well.

Kent and Gretchen Kreuter

The Hyperbole of Failure

In at least four of Fitzgerald's later short stories his feelings of both guilt and failure become abundantly clear. Each of the four —"Three Hours Between Planes," "The Long Way Out," "The Lost Decade," and "Babylon Revisited"—is a hyperbolic treatment of the author's sense of non-fulfillment and of remorse about the immediate circumstances of his own life.

"Three Hours Between Planes" is the story of Donald Plant, who pays a visit to a childhood sweetheart, exchanges confidences and kisses with her, and then discovers she has mistaken him for someone else. The success he had felt at recapturing the past and molding it to the image he had desired—the girl had cared little for him when they were both young—dissolves. Plant has failed, but not through any fault of his own. "The second half of life is a long process of getting rid of things,"[4] says Fitzgerald through Donald Plant, and the attempt to relive an earlier age in terms of later knowledge is impossible.

The author himself was attempting to get rid of a number of things and was having little success in doing so. Faced with the personal consequences of the twenties, he seemed unable to throw them off. He was still an alcoholic, still dissatisfied with his writing, still in debt. Most important, in terms of this story, he still had within him the image of his wife Zelda as she had been in the first years he knew her. He felt he had to extirpate this image and accept the fact that she would not recover from her illness.

"The Long Way Out" has a similar emphasis upon the idea of failure or lack of fulfillment, and again the protagonist is not directly responsible for the outcome. Mrs. King, a victim of schizophrenia, is sufficiently improved to be granted a few days' leave from the sanitarium to be with her husband. Mr. King however, is killed in an automobile accident and never arrives to meet her. When she is told of his death, she has a serious relapse, refuses to believe the news, and each day thereafter waits patiently and mindlessly for him to arrive.

The parallels with Zelda are obvious. Arthur Mizener, commenting upon Fitzgerald's attitude toward his wife's illness, remarks,

> Despite the doctors' assurances that Zelda's trouble went back a long way, and that nothing he could have done would have prevented it, Fitzgerald had a deep feeling of guilt about it. He knew how much he was to blame for the irregularity of their lives; he knew what he had contributed to that 'complete and never renewed break of confidence' which had occurred in Paris in 1929. . . .[5]

In these two stories the element of guilt is suggested not by the failure of the characters concerned, but rather by the author's choice of subject matter. This is somewhat true also of "The Lost Decade." Here, however, the hyperbole becomes more extravagant. Louis Trimble, an architect, is shown around New York by the point-of-view character who has the impression that Trimble has been away from the city for ten years. The latter learns finally that the architect has simply been drunk for a decade.

The sense of failure is overwhelming. The reader does not learn why this has happened to Trimble; he learns only that a promising and talented man has wasted years of his life. Again the personal parallel is clear. Mizener suggests that Trimble is intended as a personification of the lost generation of the twenties. It is more likely that Trimble represents the colossal dissipation that Fitzgerald had come to believe himself guilty of. The author's desire to dissociate the major character from any strict identification with the twenties is seen in the fact that the architect's great drunk didn't begin until that decade was nearly over. It began, in fact, just about the time of the "break of confidence" that occurred between Zelda and Scott Fitzgerald.

"Babylon Revisited" is the best of these four stories, and it deals not only with personal frustration and failure, but with the problems of money, liquor, and moral responsibility as well. Charlie Wales, a reformed pleasure-seeker, returns to Paris, hoping that his sister-in-law Marian will give him the custody of Honoria, his little daughter. Marian cannot forget, however, that Charlie had, in a drunken stupor, contributed to his wife's death by locking her out in the snow. When some carousing friends of Charlie's appear on the scene and begin to reminisce about the good old days, her mind is made up, and she refuses to permit him to take his daughter away with him.

Fitzgerald frankly admitted the personal nature of this story. In a letter to his daughter he told her that she was a character in "Babylon Revisited." What he felt had been the irresponsible treatment of his wife he expressed in terms of a situation that led to her death. His inability to fulfill what he thought were the responsibilities of fatherhood he described in terms of a parent who was believed a menace to the welfare of his child.

When Charlie Wales sees Paris again, he is moved to make some sort of moral judgment upon his actions of several years before. "He suddenly realized," Fitzgerald writes, "the meaning of the word 'dissipate'—to dissipate into thin air; to make nothing out of something. In the little hours of the night every move from place to place was an enormous human jump, an increase of paying for the privilege of slower and slower motion."[6] Thinking of what he had done to his wife, Wales concludes that in those days of waste men "locked their wives out in the snow, because the snow of twenty-nine wasn't real snow. If you didn't want it to be snow, you just paid some money"(p.402). The suffering that Wales has undergone as punishment for his past sins is made eminently clear. He believes that he had once arrived at a "condition of utter irresponsibility"(p.398), and he admits his culpability in the events that occurred because of it.

Yet Fitzgerald seems to have believed that Charlie's punishment was not proportionate to his crime. Honoria, symbol of the esteem and respect that Wales has now rightfully earned, is not given to her father for reasons that have nothing to do with what he is or does at the time. She remains with her aunt partly because Marian, with her own family in straitened circumstances, spitefully resents Charlie's financial success. Moreover, the appearance of the old friends, which confirms Marian's resentment, is something Charlie is powerless to avert. He has done everything possible to regain his lost honor, but in the end his actions are irrelevant, for it is the acts of others that finally decide the outcome.

Wales, like Scott Fitzgerald in his own life, makes no searching examination and offers no convincing explanation of the reasons for his previous misdeeds. Charlie seems to have emerged from the experience with only a feeling of guilt, a slight sense of outrage at his cruel and unusual punishment, and an understanding of the meaning of dissipation. The very fact that Fitzgerald continued to be enmeshed in the same problems he had had in the twenties is partial proof that he had not discovered why they had happened.

It was all very well to attribute the lunacies of the twenties to the war, or to too much money, or to immaturity, but for some people—Fitzgerald among them—these were not reasons but rationalizations. Unable to go further than this, the author could not give such a dimension to the character of Charlie Wales. Instead, he took refuge in a determinism that was as much a characteristic of the "New England conscience" as the guilt and remorse that plagued them both.

The Case History

A fatalistic determinism likewise marks the only novel Fitzgerald completed after 1929, *Tender is the Night*. If the short stories just discussed represent a hyperbolic treatment of some of the circumstances of Fitzgerald's own life, the novel traces the moral decline and fall of practically everyone. The men and women that inhabit the novel are no longer the daring, fun-loving throng of the author's earliest vision of the twenties. They are unsavory couples with dissolving marriages, Americans dying in barroom brawls, and decadent nobles with homosexual sons, The moral themes of the novel are the same as those in the short stories, and the resolution of moral issues is handled in the same way.

The central figure of *Tender is the Night* is Dick Diver, a psychiatrist who, one can't help noticing, is singularly unable to diagnose his own psychic ills. The book charts Diver's course downward from professional promise and personal happiness to utter obscurity and moral decay. The reader's last glimpses of

Diver find him moving to smaller and smaller towns in upstate New York; rumor has it that his last move was occasioned by an unpleasant affair he had with one of his patients.

A great deal has been written about the incest motif that dominates the book. Diver, it has been observed, is sapped of his strength because he is forced to become the father-figure first to Nicole Warren, the woman he marries, then to Rosemary Hoyt, Hollywood star of "Daddy's Girl," and finally to the whole group of immature, inebriated Americans that frequent the Riviera after the First World War. As a device for indicating both the decadence and the infantilism of the twenties this is highly successful. If the novel did nothing more than evoke a mood, critical discussion could stop with revealing the Oedipal relationships within it.

Such is not the case, however. Dr. Diver is perhaps the most appealing personality Fitzgerald ever created, and one cannot view him as merely one more indistinguishable face in the crowd or regard his fate with indifference. One wants to know why Diver meets his doom, why he has succumbed to the kinds of demands that his friends place upon him, and, above all, how this has happened to a man who knows himself as well as a man in Diver's profession must. The answers, of course, lie partly in the nature of the time Diver is living in. His self-knowledge was attained before the war and hence, to Fitzgerald, in another era; it is no longer adequate in the face of new needs. One of those new needs is a way of coping with the prosperity that came with the twenties. The problem as it is defined in *Tender is the Night* and as it is faced by Dick Diver is essentially a moral one.

It is Nicole, first Diver's patient and then his wife, who brings about his confrontation with great wealth and who is the agent of his decline. Her fortune is ever swelling, and as news of its increase is brought, throughout the novel, by one character or another, one comes to feel that money is the dynamic, inexorable force that drives Diver downward. He, like Charlie Wales, has no power over these matters. Not only does he lack the strength to give his life a purpose in the face of such wealth, but he is also unable to free himself from its enervating effects after Nicole has left him.

Fitzgerald has provided Wales with a will but deprived him of the chance to make it effective. Diver, on the other hand, acts as though he had been created without any will at all. Consequently it is virtually impossible to make any sort of moral evaluation of Diver's actions. He has been destroyed by forces he could neither control nor even fully understand, and the moral judgment he had once possessed was of no use.

The fate of Dick Diver furnishes another insight into Fitzgerald's later moralism and the nature of his contrition for past sins. To him it was believable that a man should lose his zest for work, his desire to make any contribution to society, if the profit motive is removed. And without work a man's character crumbles. This begins to sound remarkably like the Protestant ethic. If profit is, then, to some extent the measure of virtue, the fact that Fitzgerald's writing didn't sell served to aggravate the frustrations of his other personal adversities. It increased his sense of guilt without increasing his understanding.

The Confessional

In 1936 three essays by Fitzgerald—"The Crack Up," "Pasting it Together," and "Handle With Care"—appeared in *Esquire* magazine. In them the author described in directly personal terms the kind of decay that was the theme of his fictional account of Dick Diver. He wrote that he was ruined, that he had bankrupted his talent and his emotions, and that his search for some way out of the chaos was in vain. Of Catholic family and upbringing, Fitzgerald seemed to have resorted to the public prints as an instrument of confession and purgation.

But the confession was too facile. It was overlaid with the same shell of mild cynicism that marked so much of the writing he did in the twenties. It never really confronted the central issues that lurked behind the hard and glittering descriptions of his mental state. Instead, it is distinguished chiefly as an example of the way a man of no mean literary ability could unfeelingly describe his own feelings.

The reason for the tone and temper of the essays is easy to guess. Fitzgerald was very close to the events he was describing.

Always fearful of moralizing, he used the quality of cynicism in his talent to win a public for what would otherwise have seemed to be mere whining or preaching. It is a technique at least as old as Swift. Fitzgerald could achieve the benefits of confession, a momentary release from a sense of guilt, without turning his audience into a kind of collective priest.

He did, however, make one observation that is extremely revealing. "The test of a first-rate intelligence," he wrote, "is the ability to hold two opposed ideas in the mind at the same time, and still retain the ability to function. One should, for example, be able to see that things are hopeless and yet determined to make them otherwise."[7] This may appear to be merely a rationalization for things one can neither dismiss nor understand. But in Fitzgerald's case it is more than that. It is a precise statement of what he himself was doing—keeping within his mind several antithetical attitudes that muddied his moral vision. The kind of opposites that found expression in "The Crack Up," in his later short stories, and in *Tender is the Night*, emphasized the contrast between excessive guilt and excessive punishment, between failure and innocence.

Donald Plant and Mr. King couldn't help it that they were unable to fulfill the expectations of the women they loved. Charlie Wales, lost in a generation of the lost, came to responsibility too late, and though abounding in contrition and virtue was forced to continue his punishment. Surely even Henry IV would have felt a second trip to Canossa unjust! Dick Diver, imprisoned in wealth and a world of people made useless by wealth, likewise failed to live up to his early promise. His decline was as inevitable as it was innocent.

There is another factor too that serves to lighten the burden of responsibility upon Fitzgerald's shoulders and on the various fictionalized representations of him. Either the instrument of temptation or the initiating cause of failure is, in almost every case, a woman. For Diver it was Nicole's money; for Plant it was his old sweetheart's poor memory; for Charlie Wales it was a still-carousing woman from the past and a Puritanical sister-in-law. There are, of course, women in these stories who meet with disaster, but more often than not theirs is not moral or spiritual.

They merely bring about the failure of the men who love them.

Fitzgerald's own world was crumbling, and he was willing to admit that a large measure of responsibility was his. But apparently admission was not enough, for he continued to be plagued with increasing evidences of sin. It was the conflict between his own sense of justice and that which seemed to be imposed upon him from outside that helped produce "The Crack Up." In attempting to lighten the oppressive weight of what seemed to be evil of his own creation, he employed both cynicism and an almost unconscious blame of others.

The Past As Prologue

The fragment of a novel that Fitzgerald left at his death is in some ways anticlimactic. It seems almost as though the author had effectively passed judgment upon his life and work in "The Crack Up," and might have been spared the effort of a literary second coming. A casual glance at *The Last Tycoon* seems to indicate that he had, indeed, broken sharply with his earlier writing and had chosen a new and very different subject.

Yet the difference is more apparent than real. It is obviously the work of the same man, no longer preoccupied with the sparkle and then the tarnish of the twenties, but still grappling with the same kinds of problems. The setting is Hollywood; the tycoon of the title is Monroe Stahr, a young and highly talented motion picture director. It is in Stahr that the reader sees the residue Fitzgerald thought he himself had been left with after the close of the postwar decade. Though he is only in his thirties, Stahr is destined for an early death. The tycoon's doctor shakes his head dolefully after each examination and sees in his patient an urge toward total exhaustion, "a perversion of the life force . . ."[8]

This is not intended to be a novel of new beginnings or of a new point of view. Though social and economic matters intrude themselves more frequently in *The Last Tycoon* than in other of Fitzgerald's novels—problems of labor unions and depression wages, for example—the personal and moral issues remain uppermost. Perhaps it could not have been otherwise. The difficulties that the author had first faced in the twenties were not yet solved, and he was ever aware of the weight of the past. In *The Last Tycoon* this legacy is symbolized by the fact that Monroe Stahr falls in love with a woman to whom he was first attracted because she resembled his dead wife. Neither he nor Fitzgerald had broken with the past.

The world had moved on but the novelist had not. His last sizeable work was permeated with a feeling of decline and decay that hung over all its characters. It is no coincidence that Kathleen, the woman Stahr loves, should have once lived with a man whose chief interest seemed to be that she read Spengler: "Everything was for that," she tells Stahr. "All the history and philosophy and harmony was all so I could read Spengler, and I left him before we got to Spengler. At the end I think that was the chief reason he didn't want me to go." (p.91)

Then there is Cecilia, the narrator of the story, who is afflicted with tuberculosis, a disease that combines an outward appearance of health with inward decay. Finally, of course, there is the title of the novel itself. Stahr is the last of a line, not one of the new heroes of the thirties, and he is destined for early extinction. Alongside this theme of decay and futility is the central moral problem of the novel's climax. Both in the manner in which the issue is created and in which it is resolved, there are echoed the same concepts of guilt and responsibility that marked the rest of Fitzgerald's work in the 1930's.

Only the outline of the last half of *The Last Tycoon* was ever written. In it the following situation is developed: Stahr, fearful of being murdered by his evil partner Brady, resorts to Brady's techniques and hires gangsters to kill him. Stahr then leaves for New York so as to be away from the scene when the murder is done. On the plane, however, he has a change of heart and a feeling of revulsion that he has thus descended to Brady's level. He resolves to wire the hired gunmen at the next airport and call the whole thing off. But the plane crashes, Stahr is killed, and the murder goes through. (pp.132–133)

The moral framework is almost identical to that of Fitzgerald's most moralistic tale, "Babylon Revisited." There is the descent into evil, for which Stahr is not entirely responsible, having been influenced by the bad example of his partner Brady and by the accessibility of the mobsters. There is the recognition of evil and the desire to halt its consequences, which is thwarted by circumstances beyond the control of the protagonist. The only moral difference between Stahr and Wales is that the former is not permitted to meditate over the consequences and the implications of what he has done. He is spared this by being handed the fate that Fitzgerald usually reserved for his women characters, escape through death or insanity.

To say all this is not to suggest that Stahr is only a type. Fitzgerald was too good a writer to have created a mannikin. Stahr is differentiated from almost anyone else who appears in his fiction. Most distinctive is the fact that Stahr knows himself more thoroughly than Dick Diver or Charlie Wales or Donald Plant or Louis Trimble knew themselves. He is aware of the extent and limitations of his mental, moral, and physical capacities. He is a somber figure who has accepted the burden of the past, and whose actions in the present are not crippled by it.

Yet it remains true that Fitzgerald came to his last work, so different in scenario and outward characterization from most of his other writing, with essentially the same moral concepts, the same ideas of guilt and responsibility that had long marked his writing.

More important than the nature of Fitzgerald's moralism, of course, is its quality. The most serious charge that must be leveled against him is that he never made a really searching inquiry into the sources of his moral ideas or of the reasons behind the situations that moved him to render moral judgment. His own specific references to his tendency to moralize were always oblique, as though he felt he should either get rid of this predilection or make light of it. Instead of trying to understand it, he tried to direct his reader's attention to something else. When this was no longer possible, he found himself in the midst of a tangle of sometimes adolescent, sometimes senile ways of coping with the moral issues raised in his fiction and in his life.

The absence of a mature, well-defined position of moral perception in a writer is important only if it damages the effectiveness of his writing. In Fitzgerald's case it is clear that his work was damaged, and seriously so. This deficiency kept him from realizing the brilliant potentialities of some of the characters he created. It meant that even the best of them must be only pathetic creatures lost in a world they never made, a world that was hopelessly bewildering.

Only in *The Last Tycoon* did Fitzgerald approach a more sophisticated treatment, and even there he left much to be desired. The moral outlook of Monroe Stahr was that of a latter-day Stoic, better able than Charlie Wales or Dick Diver to sustain the blow of fortune, but still not entirely the master of himself. For inherent in this brand of Stoicism is the abandonment of the effort to understand—one only accepts.

For Fitzgerald himself the absence of a clear moral vision meant that he continued to be torn by an ambivalence that thrust him back and forth between the two poles of guilt and innocence.

Notes

1. *The Last Tycoon*, ed. Edmund Wilson (New York: Charles Scribner's Sons, 1941), p.158.
2. *The Crack-up*, ed. Edmund Wilson (New York: New Directions, 1945), p.305.
3. *Afternoon of an Author*, with an introduction and notes by Arthur Mizener (Princeton: The Princeton University Library, 1957), p.134.
4. *The Stories of F. Scott Fitzgerald*, with an introduction by Malcolm Cowley (New York: Charles Scribner's Sons, 1951), p.69.
5. Arthur Mizener, *The Far Side of Paradise* (Boston: Houghton Mifflin Co., 1951), p.218.
6. Cowley, ed. *Stories*, p.389.
7. *The Crack-Up*, p.69.
8. *The Last Tycoon*, p.108.

4. *Tender Is the Night*

by RICHARD D. LEHAN

Fitzgerald dedicated *Tender Is the Night* to Gerald and Sara Murphy, and it is commonly known that Fitzgerald modelled Dick and Nicole Diver, in part, on the Murphys. Murphy, whose father was president of Mark Cross (the New York leather goods store), went to Yale, was in the top fraternity (DKE), a member of Skull and Bones, and an important man in the class of 1911.

In 1922 the Murphys went to Paris where they became friends of writers, artists, and diplomats. When Stravinsky's ballet "Les Noces" premiered in 1923, they gave a party on a barge tied up to a dock in the Seine, and included in the forty guests were Picasso, Darius Milhaud, Jean Cocteau, Ernst Ansermet, Diaghilev, Tristram Tzara, and Scofield Thayer (editor of the *Dial*).[1]

In the summer of 1923, Cole Porter invited the Murphys down to his rented chateau at Cap d'Antibes. After May first, the tourists left Antibes because it was too hot. The Murphys, however, fell in love with it. Gerald dug out a corner of the beach, convinced the owner of a small hotel to stay open with a skeleton staff, and stayed on for the summer.

Fitzgerald met the Murphys in Paris the next year, and it was inevitable that Murphy would impress Fitzgerald whose imagination could warm to his social elegance, easy manner, and heightened way of life. "When I like men," Fitzgerald once wrote, "I want to be like them—I want to lose the outer qualities that give me my individuality and be like them."[2] Fitzgerald acted upon such a desire when he made Dick Diver a composite of Gerald Murphy and himself.

As *Tender Is the Night* opens, Dick Diver is really Gerald Murphy at Cap d'Antibes, raking red seaweed from the beach, keeping his guests amused, and being the emotional nucleus of the group, the object of Rosemary Hoyt's admiring eyes. Fitzgerald partly modelled Gausse's hotel on the Hotel du Cap d'Antibes. The Villa Diana, where the Divers have their garden party, is a composite of a house owned by Samuel Barlow (an American composer) and the exotic garden of the Villa American, the house the Murphys built in a garden surrounded by orange, lemon, and cedar trees. Nicole at the beginning of the novel, her brown back "set off by a string of creamy pearls," is Sara Murphy who often wore pearls on the beach because she believed the sun was good for them.

A great many of Fitzgerald's experiences went into *Tender Is the Night*. In the winter of 1924, he fought, like Dick Diver, with a group of taxi drivers, punched a policeman in the fracas, and was severely beaten. Late one night on the Riviera, Fitzgerald, like Abe North, threatened to saw a waiter in half. Also, like Abe North, Fitzgerald had his wallet stolen in a Paris night club, accused the wrong Negro, and created an unpleasant scene.[3]

Fitzgerald also brought to the Riviera a number of people who had impressed him in America. Abe North, who prefigures Dick's decline, is based on Ring Lardner. Fitzgerald wrote Maxwell Perkins in January of 1933 that "I am [Ernest Hemingway's] alcoholic just like Ring is mine,"[4] and Lardner symbolized for Fitzgerald the man of genius who had dissipated his energy and wasted his talent. When Dick learns one day during his own decline that Abe has been killed—beaten to death in a speakeasy—"Dick's lungs burst for a moment with regret for Abe's death, and his own youth of ten years ago."[5]

Rosemary Hoyt is modelled on Lois Moran, the movie star, whom Fitzgerald met in 1927 when he was working for United Artists on a story for Constance Talmadge. George Jean Nathan described Lois in much the way Fitzgerald depicted her in *Tender Is the Night*: "She was a lovely kid of such tender years that it was rumored she still wore the kind of flannel nightie that was bound around her ankles with ribbons, and Scott never visited her save when her mother was present."[6]

The *Tender Is the Night* that Fitzgerald published in 1934 is a much different novel from the one he began writing in Juan-les-Pins in 1925. The novel was originally about matricide, based on a 1925 San Francisco murder in which a sixteen-year-old girl, Dorothy Ellingson, killed her mother who objected to her daughter's wild living.[7] Fitzgerald worked on this version from 1925 to 1929. He planned to take liberties with the Ellingson case, setting the novel on the Riviera where Francis Melarky, a young motion picture technician, was to murder his mother, Charlotte Melarky. This version went through four drafts and was variously entitled *Our Type*, *The Boy who Killed his Mother*, *The Melarky Case*, and *The World's Fair.*

Sara Murphy may have had Fitzgerald's title in mind when she said of that summer in Antibes: "It was like a great fair, and everybody was so young."[8] The *World's Fair* version, which has since been published,[9] reveals that Francis Melarky is modelled on Fitzgerald himself, and the Pipers (who later become the Divers) are modelled on the Murphys. Francis, in fact, is in love with Dinah Piper, who encourages him. As Arthur Mizener pointed out, the Pipers are depicted ambiguously—favorably from Francis' point of view, unfavorably from Abe Grant's (who becomes Abe North). As in *The Great Gatsby*, the narrator analyzes a magnetic character, and we again have the bifurcated point of view with two resulting emotions—admiration and cynicism—only here the emotions are those of two men rather than one.

In the finished version of *Tender Is the Night*, Fitzgerald fused Francis Melarky (Fitzgerald himself) with Seth Piper (Gerald Murphy). This way Fitzgerald became the man that he admired and lived the heightened life that so appealed to him. Fitzgerald, in other words, created a larger world in his early drafts of the novel, and then he invited himself into this world, fulfilling in his imagination what he could not fulfill in life. Fitzgerald, however, saw himself in double context—as both success and failure—and he fused to Seth Piper's charm Francis Melarky's destructive nature. Here Fitzgerald was again using the irony that he so brilliantly developed in *The Great Gatsby*; but instead of the irony being completely a matter of point of view, he made it a matter of characterization—the ambivalence being not in the way Dick Diver is *seen* but in the way he *acts*.

Also, in the early draft, the Pipers have a dinner party, then there is the duel, and finally Francis accompanies the Pipers to see Abe Grant off to America. In *Tender Is the Night*, Rosemary becomes Francis Melarky, attending the dinner party, watching the duel, and accompanying the Divers and Norths to Paris. Fitzgerald, in other words, allowed Rosemary to stand for himself. Rosemary, whose most famous movie was called *Daddy's Girl*, is the very spirit of youth and success. She symbolizes a state of being that both Abe North and Dick Diver have known and lost. Abe North, at one point in the novel, is "happy to live in the past. The drink made past happy things contemporary with the present, as if they were still going on, contemporary even with the future as if they were about to happen again" [103]. Rosemary is the personification of this feeling—just as Ginevra King must have been the personification of this feeling for Fitzgerald. Ginevra kept the "illusion perfect," Fitzgerald once wrote;[10] and in a Josephine story ("A Nice Quiet Place," written at a time when Fitzgerald was working on *Tender Is the Night*)[11] Josephine, who is modelled on Ginevra King, is at one point mysteriously called Rosemary, a mistake that neither Fitzgerald nor his editor caught when the story was included in *Taps at Reveille*.[12]

Rosemary gives excitement to life, keeps the world alive, the bloom on the rose. Her beauty is something inviolable, something to be longed after. Fitzgerald could not live without this double focus—back toward the glory that was, forward toward the promise that might be, although the future seemed bleak in *Tender Is the Night*. If Dick Diver represents what Fitzgerald thought that he might *become*, Rosemary represents the spirit of what he once *was*. At the beginning of the novel, Dick feels that he holds Rosemary in trust, that he must guard her like a father protects a child [cf.21]. At the end, as his decline becomes more serious, he seduces her. The seduction stands in contrast to an earlier scene, one that took place at the height of Dick's career, when Rosemary asks Dick to be her lover and he refuses. When he gives in, Dick loses his sense of wonder, he loses a point of view—a way of looking at life—just as Gatsby loses a point of view when he loses Daisy. Fitzgerald associated the theme of wasted youth and of failure in *Tender Is the Night* with child seduction. At his lowest ebb, under arrest in Rome, Dick says, " 'I want to make a speech . . . I want to explain to these people how I raped a five-year-old girl' "[235]. When Dick seduces Rosemary, he betrays a trust, just as Dick Diver and Fitzgerald himself believed that they had betrayed their own youthful talent, were reckless with time's promises, and taken too many wrong paths. Fitzgerald once wrote to his own daughter, "What little I've accomplished has been by the most laborious and uphill work, and I wish now I'd *never* relaxed or looked back —but said at the end of *The Great Gatsby* 'I've found my line —from now on this comes first. This is my immediate duty—without this I am nothing.' "[13]

Fitzgerald did not begin the Dick Diver version of the novel until after Zelda's breakdown in April of 1930. Certainly Fitzgerald felt that his marriage to Zelda had taken its toll on his energy. He wrote to his daughter in 1938 that when he was young he "lived with a great dream." Zelda hindered his ambitions because she wanted him "to work too much for *her* and not enough for my dream." Zelda "was spoiled," Fitzgerald said, "and meant no good to me." When Zelda broke, Fitzgerald continues: "It was too late also for me to recoup the damage. I had spent most of my resources, spiritual and material, on her, but I struggled on for five years till my health collapsed, and all I cared about was drink and forgetting."[14]

Fitzgerald obviously brought this motion to *Tender Is the Night*, making Nicole into the spirit of Zelda, who drains Dick Diver of strength and energy. This is also what Fitzgerald must have had in mind when he wrote Edmund Wilson that he thought of Dick Diver as an "homme épuisé."[15]

Fitzgerald, however, complicated his own relationship with Zelda by making Dick the victim of the very rich. Here we are back with a Gatsby theme—in fact, the Warrens, like the Buchanans, are a wealthy Chicago family. Fitzgerald was once again venting his rage at people like Charles King and his family—or so the evidence suggests. At one point in the first edition of *Tender Is the Night*, Fitzgerald names Nicole's father Devereux Warren [166] and at another point he calls him Charles [320]. Bruccoli quotes a young writer, Charles Marquis Warren, who believed that Fitzgerald was using his name "as a friendly gesture." How one can so interpret being named after Nicole's father—a liar, a coward, a man guilty of incest—is difficult to understand. A more likely interpretation is that Charles (Devereux) Warren is a cruel distortion of Charles King—a fantasy projection of Fitzgerald's hurt feelings and his lively imagination. In this connection, it is interesting that Fitzgerald, in an early draft, named one of Dick's children Ginevra—and that he makes, in the final version, Tommy Barban, an unsympathetic character, a broker as well as a soldier of fortune [cf.274]. The invention of Baby Warren may be purely mechanical (she develops out of Charlotte Melarky, Francis' mother). Fitzgerald needed somebody to embody the ruthless spirit of the very rich, get the upper hand of Dick, reject him once he served his purpose. And yet she reveals Fitzgerald's attitude toward the rich, embodies his bitterness. "I have never been able to forgive the rich for being rich," Fitzgerald once wrote, "and it has colored my entire life and works."[16] Fitzgerald also said that he took things hard, specifying his loss of Ginevra.[17] This particular incident in his life seems most responsible for his attitude toward the very rich, most responsible for the unsympathetic Chicago families of wealth that appear in his best fiction.

If Fitzgerald took Zelda's sickness as a starting point and coupled the drain of this illness upon him with his feelings toward the very rich, he did not make Dick Diver merely the victim of Nicole and her wealthy family. Dick is complicit in his decline. He is the "spoiled priest" as Fitzgerald refers to him in his plans for the novel. One of the most astute critics of this novel, Matthew Bruccoli, believes the two views of Dick—the "homme épuisé" and the "spoiled priest"—are somewhat contradictory, but this is because he misreads what Fitzgerald means by "spoiled priest" and does not fully see Dick's dual nature—that he is *used* by others because he *allows* himself to be used and is responsible in part for his failure. A priest is a man who has dedicated himself to a heightened purpose with a serious sense of duty. The "spoiled priest" has betrayed that sense of duty, lost self-discipline, and given way to excesses. In his Notebook, Fitzgerald once said of himself that "strict self-discipline" was "the secret of his charm": "When you let that balance become disturbed, don't you become just another victim of self-indulgence?—breaking down the solid things around you and, moreover, making yourself terribly vulnerable?"[18]

The dream in Fitzgerald's fiction is betrayed from within and without. From without it hits upon the rocks of crass materialism, flounders in contact with people (the Buchanans and the Warrens) hardened by wealth and their innate superiority. From within the dream is betrayed by misjudgment and self-indulgence. Gatsby misjudges the Buchanans, Dick misjudges Nicole's influence on him, and it is an interesting coincidence that Tommy Barban's words to Dick are exactly Gatsby's words to Tom Buchanan: "Your wife does not love you," said Tommy [Barban] suddenly. "She loves me."[131]. Gatsby indulges his fantasy beliefs that he can win Daisy back with a gaudy yellow car and swindler's money. Dick Diver's self-indulgence is more physical; the good life—the life of leisure and elegance—lures him to a point where the man of discipline in him is smothered. The "carelessness" of the Warrens has to be taken in context with Dick's carelessness toward himself.

Dick's main flaw is his desire to be loved and to be the center of attention. Both Fitzgerald and Dick Diver liked to feel people dependent upon them. Fitzgerald once said of himself: "I must be loved. I tip heavily to be loved. I have so many faults that I must be approved of in other ways."[19] Dick also is the victim of his vanity, and throughout the novel he goes out of his way to help others (a girl on a battlefield cemetery who is trying to put a wreath on her brother's grave, a girl and her mother aboard an ocean-liner, Mary Willis who shot down a man at the train station, a troubled girl with an extreme case of eczema). Fitzgerald suggests that it is his desire to help Nicole that leads to their marriage. He liked to give lavishly of his strength, cater to egos, and his vanity made him vulnerable. At the very end of the novel, Nicole tells Baby Warren, her hard-hearted sister, " 'Dick was a good husband to me for six years. . . . All that time I never suffered a minute's pain because of him, and he always did his best never to let anything hurt me.' " Her sister replies, " 'That's what he was educated for' "[312]. This is the thankless rich speaking, but Dick played into their hands. Dick's desire to be needed remains with him to the end. Even as Nicole is about to discard him, Dick answers the call for help from Mary North and Lady Caroline:

> "Use me!" [he says, hanging up the phone.] He would have to go fix this thing that he didn't care a damn about, because it had early become a habit to be loved. . . . Wanting above all to be brave and kind, he had wanted, even more than that, to be loved. So it had been.[302]

When Dick falls in love with Rosemary—who represents "all the immaturity of the race"[69]—he is already used up, and this scene reveals how completely he has abandoned his self-discipline, a discipline that has obviously been open to attack from the beginning. Although Dick is thirty-three years old when he falls in love with Rosemary, Fitzgerald portrays him acting as self-indulgently and irresponsibly as an adolescent. He waits for Rosemary at the studio, for example, "with the fatuousness of one of Tarkington's adolescents"[91]. He tries to becloud the fact that Rosemary is so young, and when he first kisses her, "her youth vanish[ed] as she passed inside the focus of his eyes and he kissed her breathlessly as if she were any age at all"[63]. Just before Dick consummates his love affair with Rosemary, his father dies. Dick has been brought up by his father to believe in the old virtues—" 'good instincts,' honor, courtesy, and courage"[204]—and his father's death symbolically parallels his own loss of authority and self-discipline. Furthermore, when Nicole falls in love with Dick, he takes the place of her father. The fact that she falls out of love with him and that Dick commits symbolic incest with Rosemary, an act which leagues him with Devereux Warren, reveals Dick's failure to become a responsible "father," a position which, in this novel, Fitzgerald seems to equate with maturity. Like Fitzgerald's earlier works, *Tender*

Is the Night reveals not only a sense of regret for a past lost, but of regret for a future unfulfilled because it was irresponsibly wasted. Whereas a novel such as *The Great Gatsby* emphasizes the attempt to recapture the lost past, *Tender Is the Night* emphasizes the future that remained unfulfilled. Like Gatsby, Dick Diver felt that youth was something that could be drawn upon forever. But unlike Gatsby, he had the means, the talent, to make the dream come true. Dick is the victim of his own weak will.

If Amory Blaine wonders if the race is worth while, if Anthony Patch does not know when to begin running, if Jay Gatsby does not know when to stop running, Dick Diver does not know that the race is lost. When Tommy Barban tells Dick that Nicole is leaving him, Fitzgerald describes at the same moment the Tour de France, the cross-country bicycle race. A "lone cyclist in a red jersey" first appears, "toiling intent and confident out of the westering sun," then fifty more followed "most of them indifferent and weary," and finally a light truck took up the rear carrying "the dupes of accident and defeat"[310]. Fitzgerald establishes an obvious parallel between the descriptive detail and Dick's fate. Dick, who was once very much like the lone cyclist in the red jersey, is no longer even weary and indifferent but a "dupe" of defeat. When Dick first meets Baby Warren in the Alps, he is on a bicycle trip [cf.147–57], and when Baby Warren "dismisses" him, she remarks: " 'We should have let him confine himself to his bicycle excursions' "[312]. One of the last pieces of news about Dick from New York is that "he bicycled a lot" [314].

Dick Diver is like Anthony Patch in many ways: he is young and handsome, he likes to be the center of attention and to give himself lavishly to others, and he is essentially a weak and passive man. But where Anthony has only the hope of his grandfather's money to sustain him, Dick has committed himself to the study of psychiatry and has the promise of a brilliant career before him. The novel's thirteen-year span takes Dick from the age of twenty-six, when he is working his way to the top of his profession, to the age of thirty-nine, when he has given up the profession and given way to alcoholism and complete self-abandonment. As in *The Beautiful and Damned*, Dick has first the sense of promise and expectancy (here his hope of becoming a brilliant psychiatrist); this sense of expectancy lasts during the days and evenings of wild and riotous parties; this eventually gives way to a sense of waste; and the sense of waste is replaced by the regret that the time of youth has not been better used.

The theme of *Tender Is the Night*, in part, will be the theme of "The Crack-Up" articles, and two years later Fitzgerald will tell us that he lived

> distrusting the rich, yet working for money with which to share their mobility and the grace that some of them brought into their lives. During this time I had plenty of the usual horses shot out from under me—I remember some of their names—*Punctured Pride, Thwarted Expectation, Faithless, Show-off, Hard Hit, Never Again.* And after a while I wasn't twenty-five, then not even thirty-five, and nothing was quite as good.[20]

Fitzgerald once said, "I am part of the break-up of the times."[21] He came to believe this in a literal way. The Jazz Age, days of promise and gaiety, ended with the depression of 1929, and what Fitzgerald believed to be the pattern of human growth turned out to be the pattern of twentieth-century history. While accidental, it is nevertheless appropriate that as early as 1920 Fitzgerald thought that seventeen to thirty were the halcyon years. He had, of course, no way of knowing that what he felt to be a personal truth would become a historical fact when *The Great Gatsby* was published in 1925. But he did know it when he was writing *Tender Is the Night*, published in 1934, and it is thus significant that this story takes places—although not chronologically—between 1917 and 1930, and that it is about a brilliant young psychiatrist who in 1917 reveals great talent but who misused and dissipated it by 1930. As Dick Diver wasted his genius with riotous living and had only failure to show for it, so too, Fitzgerald came to feel, the riotous twenties led directly to the catastrophe of 1929 and the thirties. *Tender Is the Night* and "Babylon Revisited" clearly indicate that Fitzgerald believed in a one-to-one relationship between personal and historical tragedy and a causal connection between the irresponsibility that characterized the 1920's and the suffering of the 1930's. He thought of youth and of the gay twenties in exactly the same way—as a fixed quantity of time. In well-known passages from *The Crack-Up*, Fitzgerald's history of his personal demise, he talks about being "a mediocre caretaker of most of the things left in my hands, even of my talent," until one day he suddenly realized that he was involved in "an over-extension of the flank, a burning of the candle at both ends; a call upon physical resources that I did not command, like a man over-drawing at his bank."[22] As the Jazz Age drew too heavily on its financial resources, so Dick Diver drew carelessly on his emotional resources; and in both cases it led to bankruptcy—economic and personal bankruptcy.

In this context, Dick's desire to be loved becomes ironic. His contact with women throughout the novel tends to function within a father-daughter relationship, and almost all of the minor characters reveal the breakdown of natural love. *Tender Is the Night* is full of perversion and abnormal love: Campion, Dumphry, and Francisco are all homosexuals; Mr. Warren is guilty of incest; and Mary North and Lady Caroline turn out to be lesbians. Fitzgerald says that "it was as if for the remainder of [Dick's] life he was condemned to carry with him the egos of certain people, early met and early loved, and to be only as complete as they were complete themselves. There was some element of loneliness involved—so easy to be loved—so hard to love"[245]. *Tender Is the Night* is a novel about the failure of an individual—it is also a novel about the failure of society. In many ways, the world failed to come up to Dick's expectation of it. That is why the innocence of youth had such appeal for Dick, why he is so attracted to Rosemary, whose "fineness of character, her courage and steadfastness" stand in contrast to "the vulgarity of the world"[69]. When Dick violates her, he destroys his last image of innocence—of freshness, vitality, of promise and youth.

One of the novel's final ironies is that Nicole, who is twenty-four, can, thanks to Dick, salvage the remains of her youth—a time which she guards "jealously":

> She [Nicole] bathed and anointed herself and covered her body with a layer of powder, while her toes crunched another

pile on a bath towel. She looked microscopically at the lines of her flanks, wondering how soon the fine, slim edifice would begin to sink squat and earthward. In about six years [that is, at thirty], but now I'll do–in fact I'll do as well as any one I know.

She was not exaggerating. The only physical disparity between Nicole at present and the Nicole of five years before was simply that she was no longer a young girl. But she was enough ridden by the current youth worship, the moving pictures with their myriad faces of girl-children [cf. Rosemary], blandly represented as carrying on the work and wisdom of the world, to feel a jealousy of youth.

She put on the first ankle-length day dress that she had owned for many years, and crossed herself reverently with Chanel Sixteen. When Tommy drove up at one o'clock she had made her person into the trimmest of gardens.

How good to have things like this, to be worshipped again, to pretend to have a mystery! [290–91]

Fitzgerald's careful choice of words–"anointed," "crossed herself," "worshipped," "powder" [cf. *Song of Solomon*,3:6], "garden" [cf. *Song of Solomon*, 4:12–14]–puts this whole passage in double context. There is supposedly a religious quality to Nicole's beauty and youth, and Dick, like Gatsby, becomes a kind of sacrificial priest to the beauty and glamor of the very rich. The deracinated people who form a backdrop for the story of Dick Diver are very similar to the characters in *The Waste Land*. The society is sick, and these people corrupt and eventually sacrifice their high priest. This is further suggested when Dick, leaving for good the beach he had made popular, "raised his right hand and with a papal cross he blessed the beach from the high terrace"[314].

Fitzgerald often moved through metaphor from the personal to the historical level. At one point, discussing Dick's lavish behavior, Fitzgerald said that "the excitement . . . was inevitably followed by . . . [a] form of melancholy":

The reaction came when he realized the waste and extravagance involved. He sometimes looked back with awe at the carnivals

> of affection he had given, as a general might gaze upon a massacre he had ordered to satisfy an impersonal blood lust.[27]

The reference to war is picked up in the novel as a whole. Dick and Rosemary visit a cemetery for war dead. Dick sees the First World War as bringing an end to class distinction, and he nostalgically regrets the death of the old order. This was "a love battle," he says, romanticizing the relationships that existed between the classes. "This was the last love battle"[57]. Fitzgerald had been reading Spengler ("I read him the same summer I was writing *The Great Gatsby* and I don't think I ever quite recovered from him"),[23] and he agreed with Spengler that each culture passes through a cycle similar to that of human life. Dick's decline parallels the decline of the West. He abandoned the old virtues of his father and dissipated his energies, just as western culture had abandoned the old aristocratic virtues for a crass materialism.

Fitzgerald believed that the turning point in America came after the Civil War. Grant, he says in *Tender Is the Night*, "invented mass butchery"[27]. Dick Diver is torn between allegiance to past and present as he thinks back on his father—a Southern sympathizer, who has told him stories of John Singleton Mosby and his guerrilla band.[24] "The old loyalties and devotions" fought against "the whole new world in which he believed"[106]. Dick ultimately rejects his father's world, the aristocratic and "conscious good manners of the young Southerner." He "despised them because they were not a protest against how unpleasant selfishness was but against how unpleasant it looked" [194]. Yet the struggle between the two orders is real enough for Dick, who at two points in the novel [118 and 315] is connected directly with Grant's "destiny." A failure, his research days over, Dick's career, Fitzgerald tells us, "was biding its time again like Grant in Galena"[315]. After an initial failure as an army officer, Grant returned to Galena, Illinois, from where he left a grocery store (Dick "became entangled with a girl who worked in a grocery store"), to fulfill in the Civil War a destiny that was to end one order and to establish another—that of the commercial and industrial interests—the new financiers. The story of U. S. Grant—the man who came back after a bitter defeat—seems to have touched Fitzgerald deeply. While he felt that Grant had been used by the new industrialists, just as Dick Diver had been used by the very rich, Grant's story also appealed to his romantic conviction that success, like the phoenix, can appear from the ashes of the past. In the holograph copy of *The Great Gatsby*, Jordan Baker asks about Gatsby's background and Nick mentions that nobodys often came "from the lower east side of Galena, Illinois." [ms.p.55]

Dick's father died in New York state and was buried in Virginia. Dick brings the body South, and "only as the local train shambled into the low-forested clayland of Westmoreland County, did he feel once more identified with his surroundings" [204]. Fitzgerald could write these words with feeling because in 1931 his own father died in Minnesota and was buried in Maryland. And yet, like Grant leaving Galena, when Dick Diver takes leave of his father, he puts behind him an old and different way of life:

> Dick had no more ties here now and did not believe he would ever come back. He knelt on the hard soil. These dead, he knew them all, their weather-beaten faces with blue flashing eyes, the spare violent bodies, the souls made of new earth in the forest-heavy darkness of the seventeenth century.
>
> "Good-by, my father—good-by, all my fathers." (204–5)

Fitzgerald wrote these words out of his own feeling—in fact, he used in *Tender Is the Night* a passage from an unpublished (until 1951) paper that he wrote on the death of his own father:

"The Death of My Father"	Tender Is the Night
I loved my father—always deep in my subconscious I have referred judgments back to him, [to] what he would have thought or done. . . . I was born	Dick loved his father—again and again he referred judgments to what his father would probably have thought or done. Dick was born several months after the death of two

"The Death of My Father"	Tender Is the Night
several months after the sudden death of my two elder sisters and he felt what the effect of this would be on my mother, that he would be my only moral guide. . . . He came of tired stock with very little left of vitality and mental energy but he managed to raise a little for me.[25]	young sisters and his father, guessing what would be the effect on Dick's mother, had saved him from a spoiling by becoming his moral guide. He was of tired stock yet he raised himself to that effort. [203]

Dick's father died in Buffalo, and Dick returned to Buffalo after his decline. Fitzgerald lived in Buffalo from the age of two to eleven, and it was here—when Mr. Fitzgerald was fired from Procter and Gamble—that he witnessed his father's cruelest defeat. The Fitzgerald family returned sadly and without success to the Midwest. Dick also is "without success" in Buffalo, and gradually disappears into upper-state New York. Fitzgerald, in *Tender Is the Night* as in *The Great Gatsby*, chose the details of his novels out of his own catalogue of emotional experience.

Fitzgerald, perhaps forcing the comparison, saw a strange parallel between the story of Dick Diver, himself, his own father, and Ulysses Grant. They were all men who knew two ways of life—who could look back on a glorious or a proud past, but who had been defeated in various ways by life. Behind the real world in a Fitzgerald novel is a golden one that is slowly vanishing from view, and Fitzgerald felt this was true in a general as well as individual way. Dick Diver's story—which strangely included the story of Grant, Fitzgerald's father, as well as Fitzgerald himself—is also the story of Western civilization in its process of decline.

Fitzgerald published one novel about deterioration and decline in 1922 and another in 1934. *The Beautiful and Damned* is an inferior work because Fitzgerald was not fully in command of his craft, and because the matter of deterioration was not a lived experience. If *This Side of Paradise* was a form of preparation for *The Great Gatsby*, so *The Beautiful and Damned* was a kind of preparation for *Tender Is the Night*. The hurt that Fitzgerald experienced with Ginevra King and Zelda Sayre was badly embodied in *This Side of Paradise*, because it was not assimilated and because Fitzgerald handled it too literally—unwilling or unable to find imaginative ways of realizing the dramatic as well as symbolic quality of the experience. The fear of waste and decline that Fitzgerald depicted in *The Beautiful and Damned* was melodramatic because the ideas in the novel were unassimilated and because Fitzgerald was too intent on making Anthony embody the ennui of the smart set. Fitzgerald did not have to rely upon sophisticated clichés to write *Tender Is the Night*: by the thirties he knew firsthand—and all too well—the meaning of sickness, physical decline, and disappointment.

The short stories that Fitzgerald published between *The Great Gatsby* and *Tender Is the Night* reveal his change of mind and feeling, and they also give us a way to follow Fitzgerald's journey from one novel to his next.

In the March 1929 issue of the *Saturday Evening Post*, Fitzgerald published "The Last of the Belles," which has many of *The Great Gatsby* overtones. Told by a young man named Andy, the story occurs during World War I in Tarleton, Georgia, near an army camp. "It was a time," says the narrator, "of youth and war, and there was never so much love around."[26] Four young men are in love with one girl—Ailie Calhoun—the last of the belles. During Andy's first months at Tarleton, Bill Knowles disappears into the war, Horace Canby kills himself in a plane crash when Ailie refuses to marry him, and Ailie falls in love with Earl Schoen. When Earl Schoen returns to Tarleton after the war, dressed so that "the background of milltown dance halls and outing clubs flamed out at you"[268], Ailie breaks off their romance. At this point, Andy leaves to go back to Harvard, gets his law degree, eventually turns thirty, and returns to Tarleton in search of lost youth. There he proposes unsuccessfully to Ailie, and then has the taxi driver take him to his old army camp where he tries—also unsuccessfully—to recapture the romantic past. The tone at the end of this story parallels the tone of *The Great Gatsby*:

> The taxi driver regarded me indulgently while I stumbled here and there in the knee-deep underbrush, looking for my youth in a clapboard or a strip of roofing or a rusty tomato can. I tried to sight on a vaguely familiar clump of trees, but it was growing darker now and I couldn't be quite sure they were the right trees.
>
> . . . All I could be sure of was this place that had once been so full of life and effort was gone, as if it had never existed. [273–74]

When Andy loses the beautiful girl who embodies the spirit of the romantic past, he loses his youth and the sense of eternal promise which—in Earl Schoen's case—was betrayed by his lack of money. All the themes that are in *The Great Gatsby* are here—as well as the emotions of nostalgia and disappointment.

In the January and February 1926 issue of *Redbook*, Fitzgerald published "The Rich Boy," perhaps his finest short story. "The Rich Boy" is similar in several ways to *The Great Gatsby*. Like Gatsby, Anson Hunter has lost his first love, but he does not romanticize this loss; instead he feels that someone else must pay for his unhappiness and finds satisfaction in throwing over Dolly Karger and driving his aunt's lover to suicide. Others would have been added to this list if Paula Legendre—the only one to ever triumph over him—had not died in childbirth. Like Tom Buchanan, Anson Hunter is glib, hard-driving, hard-drinking, insensitive, and egotistical. He was born to believe that he is naturally superior. In fact, as the narrator tells us, he was never happy unless there were "women in the world who would spend their brightest, freshest, rarest hours to nurse and protect that superiority he cherished in his heart."[27] Like Dick Diver, Anson is a born leader; people gravitate to him; and he is proud to be of service to them—in fact, it increases his sense of superiority. Yet, seen from another perspective, Anson—who feels that others exist for his comfort and who disposes of his aunt's lover and of Dolly Karger with ruthless dispatch—is a kind of brother to Baby

Warren, and the theme of the ruthless rich establishes a bridge between *The Great Gatsby* and *Tender Is the Night.*

There are four short stories published between 1929 and 1931 which rehearse even more directly the general themes and situation of *Tender Is the Night.*

In the January 1930 issue of the *Saturday Evening Post*, Fitzgerald published "Two Wrongs." In this story, Bill McChesney, a successful Broadway producer, marries Emmy Pinkard, a young dancer from Delany, South Carolina. Three years later McChesney has drunk himself to a point where he begins to dissipate his talent. Emmy gets stronger as he gets weaker—just like Dick Diver and Nicole—until he finds that he lacks the energy to do his work, that "he had come to lean, in a way, on Emmy's fine health and vitality."[28] In the end, McChesney is stricken with T.B. and goes off, alone, to a sanitarium in the West. Emmy remains in New York where she continues, with many signs of success, her ballet dancing—"the old dream inculcated by Miss Georgia Berriman Campbell of South Carolina [which] persisted as a bright avenue leading back to first youth and days of hope in New York"[240–41]. Emmy continues to look ahead with the expectancy of youth; McChesney has only the lost past to gaze upon. Quite obviously, there is a great deal in this story—physical breakdown, man and wife separated by sickness, the desire to realize the old dream by taking up a career as ballet dancer, the sense of lost promise, and the loneliness and the regret—which comes more or less directly from Fitzgerald's and Zelda's own experience, and which was to go into *Tender Is the Night.*

Another story which treats the theme of waste and deterioration is "One Trip Abroad," published in the October 1930 issue of the *Saturday Evening Post.* Nicole and Nelson Kelly, wealthy Americans, bring their youth and enthusiasm to Europe; tour North Africa, Italy, the Riviera, Paris, and Switzerland; and three and a half years later they have wrecked themselves with foolish living and self-indulgence. The story closes in a Switzerland sanitarium, where they are trying to regain their health, and where they see a rather unpleasant couple—unwholesome and dissipated—whom they met in North Africa. Suddenly they realize that these two embody the spirit of their own decline—that they are looking at an image in a mirror:

> "Did you see?" she cried in a whisper. "Did you see them?"
> "Yes!"
> "They're us! They're us! Don't you see?"[29]

Another story, "The Rough Crossing," published in the June 1929 issue of the *Saturday Evening Post*, also depicts an American couple, Adrian and Eva Smith, sailing for Europe. They act as badly as the Nelsons—both drink and argue and are jealous and suspicious of the other, Eva to the point of being suicidal. Fitzgerald adds to the story Betsy D'Amido who, like Rosemary Hoyt in *Tender Is the Night*, represents the spirit of youth and vitality. Betsy evokes in Adrian, at a time when he no longer thought it possible, the old excitement of youth—the feeling of new life, promise, and possibility: "Her youth seemed to flow into him, bearing him up into a delicate romantic ecstasy that transcended passion. He couldn't relinquish it; he had discovered something that he had thought was lost with his own youth forever."[30] When Nicole in "One Trip Abroad" has reached the lowest point of decline, her jewels are stolen. When Eva reaches this point, she throws her pearl necklace into the sea—and "with it went the fairest part of her life"[265]. Adrian also loses his sense of renewed youth when he departs from Betsy, who is being met by her fiancé. Yet, unlike *Tender Is the Night*, Adrian and Eva are together in the end—hoping to make a new start. Four years later, Fitzgerald would know that this was impossible, and Dick Diver would slink—beaten, defeated, weak, and dissipated—into the limbo of upper-state New York.

"Babylon Revisited," published in a February 1931 issue of the *Saturday Evening Post*, is still another story that anticipates *Tender Is the Night*. In fact, as the following comparison shows, Fitzgerald even used passages from the story in the novel:

"Babylon Revisited"	Tender Is the Night
Outside, the fire-red, gas-blue, ghost-green signs shone smokily through tran-	. . . outside the taxi windows, the fire-red, gas-blue, ghost green signs began to

"Babylon Revisited"	Tender Is the Night
quil rain. It was late after-	shine smokily through tran-
noon and the streets were	quil rain. It was nearly six,
in movement; the *bistros*	the streets were in move-
gleamed. . . . The Place	ment, the bistros gleamed,
de la Concorde moved by	the Place de la Concorde
in pink majesty.[31]	moved by in pink majesty.[74]
He wasn't young any more,	He was not young any more
with a lot of nice thoughts	with a lot of nice thoughts
and dreams to have by him-	and dreams to have about
self.[407]	himself.[311]

Like Dick Diver, Charles Wales has misspent the past, lived recklessly in Paris during the twenties, and is a pathetic figure as the story opens. His wife is dead; and his daughter, Honoria (the Murphy's daughter was named Honoria, but Fitzgerald seems to be punning on the name), has been legally adopted by his sister-in-law and her husband.

The story opens with the *ubi sunt* theme: " 'And where's Mr. Campbell?' Charlie asked"[382]. Mr. Campbell is gone—and so are most of his old friends. Charles Wales has Fitzgerald's characteristic longing to relive the past, to return anew to the days of youth: "he wanted to jump back a whole generation . . ."[387]. He is overwhelmed by a sense of guilt, feels that his past was a "most widely squandered sum"[388], and gives a street tramp a twenty-franc note in the hope that he can buy away this sense of guilt. But he cannot elude the past; it trails him in the form of Duncan Schaeffer, a friend from college, and Lorraine Quarrles, a worn-out beauty of thirty—both described as "ghosts out of the past"[390]—who try to get Charles to repeat the lavish time of three years ago and who cause him to lose his daughter just when Marion Peters was on the verge of relinquishing Honoria. The past still has its toll on the present. The story closes, as it opens, at the Ritz bar, Charles pondering his own life in terms of the Crash of 1929.

Fitzgerald has here set up an equation between personal and public tragedy. Time is thought of in moral terms. As the financial recklessness of the twenties led to the Great Crash, so did

Charlie's reckless living lead to his physical and emotional breakdown, the loss of Honoria (his honor), and his feeling of regret and guilt about his misspent past. In the climactic scene, Charles accompanies Lorraine Quarrles and Duncan Schaeffer to the door; and when he goes back to the Peters' salon, "Lincoln was swinging Honoria back and forth like a pendulum from side to side"[404]. The pendulum is an obvious symbol of time; Charles is the victim of his past; and "Babylon Revisited" reveals—as much as any other story—that Fitzgerald believed that time is given to us in trust. The past lies about Charles Wales like ashes, and, because he is no longer "young," he has no dreams to buoy up the future. At the very end of the story, Charles asks the waiter " 'What do I owe you?' " There are, of course, two meanings intended here—one literal, the other metaphorical. Fitzgerald often equated time and money, and Charles must continue to pay for time misappropriated—to pay with his youth: "He wasn't young any more," Fitzgerald will use the same words to describe Dick Diver, "with a lot of nice thoughts and dreams to have by himself"[407]. Like Dick Diver, Charles stands trapped in time—between the unfulfilled past and the hopeless future.

The stories that Fitzgerald published after *The Great Gatsby* contain all the elements of *Tender Is the Night*. "One Trip Abroad" is a study of physical and moral decline; "Two Wrongs" is a study in physical and emotional transference—the woman getting stronger as the man gets weaker; "The Rough Crossing" is a study of deterioration—the process made more pathetic because it is seen in contrast to the vitality of a beautiful young girl; and "Babylon Revisited" is a study in misspent time —the moral consequences of Charles Wale's life being extended to parallel the economic decline of the thirties. To these stories, Fitzgerald added "The Rich Boy," and related Dick's decline to the habit of mind of the very rich with their sense of superiority and ownership.

Despite the fact that *Tender Is the Night* is built up from the short stories, and despite the many revisions that it went through, Fitzgerald never had this novel under control, and it gave him the utmost technical difficulty. Perhaps, as the above study suggests, he brought too many disparate elements to the novel and extended the theme too broadly beyond the story of Dick Diver to include American history and Spengler's theory of the declining West. Whatever may be the cause, Fitzgerald never really succeeded in working out a coherent and sustained point of view; was never satisfied with the inverted time sequence; and inserted a number of implausible episodes—especially the duel between McKisco and Tommy Barban, and the mysterious murder of a Negro on Rosemary's hotel bed. One has a feeling that Fitzgerald was over-reaching in this novel, trying to make the sensational believable, and never quite succeeding. Certainly he does not have the control here that he revealed in *The Great Gatsby*. The language itself gives Fitzgerald away; there are too many passages like the following—vague and badly written—in which the reader does not know what Fitzgerald is trying to say:

> To resume Rosemary's point of view it should be said that, under the spell of the climb to Tarmes and the fresher air, she and her mother looked about appreciatively. Just as the personal qualities of extraordinary people can make themselves plain in an unaccustomed change of expression, so the intensely calculated perfection of Villa Diana transpired all at once through such minute failures as the chance apparition of a maid in the background or the perversity of a cork. While the first guests arrived bringing with them the excitement of the night, the domestic activity of the day receded past them gently, symbolized by the Diver children and their governess still at supper on the terrace.[28]

Passages like this blur the clean narrative line of *Tender Is the Night*. Fitzgerald, as everyone knows, thought of revising the novel by beginning with Dick's first meeting Nicole and proceeding chronologically. The source of unity in the original novel stems from comparison and contrast. We open and close on the beach, and the man we first see is endowed with the strength of youth and the sense of life's promise. This contrasts with the debilitated man at the end who is overwhelmed by his sense of waste. Fitzgerald thought a chronological structure might better show the cause-and-effect relationship of Dick Diver's decline. He most certainly is wrong in this conclusion, because he gave far more emphasis to the *fact* of Dick's decline, which supplies the emotional tone of the novel, than he did to the reasons for his decline, which are unclearly entangled in Fitzgerald's concern over Zelda's breakdown, his attitude toward the rich, and his own sense of lost vitality and promise. Fitzgerald's attitude toward Dick is the same personal and emotional attitude that he took toward all his characters; *Tender Is the Night* is not a clinical study of deterioration; and critics—Wayne Booth, for example—miss the point when they suggest that a chronological revision would bring out more clearly the central conflict of the novel.[32]

Whereas *The Great Gatsby* was a novel about what could never be, *Tender Is the Night* is a novel about what could have been. Dick Diver had the talent and genius to succeed; he also had in his youth the necessary vision and sense of commitment. He was sidetracked by the very rich and by his own weakness, which was to feel needed and be the center of attention. Both Gatsby and Dick Diver believed that they could make time stand still; Gatsby thought he could recapture the lost past, and Dick Diver thought that his future would wait for him. Fitzgerald suggests that both were not aware of the nature of time.

The title *Tender Is the Night* comes from Keats's "Ode to a Nightingale," where the speaker longs for a state of eternality while recognizing that he is subject to a state of temporality—a state "where youth grows pale, and specter-thin, and dies." Like Keats, Fitzgerald longed for a world of arrested time where love will be "Forever warm and still to be enjoyed,/Forever panting and forever young." But like Keats, Fitzgerald also knew that no such world was possible for men. Jay Gatsby was never able to learn this, and Dick Diver learned it too late.

Notes

1. Calvin Tomkins, "Living Well Is the Best Revenge," *New Yorker*, XXXVIII (July 28, 1962), pp.43–44.

2. Ibid., p.31.

3. Morley Callaghan, *That Summer in Paris* (New York: Coward-McCann, 1963), p.191.

4. *The Letters of F. Scott Fitzgerald*, ed. Andrew Turnbull (New York: Charles Scribner's Sons, 1963), p.230.

5. F. Scott Fitzgerald, *Tender Is the Night* (New York: Charles Scribner's Sons, 1934), p.200. All further quotations are from this edition, page reference indicated in brackets after the quote.

6. George Jean Nathan, "Memories of Fitzgerald, Lewis and Dreiser," *Esquire*, L (October, 1958), pp.148–49.

7. See Matthew J. Bruccoli, *The Composition of Tender Is the Night* (Pittsburgh: University of Pittsburgh Press, 1963), p.18. Bruccoli's book is a thorough and useful study of Fitzgerald's seventeen drafts of the novel.

8. Calvin Tomkins, *New Yorker*, p.50.

9. "The World's Fair," *Kenyon Review*, X (Autumn, 1948), pp. 567–78.

10. *The Letters*, p.19.

11. "A Nice Quiet Place" was originally published in the *Saturday Evening Post*, May 31, 1930.

12. F. Scott Fitzgerald, *Taps at Reveille*, (New York: Charles Scribner's Sons, 1935), p.169.

13. *The Letters*, p.79.

14. Ibid., p.32.

15. Ibid., p.346.

16. Andrew Turnbull, *Scott Fitzgerald* (New York: Charles Scribner's Sons, 1962), p.150.

17. *The Crack-Up*, ed. Edmund Wilson (New York: New Directions, 1956), p.180.

18. Ibid., p.209.

19. Turnbull, p.261.

20. "Handle with Care," *Esquire*, March, 1936; reprinted in *The Crack-Up*, p.77.

21. Turnbull, p.265.

22. "The Crack-Up" and "Handle with Care," *The Crack-Up*, pp.71 and 77.

23. *The Letters*, pp.289–90.

24. Mosby (Fitzgerald misspelled the name "Moseby"), born in 1833 and died in 1916, organized a group of rangers which became Company A, 43rd Battalion Partisan Rangers of the Confederate army. This band created havoc with the Union troops fighting in

northern Virginia. Mosby's most famous exploits were kidnapping General Stoughton out of his own headquarters on May 9, 1863; raiding Points of Rock, Maryland, on July 4, 1864; and seizing $168,000 from Union troops on October 14, 1864.

25. *The Apprentice Fiction of F. Scott Fitzgerald 1909–1917*, ed. John Kuehl (New Brunswick: Rutgers University Press, 1965), p.67.

26. "The Last of the Belles," *Saturday Evening Post*, March 2, 1929; reprinted in *Taps at Reveille*, p.258. All further quotations from this story will be cited to this edition, page reference indicated in brackets after the quote.

27. "The Rich Boy," *Redbook*, January-February, 1926; reprinted in *All the Sad Young Men*, p.56.

28. "Two Wrongs," *Saturday Evening Post*, January 18, 1930; reprinted in *Taps at Reveille*, p.242. All further quotations from this story will be cited to this edition, page reference indicated in brackets after the quote.

29. "One Trip Abroad," *Saturday Evening Post*, October 11, 1930; reprinted in *Afternoon of an Author*, ed. Arthur Mizener (Princeton, N.J.: Princeton University Library, 1957), p.165.

30. "The Rough Crossing," *Saturday Evening Post*, June 8, 1929; reprinted in *The Short Stories of F. Scott Fitzgerald*, ed. Malcolm Cowley (New York: Charles Scribner's Sons, 1951), pp.263–64. All further quotations from this story will be cited to this edition, page reference indicated in brackets after the quote.

31. "Babylon Revisited," *Saturday Evening Post*, February 21, 1931; reprinted in *Taps at Reveille*, p.384. All further quotations from this story will be cited to this edition, page reference indicated in brackets after the quote.

32. Wayne C. Booth, *The Rhetoric of Fiction* (Chicago: University of Chicago Press, 1961), pp.192–95.

5. *Tender Is the Night*

by JAMES E. MILLER, JR.

An account of the many versions through which *Tender Is the Night* passed is a story in itself, its last event occurring only with the publication of a "final" version that Fitzgerald had prepared but was unable to see through the press. The first draft of the novel was a story of a young Hollywood technician, Francis Melarky (an early version of Rosemary Hoyt), who kills his demanding and dominating mother; a subsequent draft shifted focus to Abe Grant and Seth Piper (Abe North and Dick Diver of the published novel). Finally, Fitzgerald published the book—now mainly about Dick Diver—in 1934, first as a serial in *Scribner's Magazine* (January–April) and later, after further revision, as a book. In anticipation of republication in the Modern Library series (which never came about), Fitzgerald drastically revised his novel, shifting about entire blocks of narrative, and wrote on the inside front cover: "This is the *final version* of the book as I would like it." This version was edited and issued in 1951.[1]

There are, then, several manuscript versions and three published versions of *Tender Is the Night*—and it is doubtful that Fitzgerald ever achieved in all his revising the form of the novel that he conceived somehow as the ideal. Thus, we are in a sense dealing with an unfinished (or incompletely conceived) work—a problem not unlike that involved in dealing with *The Last Tycoon*. The major revision that Fitzgerald made in his published novel relates to the book's point of view. In its first published version, the book opened with Rosemary Hoyt as the "commanding center." All the events were filtered through her fresh, even naive, intelligence, and the readers were misled into forecasting for her a role she did not have. One reviewer's comment sums up what must have been an almost universal reaction: "In the critical terminology of Kenneth Burke, Mr. Fitzgerald has violated a 'categorical expectancy.' He has caused the arrows of attention to point toward Rosemary. Then, like a broken field runner reversing his field, he shifts suddenly and those who have been chasing him fall figuratively on their noses as Mr. Fitzgerald is off on a new tack."[2]

Fitzgerald himself must have come to believe that the primary defect of his novel was the opening. In 1938, he wrote to Maxwell Perkins with the suggestion that three of his novels, *This Side of Paradise*, *The Great Gatsby*, and *Tender Is the Night*, be published in a single volume: ". . . I am especially concerned about *Tender*—that book is not dead. The *depth* of its appeal exists—I meet people constantly who have the same exclusive attachment to it as others had to *Gatsby* and *Paradise*, people who identified themselves with Dick Diver. Its great fault is that the *true* beginning—the young psychiatrist in Switzerland—is tucked away in the middle of the book."[3] Although the proposed volume was never published, Fitzgerald continued to brood over the order in which the events should be related, and on one occasion he wrote in his notebooks:

> *Analysis of Tender*:
> I Case History 151–212 61 pp. (change moon) p.212
> II Rosemary's Angle 3–104 101 pps. P.3
> III Casualties 104–148, 213–224 55 pps. (−2) (120+121)
> IV Escape 225–306 82 pps.
> V The Way Home 306–408 103 pps. (−8) (332–341)[4]

Malcolm Cowley followed this scheme when he edited the new version of the novel, except for Fitzgerald's intended omissions in Books III and V: Cowley could not bring himself to eliminate the episode of the Divers' visit to Mary Minghetti in Book V. The fact that dropping either of these episodes tends to render subsequent events inexplicable strongly suggests that Fitzgerald had never really finished the revision he so long wanted to make of his novel. We may well assume that had he actually published the novel again before his death, it would differ, and perhaps markedly, from all three versions that we now have in print.

Cowley himself had doubts about the novel as he edited it from Fitzgerald's notes and manuscripts, particularly about the opening scenes: "The beginning of the first edition, with the Divers seen and admired through the innocent eyes of Rosemary Hoyt, is effective by any standards. Some of the effectiveness is lost in the new arrangement, where the reader already knows the truth about the Divers before Rosemary meets them." But Cowley finally concludes that the revision is superior: "By rearranging the story in chronological order Fitzgerald tied it together. He sacrificed a brilliant beginning and all the element of mystery, but there is no escaping the judgment that he ended with a better constructed and more effective novel."[5]

If, indeed, there is no escaping the judgment, there may still be some lurking doubts as to the ultimate superiority of *either* version, each having its special virtue, both still defective, somehow, in point of view. *Tender Is the Night* relates the decline and disintegration of its hero, Dick Diver, from a position of great promise in clinical psychology to the level of a pitifully inept general practitioner, moving from town to town in upstate New York in search of his lost self—a decline whose causes are both complex and obscure. Dick Diver has all of the weaknesses of Anthony Patch of *The Beautiful and Damned* together with some of the capacity for vision (but not the illusion) of Jay Gatsby.

In the original published version, Fitzgerald, in Conradian fashion and surely for artistic purposes, arranged the events of his story out of their chronological order. In this disarranging or "re-ordering," the protagonist Dick Diver, like Gatsby and Lord Jim, was "gotten in" with a "strong impression" by his introduction through the youthful but sophisticated consciousness of Rosemary. In other words, Fitzgerald was originally following a technique he had successfully used before in *The Great Gatsby*. The defect of the later novel, perhaps, lay not in the opening, but in the subsequent passages. Rosemary Hoyt, instead of continuing to function in a significant way (like Nick Carraway) in the technique and theme, appears to loom large in the action—and then fades away. The difficulty with Rosemary runs too deep to be evaded by a mere reshuffling of narrative blocks. Putting events back in their chronological order sacrifices far more in dramatic effect and suspense than it gains in lucidity. And it does nothing to dispel the sense of wastefulness we feel in Fitzgerald's technical use of one of his most fully drawn young innocents.

But since neither the original nor the revision is obviously superior, it seems appropriate to accept the version that Fitzgerald himself finally settled on, even though he never saw it in print. The following analysis will concentrate, therefore, on that version. Inasmuch as most critical commentary on the book centers on its point of view, it is perhaps useful to begin with an examination of the point of view as it appears in the final version.

The novel opens with "Case History, 1917–1919," a summary account of the events in the life of Doctor Richard Diver that led up to his marriage with Nicole Warren, "disturbed" daughter of a Chicago millionaire and patient in a psychiatric clinic in Switzerland. The opening chapter reads, as the author admits, like a biography of Dick Diver, Rhodes scholar, graduate of Johns Hopkins, student of the new science of psychiatry flourishing in the cities of Switzerland. The remaining chapters of "Case History" adhere largely to Dick Diver's point of view and relate Nicole's "transference" to him, his futile attempt, made for medical reasons, to disentangle himself from her emotions, and, finally, his involvement and commitment, partly through accidental encounter, partly through the plotting of Nicole's older sister, Baby Warren. Fitzgerald's skill in handling rather complicated exposition in these opening chapters is exhibited in his use of letters written by Nicole to Diver to dramatize her gradual mental improvement, and in his use of an internal narrator, a psychiatrist, to reveal to Dick and the reader the terrible events that lay behind Nicole's illness—the sordid seduction by her own father.

"Rosemary's Angle, 1919–1925" begins with an opening chapter that uses a mélange of techniques (most notable, Nicole's stream-of-consciousness) to carry Dick and Nicole through marriage into parenthood and out onto the beaches of the French

Riviera. Then the story abruptly shifts away from the Divers to Rosemary Hoyt, Hollywood starlet fresh from her triumph in "Daddy's Girl" and touring Europe with her possessive mother. "Her body hovered delicately on the last edge of childhood—she was almost eighteen, nearly complete, but the dew was still on her" (59).[6] In short, she is at the right moment of her life to invest what she sees about her on the Riviera with a glamour and a significance that are all youth's. It is through her shining eyes that we see Dick Diver anew—the man in the jockey cap who seems to generate all the genuine excitement on the Riviera. And, too, she serves as a tenuous link between two worlds on the beach—the rather gauche world of the petty McKiscos and the effeminate young men, Royal Dumphry and Luis Campion, and the urbane, sophisticated world of the Divers, including by now the Abe Norths and Tommy Barban. Much of Book II is given over to the Divers' elaborate party bringing together all these people, with Dick in full command of the evening's rich possibilities—until Nicole has one of her attacks of schizophrenia and retires to the bathroom, where she is unfortunately observed by Mrs. McKisco. In trying to prevent Mrs. McKisco from gossiping about what she has seen, Tommy Barban, clearly in love with Nicole, precipitates a duel with her husband—which takes place with consequences more ludicrous than serious. Rosemary remains throughout the sensitive, impressionable mirror in which all these slightly tarnished events are glitteringly reflected. The skill with which Fitzgerald maintains and exploits the value of her point of view is seen, for example, in the way in which he maneuvers her presence at the duel, hidden in the shadows with the emasculate and overexcited Luis Campion, the two together providing a counterpoint to the action that is just the right mixture of romance and comedy.

In Book III, "Casualties, 1925," the point of view becomes Dick Diver's. Having seen him for many pages through the naive and loving eyes of Rosemary, we now move up to and inside him and see what lies beneath that apparently perfect self-containment. Although his exterior behavior continues to exhibit a supreme self-possession—he refuses to take Rosemary when she offers herself to him, he remains sober during the wild drunken bouts of Abe North—there are interior signs of weakening and collapse. To suggest this gradual loosening of the grip on the essential self, Fitzgerald has hit upon an extremely effective device. Out of a casual conversation with a friend about Rosemary's past, relating an episode in which she was discovered with a boyfriend in a locked train compartment, the blinds pulled down, a phrase emerges to haunt Dick Diver: "Do you mind if I pull down the curtain?" As event tumbles on event, the phrase recurs, floating up out of nowhere into Dick's consciousness, undermining his will to resist the siren voices of his whimsical desires. The "casualties" of the title of this book are not Dick Diver's, but serve more as omens of what waits in store for him. Death, like the phrase, recurs with the insistence of a refrain. The book opens on the bleak battlefields of World War I, including a cemetery, where the principals pass in momentary observation. There are two senseless murders related only in a peripheral way to the central action. It is always Dick's efficiency that arranges for a minimum involvement of his companions in these sordid affairs. But clearly the management takes its toll, and his talent for shaping events seems to be leaking away. Book III closes ominously on a trapped man: "He stayed in the big room a long time, listening to the buzz of the electric clock, listening to time"(183).

Book IV, "Escape, 1925–1929," exposes in detail Dick Diver's sickened soul, and we gaze in fascination as all the fissures widen and the splits deepen. The title itself turns out to be ironic, as Dick's only escape is into the greater imprisonment of his senseless degradation. In a desperate move to divert the drift of his life into useful channels, he acquires a clinic in Switzerland and throws himself into the activities of his profession. But his relationship with Nicole deteriorates as her old sickness flares up anew, fired by the jealousies she feels for Dick's every casual encounter. After Nicole in a moment of madness deliberately wrecks the car, almost killing the entire family, Dick decides to take a trip—in search of a road he had long ago missed. In Munich, he learns of the death of Abe North. In Innsbruck, he receives word that his father has died. The quick trip to America to bury his father proves the turning point in Dick's life; somehow the event seems to extinguish the last impulse to hold on to the old goals. On his return to Europe, Dick does not hesitate to take Rosemary when the opportunity arises. And on an evening out in Rome, he drinks himself into a belligerent state that ends in meaningless violence and a night in jail. For a time in this last episode, we see Dick through the ruthless eyes of Baby Warren as she comes to the rescue with all the efficiency of her vast wealth—taking over what remains of Dick's soul.

Briefly at the opening of Book V, "The Way Home, 1929–1930," Dick appears through the petty vision of his clinic partner's wife, gossiping to her husband about his drinking. Later he emerges in all the weakness of his own inward gaze, no longer believing in his half-hearted self-deceptions: his drinking *has* become an embarrassment to the clinic. Released from their entanglement with the partner, the Divers drift back to the Riviera and pick up the threads of their old life. But all the charm seems gone and all the relationships strained and tense. As minor social disasters follow one on another, Nicole and Dick turn away from each other, Nicole to Tommy Barban, Dick (but only momentarily) to Rosemary. For a time we see the world from Nicole's point of view and are perhaps surprised at the self-composed balance of her vision. Her poise contrasts sharply with Dick's fumbling uncertainty—a precise reversal of their positions at the beginning of the novel. When Tommy claims Nicole for himself, everyone sensibly remains friendly—and Dick departs the Riviera and disappears from view. The last brief chapter poignantly summarizes the little that is known of Dick's subsequent fate as a general practitioner in a succession of small towns in upstate New York. The style and tone are those of the opening pages of the novel, reportorial and biographical, and they impersonally dismiss Dick to his anonymous fate: ". . . in any case he is almost certainly in that section of the country, in one town or another" (334).

In *Tender Is the Night* Fitzgerald's technique, especially his manipulation of point of view, is highly varied and sophisticated. Indeed, it might be said to suffer from an embarrassment of riches. It has all the variety of the technique of *This Side of Paradise*, but without that novel's ring of exuberant experimentation. It is more complex in conception than the technique of *The Great*

Gatsby—but *Tender* never gives the impression of absolute certainty of control that *Gatsby* gives. Fitzgerald seems sure of his craft, and the craft seems always on the verge—but never quite—of bringing all the disparate materials of the novel into clear, thematic focus. Most readers finish *Tender* with a vivid impression of its ambitious complexity. It is a novel about the decline and fall of Dick Diver, but it is also about much more than that. A closer examination, first, of the nature of Dick's malaise and, next, of the reverberations set off by the disasters that seem to mark his doom should prove valuable.

Fitzgerald wrote to Edmund Wilson in 1934, ". . . by the way, your notion that Dick should have faded out as a shyster alienist was in my original design, but I thought of him, in reconsideration as an 'homme épuisé' not only an 'homme manqué.' "[7] The extent of the vacuum that displaces Dick's vitality is detailed clearly in the novel. In Innsbruck, before he receives word of his father's death, he gropes toward some self-awareness: "He had lost himself—he could not tell the hour when, or the day or the week, the month or the year. Once he had cut through things, solving the most complicated equations as the simplest problems of his simplest patients. Between the time he found Nicole flowering under a stone on the Zurichsee and the moment of his meeting with Rosemary the spear had been blunted" (218). And when Dick reflects on his father's death, he makes the inevitable comparison: ". . . his father had been sure of what he was, with a deep pride of the two proud widows who had raised him to believe that nothing could be superior to 'good instincts,' honor, courtesy, and courage" (221).

In short, Dick's story is a story of the losing of a self, the disappearance of an identity. The structure of *Tender* may be conceived as a large X, with the one line marking Dick's decline, the other Nicole's rise. There is a kind of spiritual cannibalism or vampirism going on in the novel. As Nicole imbibes Dick's overflowing vitality, she rises from the depths of her soul-sickness to new heights of stability and self-possession—while Dick descends into spiritual exhaustion and emptiness below the level even of despair. It is as though for Dick and Nicole there is only one soul, first in Dick's possession, finally in Nicole's. The tragedy lies in the attempt, by these two people, to share what they cannot by their very nature share. In the attempt, as the marriage hangs precariously in the balance, there are only suspicion and fear, antagonism and bitterness. Possession must be all or none.

It is easy to blame the entirety of Dick's fall on the sophisticated cannibalism of the fabulous Warren world, so careless of other people's lives, or on the magnetic attraction of the fresh, young world of Rosemary Hoyt. But these answers are too simple; Dick's sickness lies hidden in lower depths than these. The self that in the progress of the novel he loses is infirmly anchored from the very beginning in the shifting, shallow sands of his being. The trait that he most notably displays is his innocence—a sinister kind of innocence that is debilitating in the face of evil, an innocence capable of transmogrification into corruption without passing through intermediate steps of deliberate commitment, of conscious moral choice.

In the opening pages of the novel (that is, in the final version), we are informed of his essential nature: "Dick got up to Zurich on fewer Achilles' heels than would be required to equip a centipede, but with plenty—the illusions of eternal strength and health, and of the essential goodness of people—they were the illusions of a nation, the lies of generations of frontier mothers who had to croon falsely that there were no wolves outside the cabin door"(5). The trouble with the world, of course, is that it is filled with wolves, and the most terrible truth of all is the wolf within. Such innocence, blind to the deceptions of the world and the self, is a constant flirtation with disaster.

Diver's innocence takes its most characteristic outlet in his perpetual charm, which, as long as it remains amusing, is harmless enough, but which can, when the mood changes or the winds shift, suddenly turn repulsive and even sinister. Like a child, Dick squanders his charm and himself on all whom he meets. And when he has used himself up and finds only emptiness within, he reacts like a child-man unaware of his full-grown body and his brute strength. The gesture that once evoked laughter begins in its grossness to provoke violence.

It is this quality of innocence in Dick that never permits us to believe deeply in him as a scientist or an author. There is no mature commitment in him. His interest in his profession seems weak and, at bottom, insecurely motivated. His writing—"A Psychology for Psychiatrists"—seems to be not a product of original research or thinking but a rather superficial compilation and condensation of his scattered reading. Never does he seem driven by a search for knowledge or ideas nearly so strong as his occasional drive to render a party romantic and charming. He appears most fully committed when he is assuring through his excessive charm the exhilarating gaiety of some enchanting evening.

Re-enforcing this theme of innocence is the child-imagery recurring throughout the novel. Most notable is the name used for Nicole's sister—Baby Warren: her trouble is that she has never gotten beyond the supremely self-centered world of childhood. But the imagery becomes particularly manifest in the world of Rosemary Hoyt, her strong attachment to her mother, and her starring role in a motion picture entitled "Daddy's Girl." Indeed, it is after Nicole has matured from the child-like state of her illness that Dick finds the attraction of the immature Rosemary so strong. The gap in their ages is enormous—so great, indeed, as to render their embrace a kind of reenactment of the incestuous affair between Nicole and her father. Throughout the novel, Dick's behavior becomes more and more regressive and childish ("A part of Dick's mind was made up of the tawdry souvenirs of his boyhood" [212]), until, finally, he seems to have departed entirely the world of adult moral responsibility. In the latter books of the novel, his unnatural interest in his children and the minutiae of their daily lives reveals a longing deeper than he knows.

In his quest for identity, Dick is confronted at every turn with reflections of the self, and it is here that the novel seems to achieve much of its rich and complex texture. The book may be said to have a mirror or echo structure: a number of the characters who revolve about Dick Diver reflect one or another of his weaknesses in isolation. As he looks about him, he can see not the self he is in process of dissipating, but the several selves warring like vultures to take over the carcass of his soul. In a way, the book with its mirror structure may be read as an allegory, with Everyman (or at least American Everyman) Diver journeying through a multitude of temptations—and succumbing to all of them: Money, Liquor, Anarchy, Self-Betrayal, Sex. These abstractions take carnal embodiment in Baby Warren, Abe North, Tommy Barban, Albert McKisco, and Rosemary Hoyt. But each of these characters is supplemented with additional figures who echo and re-echo the vice set to trap the selfhood of the unwary wayfarer.

Baby Warren represents the brittle sterility of a life dedicated to the bitch goddess Money—"there was something wooden and onanistic about her"(44). The only pleasure money can bring her is incestuously itself, not what it can buy. Although the press is always romantically linking her name with some European duke or count, clearly she is already and permanently wedded to her father's fortune. For Dick she plays the role of evil genius, mysteriously materializing at all the crucial moments of his life and subtly dictating his every important decision. Her disclosure to Dick, at their first meeting, that "the Warrens were going to buy Nicole a doctor"(45), for her father controls certain chairs at the University of Chicago, whetted his appetite for an affair from which he had been trying to escape; and her scheme throws Dick and Nicole together at just the moment to make marriage inevitable. But Baby Warren could not have achieved her nefarious ends without a responding chord in Dick—his fascination with and weakness for the glitter of vast riches. At another decisive moment in Dick's career, when Franz Gregorovius proposes partnership in a psychiatric clinic, it is Baby Warren's presence with her tempting ready cash that settles the affair and puts Dick even further in her debt. And when Dick is in jail in Rome, it is Baby who uses her influence to free him for her own possession. Finally, it is Baby who hovers in the background on the Riviera beach when Dick is dismissed from Nicole's life, his usefulness to the Warren family spent.

But Baby is only a symptom of a profound illness in the society which she epitomizes. The illness takes its most acute form in the American, and particularly the American abroad. But it infects society everywhere. Even the Swiss psychiatric clinics, dedicated as they are to serious science, batten and flourish on American fortunes. And although Dick Diver approaches the world of vast wealth with some wariness of its seductive power, gradually his point of view moves closer and closer to the Warrens'. He adapts too readily and easily to the meaningless life of the rich, drifting from one casual amusement to another, from one smart place in Europe to another. Not only is Dick slowly seduced by money—he even seems castrated by it, rendered impotent in his profession: "His work became confused with Nicole's problems; in addition, her income had increased so fast of late that it seemed to belittle his work"(183); ". . . he had been swallowed up like a gigolo and had somehow permitted his arsenal to be locked up in the Warren safety-deposit vaults"(218–19). Money infiltrates every action of the novel like a poisonous green fog, tainting everything it touches. From the ludicrous brawl Dick starts over his taxi fare in Rome to the momentary encounter with the hawker, near the end of the novel, out to get his share from the "millions of Americans pouring from liners with bags of gold" (328), the ring of coin reverberates mockingly throughout the novel.

Abe North with his drinking, Tommy Barban with his anarchic views, Albert McKisco with his corrupted talent—all represent some facet of Dick Diver's potential for damnation. Abe has had some success with musical comedy, but he has lost all sense of serious purpose and can suffer existence only in an alcoholic daze. When Abe North's death removes him from the novel, Dick takes over his role as senseless and destructive drinker. Tommy Barban (the temptation is to say Barbarian) is a soldier of fortune, willing to fight in any man's army—for action and coin. His contempt for ideas and ideals makes him ruthless—but no more destructive than Dick after he has thrown over all serious pursuit of his profession and given himself up to self-indulgence. Albert McKisco becomes a successful writer whose novels are "pastiches of the work of the best people of his time, a feat not to be disparaged, and in addition he possessed a gift for softening and debasing what he borrowed, so that many readers were charmed by the ease with which they could follow him"(223). The enormous irony in McKisco is that his work is simply a pale reflection of Dick's own "serious" books in his professional field: they too are pastiches and popularizations, representing no genuine contribution.

Although Rosemary Hoyt looms large in the novel as the object of Dick's vague desire, she remains but one variation on the complex sexual theme of the novel. Indeed, the consummation of the affair between Dick and Rosemary seems to provide them less genuine satisfaction than Tommy and Nicole take from their illicit embrace. There is some deficiency in the intense passion Dick feels for Rosemary, and the key to that deficiency seems to be provided by the recurring theme of perversion in the novel. But, it should be noted, sexual perversion is but one variation of the other perversions that pervade the action—the perversion of money, the perversion of play, the perversion of ideas, the perversion of talent.

Incidents of incest, homosexuality, and lesbianism recur so frequently throughout the book as to assume the proportions of a major theme. There is, to begin with, Mr. Devereux Warren's violation of his own daughter, Nicole, which sets off the chain of events that leads to the book's major disasters. And there is Baby Warren, forever flirting but forever frigid, her passions imprisoned by the family money. As the action moves out onto the beaches of the Riviera, we encounter the effeminate Royal Dumphry and Luis Campion and follow them (via Rosemary) through some obscure love spat that brings tears to Campion's eyes. Sometime later in the novel, when Dick goes as a doctor to Lausanne to advise on the "treatment" of a proud and desperate Chilean's homosexual son, he discovers him in the company of this same Royal Dumphry, a case apparently beyond hope. This recurring note in the novel reaches something of a climax in the tragicomic scene near the end, in which Mary North, now the Contessa di Minghetti, and Lady Caroline Sibley-Biers, both dressed as sailors, are caught picking up two girls. Although everyone pretends that the incident was an innocent escapade, Dick and the others realize that the innocence is pretense.

All these happenings provide a backdrop for Dick Diver's own ambivalent sexual impulses. There is a strange element in Nicole's relationship to him that is suggested at the very beginning. In one of her immature love letters, she says: ". . . you seem quieter than the others, all soft like a big cat. I have only gotten to like boys who are rather sissies. Are you a sissy?"(10). Later, on the Riviera, a small, seemingly casual incident recalls these earlier lines: "Nicole handed her husband the curious garment on which she had been working. He went into the dressing tent and inspired a commotion by appearing in a moment clad in transparent black lace drawers. Close inspection revealed that actually they were lined with flesh-colored cloth." This "pansy trick" (as Mr. McKisco calls it) appears innocently silly—but it strikes a slightly dissonant note in the context of Nicole's earlier letter. The restlessness in Dick that moves him to kiss one of his patients ("In an idle, almost indulgent way, he kissed her"[203]) and to be sexually attracted to another (who is "a living, agonizing sore" [199]) runs in deeper, darker channels than he knows. Near the end of the novel, when Lady Caroline Sibley-Biers accuses Dick, in the hearing of others, of "associating with a questionable crowd in Lausanne"(291), there are several levels of irony, the clearest of which derives from the character of the accuser. But Dick's certain innocence of the charge is to some extent eroded by the accumulated sexual perversion in the novel, which, even when it does not embrace Dick, seems to brush against him, leaving its indelible mark.

Tender Is the Night tends in its thematic complexity to move rhythmically both inward and outward, inward to an exploration in depth of the spiritual malaise of Dick Diver, outward to an examination in breadth of the sickness of a society and a culture. A brilliant example of the novel's outward movement will suggest something of the nature of Fitzgerald's unique perspective on the rich:

> Nicole was the product of much ingenuity and toil. For her sake trains began their run in Chicago and traversed the round belly of the continent to California; chicle factories fumed and link belts grew link by link in factories; men mixed toothpaste in vats and drew mouthwash out of copper hogsheads; girls canned tomatoes quickly in August or worked rudely at the Five-and-Tens on Christmas Eve; half-breed Indians toiled on Brazilian coffee plantations and dreamers were muscled out of patent rights in new tractors—these were some of the people who gave a tithe to Nicole and, as the whole system swayed

> and thundered onward, it lent a feverish bloom to such processes of hers as wholesale buying, like the flush of a fireman's face holding his post before a spreading blaze. She illustrated very simple principles, containing in herself her own doom, but illustrated them so accurately that there was grace in the procedure . . . (113–14).

The vision here is deceptively simple, stubbornly dispassionate, where one, especially in 1934, might expect severe censure of a "system." But the criticism is there like an undercurrent, and Nicole is made symbolic of a class without sacrificing any of her individual personality. Two words leap out of the closing sentence to fix their place in the mind—"doom" and "grace." These sum up Nicole and all her fabulous class, and they combine to create a poignant charm that Fitzgerald examines in all its magnetism and repulsion.

It is in this world, represented by Nicole, that Dick Diver meets his fate. He is both created by this world to serve its selfish ends and destroyed by it when his usefulness is squandered. He is a victim—but he is victim not only of these outside forces but also of his inner weaknesses and compulsions. It is impossible—and pointless—to apportion the blame. But it is useful to remember that Fitzgerald took his title from Keats's "Ode to a Nightingale":

> Away! away! for I will fly to thee,
>   Not charioted by Bacchus and his pards,
> But on the viewless wings of Poesy,
>   Though the dull brain perplexes and retards:
> Already with thee! Tender is the night,
>   And haply the Queen-Moon is on her throne,
>   Clustered around by all her starry Fays;
>   But here there is no light,
> Save what from heaven is with the breezes blown
>   Through verdurous glooms and winding mossy ways.

There are many possible ways of connecting Keats's words with Fitzgerald's book. One way, perhaps ironically, is to identify Nicole (as Dick sees her) and the nightingale, her world (as Dick conceives it) with the world that Keats so vividly imagines. It is the fairy world of fulfilled romance—but it is also the world of night, silence, and repose. In short, it has the attraction of death. Like Keats, Dick seems to be "half in love with easeful Death." Unlike Keats, he finds no "bell" to toll him back to his "sole self." He loses that self, not through literal death, but through profligacy of the spirit. His sole self is squandered on all the others, and at the last nothing remains for him.

Notes

1. For an account of the several versions, see Malcolm Cowley, "Introduction," *Tender Is the Night* (New York: Charles Scribner's Sons, 1951). See also Matthew J. Bruccoli, *The Composition of "Tender Is the Night"* (Pittsburgh: University of Pittsburgh Press, 1963), published after this book was in press.

2. John Chamberlain, "Tender Is the Night," *F. Scott Fitzgerald: The Man and His Work* (New York: Collier Books, 1962), p.96.

3. Quoted by Malcolm Cowley, "Introduction," *Tender Is the Night*, p.xi.

4. Ibid., p.xii.

5. Ibid., pp.viii, xix.

6. Numbers after quotations refer to page numbers in the 1951 edition of *Tender Is the Night*, ed. Malcolm Cowley.

7. Fitzgerald, "Letters to Friends," *The Crack-Up*, p.278.

6. *Tender Is the Night*

by ARTHUR MIZENER

F. Scott Fitzgerald was the first of the gifted American novelists of the 1920's to become famous; he had a Byronic, overnight success with his first novel, *This Side of Paradise*, which was published in the first year of the decade. It was a brash, immature novel that Fitzgerald's lifelong friend Edmund Wilson called "one of the most illiterate books of any merit ever published." Later in his life Fitzgerald himself said of it, with the queer impersonality he could always give his considered judgments of himself, "A lot of people thought it was a fake, and perhaps it was, and a lot of others thought it was a lie, which it was not."

The essential quality of Fitzgerald's insight is shown by that comment. Looked at objectively, *This Side of Paradise* was in many ways a fake; it pretended to all sorts of knowledge and experience of the world its author did not in fact have. But it was not a lie; it expressed with accuracy and honesty its author's inner vision of himself and his experience, however false to literal fact that vision might be at certain points. Fitzgerald's reality was always that inner vision, but he had a deep respect for the outer reality of the world because it was the only place where his inward vision could be fulfilled, could be made actual. The tension between his inescapable commitment to the inner reality of his imagination and his necessary respect for the outer reality of the world is what gives his fiction its peculiar charm and is the source of his ability to surround a convincing representation of the actual world with an air of enchantment that makes the most ordinary occasions haunting.

The success of *This Side of Paradise* did not do Fitzgerald any good. It gave him the fame and money to plunge into the gay whirl of New York parties that in postwar America somehow seemed to be a more significant life than the provincial one prewar America had lived. Fitzgerald and his beautiful wife, Zelda, rode through New York on the tops of taxis, jumped fully clothed into the Pulitzer Fountain in front of the Plaza, and quickly became leaders among the bright spirits of postwar New York. It was all harmless enough in itself, but it left very little time for serious writing, particularly for a man to whom alcohol was very damaging, almost a poison.

Yet all the time Fitzgerald was busy being the handsome hero of the Younger Generation, there was a serious writer inside him struggling to get out. That serious writer got control for a moment when he wrote *The Great Gatsby* (1924). But then the Fitzgeralds fell back into the life of parties—now mostly in Paris and on the Riviera—that gradually became for them a more and more desperate and self-destructive effort to be happy. It ended in 1930, when Zelda became a serious schizophrene and Fitzgerald, pulled up short by this disaster, found himself an alcoholic. He spent the rest of his brief life—he died in 1940, shortly after his forty-fourth birthday—fighting a grim battle to save Zelda, to cure his own alcoholism, and to fulfill his promise as a writer. "I have been a poor caretaker of everything I possessed," he said at this time, "even of my talent." He lost Zelda—she never grew better—and he was only partly successful in his fight against alcoholism. But, sick and discouraged though he was, he managed before he died to write *Tender Is the Night*, published in 1934, and a marvelous fragment of another novel called *The Last Tycoon.*

Tender Is the Night has certain defects traceable to the conditions in which it was written. As Fitzgerald himself said of it with his remarkable honesty, "If a mind is slowed up ever so little, it lives in the individual parts of a book rather than in a book as a whole; memory is dulled. I would give anything if I hadn't had to write Part III of 'Tender Is the Night' entirely on stimulant." Despite these defects, *Tender Is the Night* is the most mature and moving book Fitzgerald ever wrote.

It is not, however, an easy book to understand. Its difficulty is at least partly due to the odd discrepancy in it between the almost frivolous insignificance—by conventional standards anyhow—of the hero's life and the importance Fitzgerald obviously means us to attach to it. This difficulty in *Tender Is the Night* is only a particular instance of the general problem created in American fiction by the subjective novel as distinguished from the objective novel of social history such as Dos Passos wrote.

Fitzgerald and Dos Passos were friends, but it is evident that neither could understand what the other was up to. In 1933, the year before Fitzgerald completed *Tender Is the Night*, he wrote a mutual friend, "Dos was here, & we had a nice evening—we never quite understand each other & perhaps that's the best basis for an enduring friendship." As if to prove how right Fitzgerald was, Dos Passos wrote him, when he published the revealing essays called "The Crack-Up" that describe the personal experience underlying *Tender Is the Night*, "I've been wanting to see you, naturally, to argue about your *Esquire* articles—Christ, man, how do you find time in the middle of the general conflagration to worry about all that stuff? . . . most of the time the course of world events seem so frightful that I feel absolutely paralysed." Clearly, Dos Passos is baffled by Fitzgerald's preoccupation "with all that stuff" about the meaning of his personal experience. Fitzgerald was equally baffled by Dos Passos' obsession with "the course of world events."

There was of course a subjective novelist somewhere in Dos Passos, but Dos Passos relegated this novelist to the Camera Eye passages of *U.S.A.* and he affects the narrative only indirectly. There was also a man with a considerable sense of history in Fitzgerald: as Malcolm Cowley once put it, Fitzgerald lived in a room full of clocks and calendars. But Fitzgerald's knowledge of history, astonishing as his memory for it was, gets into his novels almost entirely as metaphors for the life of his consciousness, for the quality of his private experience. His summary of the year 1927—the year in which the slow decline of Dick Diver, the hero of *Tender Is the Night*, becomes clearly evident—is characteristic:

> By 1927 a wide-spread neurosis began to be evident, faintly signalled, like a nervous beating of the feet, by the popularity of cross-word puzzles. I remember a fellow expatriate opening a letter from a mutual friend of ours, urging him to come home and be revitalized by the hardy, bracing qualities of the native soil. It was a strong letter and it affected us both deeply, until we noticed that it was headed from a nerve sanitarium in Pennsylvania.

Fitzgerald tended to notice only those events that had this kind of meaning for him, that came to life for him as images of his personal feelings. The advantage of knowing the world in this way is that anything you notice at all takes on the vividness of your strongest private emotions. But because Fitzgerald knew the world this way, he had little capacity for sharing the common, public understanding of it. For readers to whom a novel is a dramatic representation of the world as that understanding knows it, Fitzgerald often appears to be treating with ridiculous seriousness characters and situations that "everyone knows" are insignificant.

One can frequently see in Fitzgerald's actual life, where conventional judgments are more important—or at least more difficult to ignore—how little such judgments really counted for him. All his life, for instance, he remembered bitterly his failure to achieve social success as an undergraduate at Princeton. The conventional judgment is that undergraduate social life is trivial, but Fitzgerald's failure at Princeton—whatever common sense may say of its circumstances—involved his deepest private feelings. Princeton was his first independent experience of the world, and he threw himself into realizing his ambitions there exactly as if Princeton had been the great world itself. For him the common judgment of Princeton's unimportance did not count; what counted was what he felt. He came very close to succeeding at Princeton, except that he neglected what was to him the trifling business of passing his courses, which seemed to him a great bore, and just as he was about to come into his kingdom as a big man on campus, he was forced to leave the university.

He tried for the rest of his life to tell himself that society always has this power to enforce its own values and that it was foolish of him to ignore the university's academic requirements simply because they were insignificant to him. But he never could really believe it, and gradually this experience at Princeton became for him—despite the objective insignificance of its occasion—one of his two or three major images for the unjust suffering that is the essence of human defeat.

This typical episode makes it evident that Fitzgerald, subjective novelist though he was, was not the kind of man who could commit himself wholly to the life of inner reality or be content as a novelist "with a very slight embroidery of outward manners, the faintest possible counterfeit of real life." In his life Fitzgerald strove to achieve in the actual world the ideal life he could so vividly imagine, and he was intent as a writer on producing the most lively possible counterfeit of real life.

But if this episode shows us that both in his life and his work he was determined to live in the actual world, as he often did quite dazzlingly, it also shows us that for him the meaning and value of the world were something that was determined by his private feelings, which operated independently of the established, conventional understanding of the world, not because he was consciously defying that understanding—his desire to realize the good life as he conceived it made him struggle to conform—but because the subjective life of his imagination was so intense, so overwhelmingly real for him, that even his efforts to conform to conventional ideas transformed them into something personal and queer.

Fitzgerald's first mature novel, *The Great Gatsby*, for example, is a brilliant picture of Long Island society in the 1920's. But that is only one aspect of it, the image Fitzgerald creates for a feeling too complex to be expressed in any other way. *The Great Gatsby* is a fable, marked at every important point by the folklore qualities of fables and charged with meaning by a style that is, despite the sharpness of its realistic detail, alive with poetic force. At the crisis of the story, the heroine, Daisy Buchanan, unintentionally reveals to her husband by the unguarded tone of her beautifully expressive voice that she loves Gatsby. The narrator says anxiously to Gatsby, "She's got an indiscreet voice. It's full of—" and when he hesitates Gatsby says suddenly, "Her voice is full of money." And the narrator thinks, "That was it. I'd never understood before. It was full of money—that was the inexhaustible charm that rose and fell on it, the jingle of it, the cymbals' song of it . . . High in a white palace the king's daughter, the golden girl. . . ."

This passage is resonant with an irony that echoes back and forth between the gross actual fact of money jingling in the pocket and the romance of beauty adorned, of the golden girl. On the surface Daisy Buchanan is a convincing, historically accurate portrait of the charming and irresponsible upper-class girl of the American twenties. But she is also the princess, high in a white palace, for whom the disregarded younger son longs hopelessly, until the great moment when he astonishes everyone by performing the impossible feat that wins her hand.

One of the things that has certainly helped make *Tender Is the Night* less popular than *The Great Gatsby* of ten years earlier is that the image it uses, its story, is not, as social history, so significant as Gatsby's. Its story describes the life of well-to-do American expatriates on the Riviera during the 1920's, and such people are usually thought to be about as insignificant as Princeton undergraduates. They were especialy thought to be so when the novel was published in 1934 at the depth of the Great Depression, and the idea that Fitzgerald was naively impressed by rich people became widely accepted. This is one of those foolish ideas put about by people who cannot read. Fitzgerald was no more a mere worshiper of rich people than Henry James was a snob. He was a man who dreamed of actually living the good life men can imagine. He had, as did Jay Gatsby, "a heightened sensitivity to the promises of life," and he had the elementary common sense to see that in real life the rich have an opportunity to live the good life that the rest of us do not.

One consequence of his seeing they do was that he felt the deepest scorn—what he called "the smouldering hatred of the peasant"—for rich people who did not take full advantage of the opportunity their wealth gave them. About rich people of this kind *Tender Is the Night* is devastating. Another consequence of it was his fascination with the intelligent and sensitive among the rich, like Dick Diver, who could see that opportunity. With his Irish sense of the absurd aspect of what he believed most deeply, Fitzgerald could make fun of this ideal as he had formulated it for himself, what he called "the Goethe-Byron-Shaw idea, with an opulent American touch—a sort of combination of Topham Beauclerk, St. Francis of Assisi, and J. P. Morgan"; and in the end he came to feel that the unimaginative brutality and organized chaos of the life of the rich always defeated men like Dick Diver. In Dick's best moment, *Tender Is the Night* shows us how beautiful the realized ideal life is; but in the end it shows us that people with the sensitivity and imagination to conceive that life cannot survive among the rich.

Tender Is the Night begins with the arrival of a young movie star named Rosemary Hoyt at Cap d'Antibes on the Riviera.* When Rosemary goes down to the beach she finds herself between two groups of expatriates. The first is an incoherent mixture. There is "Mama" Abrams, "one of those elderly 'good sports' preserved by an imperviousness to experience and a good digestion into another generation." There is a writer named Albert McKisco who, according to his wife, Violet, is at work on a novel "on the idea of Ulysses. Only instead of taking twenty-four hours [he] takes a hundred years. He takes a decayed old French aristocrat and puts him in contrast with the mechanical age. . . ." There is a waspishly witty young man named Royal Dumphry and his companion, Luis Campion, who keeps admonishing Mr. Dumphry not to "be too ghastly for words." The other group consists of Dick Diver and his wife, Nicole, their friends Abe and Mary North, and a young Frenchman named Tommy Barban.

Rosemary is instinctively attracted to the second group but

* There are two versions of *Tender Is the Night* in print, the original one described here and a revision based partly on a letter Fitzgerald wrote his editor late in his life and partly on a copy of the book found among his papers after he died, in which, along with some minor revisions in Book I, he had placed the original Book I after Book II Chapter 2.

she is quickly picked up by the first group, who cannot wait to tell her they recognize her from her film. It is not a very happy group. For one thing, it is clearly jealous of the second group. "If you want to enjoy yourself here," Mrs. McKisco says, "the thing is to get to know some real French families. What do these people get out of it? They just stick around with each other in little cliques. Of course we had letters of introduction and met all the best French artists and writers in Paris." For another thing, Mr. McKisco is being difficult, as if, in spite of his extensive collection of secondhand attitudes from the best reviews, he does not quite know who he is or where he is going. When his wife makes a harmless joke, he bursts out irritably, "For God's sake, Violet, drop the subject! Get a new joke, for God's sake!" and when she leans over to Mrs. Abrams and says apologetically, "He's nervous," McKisco barks, "I'm not nervous. It just happens I'm not nervous at all."

It is the poverty of ideas and the mediocrity of imagination in these people, the shapelessness of their natures, that depresses and discomforts Rosemary and makes her dislike them. It is her glimpses of the opposite qualities in the second group that attracts her. What Rosemary sees in Dick Diver is his consideration, his grace, his sensitivity to others, and—behind them all—his intense vitality. No wonder she falls in love with him.

At this point Fitzgerald goes back to trace Dick's history. He is the son of a gentle, impoverished clergyman in Buffalo, from whom he had inherited his old-fashioned, formal manners and what Fitzgerald calls " 'good instincts,' honor, courtesy, courage." He has gone to Yale, been a Rhodes Scholar, and been trained as a psychiatrist at Johns Hopkins, in Vienna, and in Zurich. After the war, he returns to Zurich, where he meets again a young mental patient named Nicole Warren, who has clung to their slight relation all through the war and her slow recovery from an illness that is not congenital but has been brought on by her father's seducing her.

Dick falls in love with Nicole, and in spite of his professional knowledge that she may be a lifelong mental problem, despite the unconscious arrogance with which the Warrens make it clear they are buying a doctor to take care of Nicole, he marries her. This act reveals the defect of uncontrollable generosity in Dick's character. "He wanted," Fitzgerald says, "to be good, he wanted to be kind, he wanted to be brave and wise . . . ; [and] he wanted to be loved, too. . . ." He had an "extraordinary virtuosity with people . . . the power of arousing a fascinated and uncritical love." This power was a kind of imaginative unselfishness; "it was themselves he gave back to [people]," as Fitzgerald says, "blurred by the compromise of how many years." This power he could not resist exercising, not merely to give Nicole back her self but to make everyone he came close to feel once more the self he had been at his best.

Dick knows from the start that in taking up his life with Nicole among the Warrens and their kind he is making the task he has set himself as difficult as possible, but with his youthful vitality intact, that seems to him only to make it more challenging and interesting. For five years he meets that challenge effortlessly. Then, at first imperceptibly, his life begins to slip from his control. Something within him, some essential vitality, is beginning to decline, and he slowly realizes that he has exhausted the source of energy for the superb self-discipline that makes it possible for him to perform for others what he calls his "trick of the heart."

This change occurs very deep in his nature. Fitzgerald is careful to prevent the reader from thinking it is some change controllable by the will, some drift into dissipation or the idleness of the rich. Dick does begin to drift in these ways, but that is only a symptom of his trouble, a desperate search for something to fill the time and stave off boredom after the meaning and purpose have gone out of his life. What destroys Dick is something far more obscure and difficult to grasp, some spiritual malaise that is anterior to any rational cause and is—as has become much plainer since Fitzgerald noticed it—as widespread among sensitive people in our time as was accidie in the middle ages or melancholia, the "Elizabethan malady," in Shakespeare's. Dick Diver is, as Fitzgerald put it in one of his notes for the book, not simply an *homme manqué*, but an *homme épuisé*. He is in a state of terrible spiritual ennui that is without visible cause and yet makes men like him—talented, attractive, successful—feel quite literally that *all* the uses of the world are weary, stale, flat, and unprofitable. "I did not manage, I think in retrospect," Fitzgerald once said of Dick Diver, "to give Dick the cohesion I aimed at. . . . I wonder what the hell the first actor who played Hamlet thought of the part? I can hear him say, 'The guy's a nut, isn't he?' (We can always find great consolation in Shakespeare)."

Perhaps he did not manage to give Dick all the cohesion he might have, but the real difficulty is that the source of Dick's disaster is indescribable. It can be shown and felt, but it can no more be analyzed than Hamlet's disaster can. As a result the main action of *Tender Is the Night* is, for all its haunting emotional appeal, as puzzling and unparaphrasable as is the famous passage from Keats's *Ode to a Nightingale* from which its title comes.

What Fitzgerald can—and does—do is to create for the reader a group of characters who, as dramatic parallels or contrasts with Dick, show what he is. The first of these we learn all about is Abe North, a musician who, after a brilliant start, has done nothing for the last seven years except drink. When Mary North says, "I used to think until you're eighteen nothing matters," he says, "That's right. And afterwards it's the same way." And when Nicole, frightened at what he is doing to himself and irritated by his lack of any visible reasons for doing it, says to him, "I can't see why you've given up on everything," he can only say, "I suppose I got bored; and then it was such a long way to go back in order to get anywhere." Dick has understood from the beginning what has happened to Abe, even though he will not know what it feels like until later. "Smart men," he has said of Abe, "play close to the line because they have to—some of them can't stand it, so they quit." Thus, at the very start of the novel, Abe North has reached the point Dick will reach at its end.

About halfway through the novel, just as Dick is beginning his own desperate battle with the impulse to quit, he hears—in fact, he overhears, as a piece of idle, feelingless gossip—that Abe has been beaten up in a New York speakeasy and crawled to the Racket Club to die—or was it the Harvard Club? The gossips' grumbling quarrel over where it was Abe died fades out around Dick as he tries to face the meaning of Abe's death, a death more shocking—more grubby and humiliating as well as more terrifying to him—than anything he had dreamed of.

There is also Tommy Barban, a sophisticated and worldly barbarian of great charm, who stands for everything Dick Diver most disapproves of. The carefully ordered life that Dick first constructed for Nicole and himself because it was necessary to Nicole's health has, as Nicole's need for it has slowly decreased, been gradually transformed to another purpose, until it has became an alert but elaborate, almost ritualized ordering of the pleasures of a highly cultivated existence. The whole business irritates Tommy, partly because it is all strictly under Dick's control and holds Nicole, with whom Tommy has been in love for years, a prisoner, but partly too because it represents in itself a way of life that offends him deeply. When he is about to leave the Riviera, Rosemary Hoyt asks him if he is going home. "Home?" he says, "I have no home. I am going to a war," and when Rosemary asks him what war, he says, "What war? Any war. I haven't seen a paper lately but I suppose there's a war—there always is." A little shocked by this, Rosemary asks him if he doesn't care at all about what he may find himself fighting for, and he says, "Not at all—so long as I'm well treated. When I'm in a rut I come to see the Divers, because I know that in a few weeks I'll want to go to war."

The novel's central group of characters consists of Dick, Nicole, Rosemary, and these two. It is surrounded by a larger group of minor characters, each of whom shows us an aspect of the world Dick Diver lives in. There is Lady Caroline Sibley-Biers, the latest wild woman from London, petulant and stupid, whose idea of amusement is to dress up as a French sailor and pick up a girl in Antibes. There is Baby Warren, Nicole's sister, "a tall fine-looking woman deeply engaged in being thirty" who "was alien from touch" and for whom "such lingering touches as kisses and embraces slipped directly through the flesh into the forefront of her consciousness." She is supremely confident that the most dehumanized routines of British social life are the ideal existence and that her series of engagements to socially eligible Englishmen, which even she no longer really expects will come to anything, constitutes a full life. There is Albert McKisco, the confused but proud possessor of a host of secondhand ideas that safely insulate him from experience. Such characters define for us the chic grossness, the neurotic orderliness, the lifeless intellectuality of the world Dick Diver lives in. They are not what they are because they are rich, though, being rich, they are able to be what they are with a freedom and completeness that ordinary people cannot. Still, they are not what they are merely because they are rich; they are so because the world is.

In this world Dick Diver's need to reach out to people, to galvanize them into life by reminding them of the selves they originally were, is like a wound, a "lesion of vitality" as Fitzgerald calls it, from which his spiritual energy slowly drips away until there is nothing left. At the beginning of the novel, "one June morning in 1925" when Rosemary meets Dick, the first faint signs of the loss have begun to show. He is still able to produce for people such enchanted moments as the one on the beach that Rosemary has watched with delight, when he holds a whole group of people enthralled, not by what he does—what he does is almost nothing—but by the quality of his performance, the delicate sense of the tone and feeling of occasion and audience by which he can make a small group of people feel they are alone with each other in the dark universe, in some magically protected place where they can be their best selves. He performs this trick of the heart once again for Rosemary when she goes to dinner with the Divers just after she has met them. At the climax of that dinner, the table seemed for a moment "to have risen a little toward the sky like a mechanical dancing platform" and

> the two Divers began suddenly to warm and glow and expand, as if to make up to their guests, already so subtly assured of their importance, so flattered with politeness, for anything they might still miss from that country well left behind. Just for a moment they seemed to speak to every one at the table, singly and together, assuring them of their friendliness, their affection. And for a moment the faces turned up toward them were like the faces of poor children at a Christmas tree.

But now, each such moment is followed for Dick by a spell of deep melancholy in which he looks "back with awe at the carnival of affection he had given, as a general might gaze at a massacre he had ordered to satisfy an impersonal blood lust." Rosemary catches a glimpse of that melancholy, without recognizing it, her very first morning on the beach when, after all the others have gone, Dick stops to tell her she must not get too sunburned and she says with young cheerfulness, "Do you know what time it is?" and Dick says, "It's about half-past one."

> They faced the seascape together momentarily.
> "It's not a bad time," said Dick Diver. "It's not one of the worst times of the day."

These periods of melancholy are one consequence of his decreasing vitality; another is his inability to maintain the self-discipline he has heretofore exercised almost unconsciously because it is only by not yielding to his momentary impulses that he can fulfill his central need to make the world over for others. The first failure of this discipline—and the major one—is allowing himself to fall in love with Rosemary. Though he cannot control that impulse, he knows that it "marked a turning point in his life—it was out of line with everything that had preceded it—even out of line with what effect he might hope to produce on Rosemary." Then he finds himself drinking just a little too much in a carefully controlled way—"an ounce of gin with twice as much water" at carefully spaced intervals. The book on psychiatry he has been working on for years begins to seem to him stale and unimportant and his work at the clinic tiresome. "Not without desperation he had long felt the ethics of his profession dissolving into a lifeless mass." When Nicole has a third serious breakdown, the long months of "restating the universe for her" leave him exhausted in a way he has never known before.

He goes off alone to try to rest and get himself together and discovers to his horror that he cannot stop yielding to every vagrant impulse of his nature—to charm a pretty girl, to blurt out without regard for his listeners the bitterness in his heart. He sees more clearly than anyone what is happening to him, but since it is happening somewhere below the level of reason, beyond the control of his will, he can only watch helplessly. "He had lost himself—he could not tell the hour when, or the week, the month, or the year. . . . Between the time he found Nicole flowering under a stone on the Zurichsee and the moment of his meeting with Rosemary the spear had been blunted."

The first faint signs of this loss of self had appeared at that first meeting with Rosemary Hoyt on the beach at Antibes. When, five years later, he and Rosemary meet again on the same beach, now crowded with dull, fashionable people, he says to her, "Did you hear I'd gone into a process of deterioration? . . . It's true. The change came a long way back—but at first it didn't show. The manner remains intact after the morale cracks." By a desperate effort he can still force himself at moments to exercise that manner, but these moments come more and more rarely and require him to be drunker and drunker, a condition in which he is as likely to assert the black despair in his heart in some outburst of incoherent violence, as he does when he picks a fight in Rome with a detective and is beaten up and thrown in jail, or when at Antibes he gets into a drunken, confused argument with Lady Caroline Sibley-Biers and even she is able to make him look foolish. These scenes are almost intolerably moving, for Fitzgerald's lifelong habit of giving events the value they have for the person who suffers them rather than their conventional public value makes us feel these trivial misfortunes as what they are, the loose ends of life, as Zelda once said, with which men hang themselves.

Finally Dick accepts the exhaustion of his vitality and its consequences, his inability to control himself to any purpose, his inability to love and be loved by others. He sets himself to cut his losses—his responsibilities for Nicole and the children and his friends—and to bury his dead—himself. The task is made simpler by the fact that Nicole has now recovered completely. Though she still depends on Dick, her dependence is now only old habit, not necessity. As she has recovered she has become more and more the superficially orderly, inwardly anarchic barbarian that has always been her true Warren self. As such, she turns instinctively away fom Dick and toward Tommy Barban. Dick therefore sets himself to break her dependence on him and to push her toward Tommy. At the last moment he deliberately provokes a quarrel with her and then watches silently while she struggles to deny him and assert her independence. When she succeeds, "Dick waited until she was out of sight. Then he leaned his head forward on the parapet. The case was finished. Doctor Diver was at liberty."

Dick stays at Antibes just long enough to make sure Nicole is safe in Tommy's hands and then leaves for America, taking with him nothing, least of all himself.

> Nicole kept in touch with Dick after her marriage [to Tommy]. . . . [He] opened an office in Buffalo, but evidently without success. Nicole did not find what the trouble was, but she heard a few months later that he was in a little town named Batavia, New York, practicing general medicine, and later that he was in Lockport, doing the same thing. . . . He was considered to have fine manners and once made a good speech at a public health meeting on the subject of drugs; but he became entangled with a girl who worked in a grocery store, and he was involved in a law suit about some medical question; so he left Lockport. After that he didn't ask for the children to be sent to America and didn't answer when Nicole wrote asking him if he needed money. . . . His latest note was post-marked from Hornell, New York, which is some distance from Geneva and a small town; in any case he is certainly in that section of the country, in one town or another.

7. The "Intricate Destiny" of Dick Diver

by EUGENE WHITE

The usual reading of F. Scott Fitzgerald's *Tender Is The Night* makes the hero, Dr. Richard Diver, something less than heroic and considerably less than a tragic figure. He is a brilliant psychiatrist whose life is ruined because he falls in love with the wrong woman and because his vitality is sapped by the abundance of the Warren money.[1] It seems to me, however, that another and more satisfying reading is possible and that careful attention to certain key passages in the novel makes such a reading plausible, if not inevitable. Therefore, I should like to offer support for the theory that Dick Diver is a man who because of his deep love for Nicole Warren makes a deliberate choice with full realization of the dilemma which it will eventually force upon him. And when the dilemma must be resolved, he chooses what is best for Nicole even though it brings heartbreak to him.

As a psychiatrist he knows the pattern which Nicole's life will follow, he knows what marriage to her would mean. Moreover, to make certain that there is no illusion, his colleagues and mentors Franz and Dohmler are there to tell him bluntly that he must break with her. When they force him to face the fact that Nicole is in love with him and that this "transference" must be terminated if she is to be spared what might appear as a tragedy to her, he admits that he is half in love with her, that the question of marrying her has passed through his mind. (p.153)[2] Franz exclaims: " 'What! And devote half your life to being doctor and nurse and all—never! I know what these cases are. One time in twenty it's finished in the first push—better never see her again!' " (p.154). Dohmler agrees and they work out a plan for what Dick must do—"he must be most kind and yet eliminate himself."

Dick attempts the break but cannot go as far with it as he had intended because of the agony of watching the stricken girl as her "flimsy and scarcely created world" goes to pieces. He is puzzled and distraught as he leaves the hospital and returns to Zurich, and the next weeks are filled with a vast dissatisfaction: "The pathological origin and mechanical defeat of the affair left a flat and metallic taste. Nicole's emotions had been used unfairly—what if they turned out to have been his own?" (p.159).

At sight of her once in a car as he walked down the street in Zurich, "the air around him was loud with the circlings of all the goblins on the Gross-Munster." He goes home and tries "to write the matter out of his mind in a memorandum that went into detail as to the solemn regime before her," but it is a "memorandum that would have been convincing to any one save to him who had written it." He knows how deeply his emotions are involved. He attempts to find antidotes. He is all too aware that "the logic of his life tended away from the girl." But after encountering her on a trip to the mountains and riding back to Zurich with her on the train from Caux, he knows that "her problem was one they had together for good now"(p.173).

All of this detailed analysis of his emotional involvement and his resistance to it shows two things, of course: his powerful love for Nicole and his realization of what marriage to her will mean to his future. One might simply say that it is a battle between reason and emotion and that emotion wins. If Diver had been a stronger man, he would not have ruined his life. But this is only part of the truth. It may well be that he is a greater man because he does have the capacity for great love, for sacrificial love that knows what it is sacrificing.

The love which Dick has for Nicole must not be underestimated. Indeed, Fitzgerald will not let us underestimate it. Over and over again he insists upon it, never more so than in the scenes with Rosemary, the symbol of what he has renounced for it: the dreams, the ambitions, the creative energy of his youth. Rosemary is a romantic dream. In reality she has nothing for him as he has nothing for her. And in his yearning away from the difficult path which he has chosen he never really fools himself.

Early in their relationship, when Rosemary begs Dick to take her and he refuses, he attempts to tell her something of what his love for Nicole means, an attempt foredoomed to failure. "Active love," he says, "–it's more complicated than I can tell you"(p.81). And four years later, after he meets her in Rome and "what had begun with a childish infatuation on a beach was accomplished at last," he thinks of his feelings for Rosemary:

> He supposed many men meant no more than that when they said they were in love–not a wild submergence of soul, a dipping of all colors into an obscuring dye, such as his love for Nicole had been. Certain thoughts about Nicole, that she should die, sink into mental darkness, love another man, made him physically sick. (p.239)

It is only if we understand the greatness of his love that we can understand the tragic proportions of the dilemma with which he is faced. If he is to save her, he must give her up. This is the knowledge which Dick Diver the psychiatrist must carry with him perhaps from the moment he decides to marry Nicole. Certainly it is a knowledge which he must face squarely long before the break is accomplished.

We get one clear indication of the professional side of his relationship to Nicole following her collapse in Paris as a result of the murder of the Negro and the appearance of his body in Rosemary's room:

> It prophesied possibly a new cycle, a new *pousse* of the malady. Having gone through unprofessional agonies during her long relapse following Topsy's birth, he had, perforce, hardened himself about her, making a cleavage between Nicole sick and Nicole well. This made it difficult now to distinguish between his self-protective professional detachment and some new coldness in his heart. As an indifference cherished, or left to atrophy, becomes an emptiness, to this extent he had learned to become

> empty of Nicole, serving her against his will with negations and emotional neglect. (p.185)

And we should not forget that it is against his will that he continues to serve her by forcing her step by painful step to a completeness that can come only with independence of him. His love for her cries out to him to protect her, to shield her, to support her. At the same time his love is great enough to make him do what he knows he must do if she is ever to be a whole person again.

> Many times he had tried unsuccessfully to let go his hold on her . . . but always when he turned away from her into himself he left her holding Nothing in her hands and staring at it, calling it many names, but knowing it was only the hope that he would come back soon. (p.198)

This is the torment which racks him as he continues in his double role of Dick Diver, husband, and Dr. Richard Diver, psychiatrist. It is stated explicitly after Nicole's running away from him and the children at the Agiri Fair. Recovering, she begs, " 'Help me, help me, Dick!' A wave of agony went over him. It was awful that such a fine tower should not be erected, only suspended, suspended from him"(p.210). It is Tommy Barban who becomes the final instrument of release. And Dick knows it even before Nicole does, knows it, fights his inward battle and comes out the victor and the loser.

Nicole is vaguely aware that something beyond her understanding and beyond her control is developing. She senses that it is willed by her husband and forced inexorably to its conclusion as he drains his own heart's blood to give her life. "It was as though an incalculable story was telling itself inside him, about which she could only guess at in the moments when it broke through the surface"(p.292).

It comes close to the surface when they board the Golding yacht and Nicole meets Tommy Barban. "In the moment of meeting she lay on his bosom, spiritually, going out and out. . . . Then self-preservation reasserted itself and retiring to her own world she spoke lightly"(p.294). The evening goes badly. Dick fights with the vicious Lady Caroline Sibley-Biers. For a moment alone on the deck his despair brings him almost to the point of carrying Nicole with him in a suicidal leap into the water below, and she yields to him "in one moment of complete response and abnegation." Instead, he lets her go, Tommy joins them, and never again is she completely his.

Next morning Nicole is happy knowing that two men, Dick and Tommy, are in a sense in combat for her: "She did not want anything to happen, but only for the situation to remain in suspension as the two men tossed her from one mind to another; she had not existed for a long time, even as a ball" (p.301). She begins to think of an affair with Tommy. "If she need not, in her spirit, be forever one with Dick as he had appeared last night, she must be something in addition, not just an image on his mind, condemned to endless parades around the circumference of a medal"(p.302). She has reached the first real point of independence. For the first time she can defy Dick, as she does a few moments later when, against Dick's express command, she tosses the whole jar of camphor-rub to the departing Tommy and then turns "to take her own medicine."

Following him upstairs, where he lies down on his own bed without saying anything, she asks if he wants lunch brought up.

> He nodded and continued to lie quiescent, staring at the ceiling. Doubtfully she went to give the order. Upstairs again she looked into his room–the blue eyes, like searchlights, played on a dark sky. She stood a minute in the doorway, aware of the sin she had committed against him half afraid to come in. . . . She put out her hand as if to rub his head, but he turned away like a suspicious animal. Nicole could stand the situation no longer; in a kitchenmaid's panic she ran downstairs, afraid of what the stricken man above would feed on while she must still continue her dry suckling at his lean chest. (p.304)

How dark the sky on which his blue eyes played Nicole can not guess. It is a sky darkened by a loss which only Dick foresees and must not stop. She has only an "apprehension that Dick was contriving at some desperate solution."

> Since the evening on Golding's yacht she had sensed what was going on. So delicately balanced was she between an old foothold that had always guaranteed her security, and the imminence of a leap from which she must alight changed in the very chemistry of blood and muscle, that she did not dare bring the matter into the true forefront of consciousness. . . . For months every word had seemed to have an undertone of some other meaning, soon to be resolved under circumstances that Dick would determine. (p.305)

Dick, the physician, is certainly aware of this delicate balance and aware that he controls it. The torture, the disintegration of these last months is fully understandable only if we are aware of the agony of such dread control.

As Nicole comes gradually to a realization that she can stand alone, a new sense of freedom develops within her:

> She had a sense of being cured and in a new way. Her ego began blooming like a great rich rose as she scrambled back along the labyrinths in which she had wandered for years. She hated the beach, resented the places where she had played planet to Dick's sun.
>
> "Why, I'm almost complete," she thought. "I'm practically standing alone, without him." And like a happy child, wanting the completion as soon as possible, *and knowing vaguely that Dick had planned for her to have it* [italics mine], she lay on her bed as soon as she got home and wrote Tommy Barban in Nice a short provocative letter.
>
> But that was for the daytime—toward evening with the inevitable diminution of nervous energy, her spirits flagged, and the arrows flew a little in the twilight. She was afraid of what was in Dick's mind; again she felt that a plan underlay his current actions and she was afraid of his plans—they worked well and they had an all-inclusive logic about them which Nicole was not able to command. (p.316)

But the cure is not yet complete, the darkest hour has not yet arrived for Dick. It follows swiftly after Nicole's rendezvous with Tommy Barban.

As she wanders about the house remembering the details of the day before and trying to arrive at some kind of justification of her action, "remorse for this moment of betrayal, which so cavalierly belittled a decade of her life, turned her walk toward Dick's sanctuary."

> Approaching noiselessly she saw him behind his cottage, sitting in a steamer chair by the cliff wall, and for a moment she regarded him silently. He was thinking, he was living a world completely his own and in the small motions of his face, the brow raised or lowered, the eyes narrowed or widened, the lips set and reset, the play of his hands, she saw him progress from phase to phase of his own story spinning out inside him, his own, not hers. Once he clenched his fists and leaned forward, once it brought into his face an expression of torment and despair—when this passed its stamp lingered in his eyes. For almost the first time in her life she was sorry for him—it is hard for those who have once been mentally afflicted to be sorry for those who are well, and though Nicole often paid lip service to the fact that he had led her back to the world she had forfeited, she had thought of him really as an inexhaustible energy, incapable of fatigue—she forgot the troubles she caused him at the moment when she forgot the troubles of her own that had prompted her. That he no longer controlled her—did he know that? Had he willed it all? (p.329)

Nicole has unknowingly been present at Gethsemane. Through her eyes we have seen Dick in the struggles of his darkest hour, the hour when he knows that he has saved Nicole and must now try to save himself. He rebuffs her tentative gesture toward him. He forces her to anger. She struggles to free herself from the power she still responds to in him.

> And suddenly, in the space of two minutes she achieved her victory and justified herself to herself without lie or subterfuge, cut the cord forever. Then she walked, weak in the legs, and sobbing coolly, toward the household that was hers at last.
>
> Dick waited until she was out of sight. Then he leaned his head forward on the parapet. The case was finished. Doctor Diver was at liberty. (p.330)

At liberty for what? Can the doctor of ten years ago, the doctor with the brilliant future, take up again where he left off, as if those intervening years had not taken their toll? Of course not. The toll has been too much. He is sapped, drained emotionally. His energy, his strength, his love have been expended in the one passion of his life. "The layer of hardness in him, of self-control and of self-discipline" which Rosemary had felt in him at their first meeting had served him well. It will serve him still as he moves from one small town practice to another, but it cannot wipe out what has been or compensate for what can never be again.

Such a reading obviously makes Dick Diver a more admirable character and a more heroic one. His story assumes the dimensions of tragedy if one accepts his choice to marry Nicole and his choice to free her as deliberately made because of his love for her. But Fitzgerald is too good a writer to make it quite that simple. He is aware of the complexities of human motivations and personal relationships. He makes his character believable by showing the less admirable qualities in him and the selfish motives which complicate the altruistic.

A conscious decision to marry a mental patient, to devote one's life to her cure; a calculated plan to force her to completion by forcing her to renounce her savior—this is too cold, too incredible, too inhuman. The choices must be blurred, must be softened, must be less starkly rational. The plan of "redemption" must not be conceived in its entirety but must evolve from the partly unforeseeable circumstances which arise. In attempting to trace a dimension of the novel which I believe has been neglected and which I believe to be essential to a recognition of its real merit, I have presented it more baldly than it appears in the total work and removed it from the qualifying colorations which act to soften its edges and humanize it.

We are told before Dick knows whether he will marry Nicole or not, before he has to make any decision about her, something about his nature which is crucial to an understanding of his subsequent actions: "In the dead white hours in Zurich staring into a stranger's pantry across the upshine of a street lamp, he used to think that he wanted to be good, he wanted to be kind, he wanted to be brave and wise, but it was all pretty difficult. He wanted to be loved, too, if he could fit it in" (p.145).

And in a passage which comes, significantly, immediately after the final break with Nicole, the passage in which she gains completeness and with it independence of Dick, he receives a telephone call at two o'clock in the morning and responds to it by going to Antibes to help get Mary North and Caroline Sibley-Biers out of jail—two women whom he despises and who have publicly humiliated him. His response is described in these words:

> He got up and, as he absorbed the situation, his self-knowledge assured him that he would undertake to deal with it—the old fatal pleasingness, the old forceful charm, swept back with its cry of "Use me!" He would have to go fix this thing that he didn't care a damn about, because it had early become a habit to be loved.... On an almost parallel occasion, back in Dohmler's clinic on the Zurichsee, realizing this power, he had made his choice, chosen Ophelia, chosen the sweet poison and drunk it. Wanting above all to be brave and kind, he had wanted, even more than that, to be loved. (p.331)

This is the selfish element, this is the fatal weakness which underlies the pattern of his life. There is an incompleteness in him which is covered over by the charm which he has cultivated and used to draw people to him, to sweep them up and manipulate them, to use himself to attempt their fulfillment. "He was condemned to carry with him the egos of certain people, early met and early loved, and to be only as complete as they were complete themselves" (p.268).

During his studies in Vienna, sharing a flat with Ed Elkins, "who would name you all the quarterbacks in New Haven for thirty years," he begins to doubt that his mental processes are in any profound way different from the thinking of Elkins. And he has a vague perception of the incompleteness within him:

> "—And Lucky Dick can't be one of these clever men; he must be less intact, even faintly destroyed. If life won't do it for him it's not a substitute to get a disease, or a broken heart, or an inferiority complex, though it'd be nice to build out some broken side till it was better than the original structure."
>
> He mocked at his reasoning, calling it specious and "American".... He knew, though, that the price of his intactness was incompleteness. (p.126)

Mingled thus with the elements in his character which make for greatness, for love and sacrifice and discipline and control, are the elements of weakness and insufficiency, the elements which blur the actions of love and selflessness and confuse them with suggestions of self-gratification and deep-seated need. But it is this very complexity of character and of motive that enriches the story and raises it to the level of the tragic. Dr. Richard Diver is a man who "is ready to be called to his intricate destiny."

Notes

1. This is essentially the interpretation accepted by most of the members of a Danforth Seminar on Literature and Religion at the University of Chicago in the summer of 1959. See also articles by Arthur Mizener, Alfred Kazin, John Chamberlain, and C. Hartley Grattan in *F. Scott Fitzgerald, The Man and His Work*, ed., Alfred Kazin (Cleveland and New York: The World Publishing Co., 1951); Malcolm Cowley's introduction to *Tender Is the Night* in *Three Novels of F. Scott Fitzgerald* (New York: Charles Scribner's Sons, 1953); Arthur Mizener, *The Far Side of Paradise* (New York: Vintage Books, 1959). Mr. Mizener says that "what really destroys Dick is emotional bankruptcy. . . . Dick uses up the emotional energy which is the source of his personal discipline and of his power to feed other people." While I agree with this statement, my purpose is to examine the cause of this bankruptcy in order to show the conscious element in the expenditure.

2. This and all subsequent references are to the Bantam edition.

8. Fitzgerald's Fragmented Hero: Dick Diver

by JAMES ELLIS

Critics who examine *Tender Is The Night* usually agree that the motivation for Dick Diver's collapse is vague. Though the novel, they say, describes his destruction, it does not satisfactorily explain the causes for the deterioration of a man so gifted as he has been made to appear. Arthur Mizener's remark about Dick Diver is illustrative of this: "It is not easy to say . . . what, in the immediate and practical sense, happens to cause the collapse."[1] William Troy's criticism is in the same vein as Mizener's: "We are never certain whether Diver's predicament is the result of his own weak judgment or of the behavior of his neurotic wife. At the end we are strangely unmoved by his downfall because it has been less tragedy of will than of circumstance."[2]

If Mizener's and Troy's observations are valid, then *Tender Is The Night* must be artistically flawed. It seems to me, however, that motivation for Dick Diver's collapse exists within the novel and that this motivation, once discovered, indicates that his tragedy is to be traced, not to circumstance, but to his own being. To understand this motivation, the early life of Dick Diver must be examined, for his destruction is no sudden matter, having as it does its origin in his early desires and in the turmoil that he suffers as he begins to doubt his choice of profession. It is only by exploring the psychological state of Dick Diver both before and

From *The University Review*, XXXII (October 1965).

after his marriage that one can come to understand the reasons for his seemingly sudden collapse.

The son of a poor clergyman, Dick at an early age "had wedded a desire for money to an essentially unacquisitive nature."[3] After graduating from Yale and studying at Oxford as a Rhodes Scholar, he had received his degree from Johns Hopkins. At Vienna, where he has gone to study with Freud, Dick proves himself clinically adept but begins to question whether or not he really desires to be a psychiatrist. He realizes that in order to fulfill himself as a doctor, he must reject a hedonistic side of himself for whom the meaning of life is *la joie de vivre*.

At the same time that he realizes this, he also suspects (and is troubled by his suspicion) that should he reject his hedonistic self, he might be denying a part of himself that is more important to the fundamental Dick Diver than is his psychiatry.[4] Fitzgerald describes Dick as he begins to question his giving of himself to psychiatry.

> His contact with Ed Elkins [his worldly roommate in Vienna] aroused in him a first faint doubt as to the quality of his mental processes; he could not feel that they were profoundly different from the thinking of Elkins–Elkins, who would name you all the quaterbacks in New Haven for thirty years.
>
> "–And Lucky Dick can't be one of these clever men; he must be less intact, even faintly destroyed. If life won't do it for him it's not a substitute to get a disease, or a broken heart, or an inferiority complex, though it'd be nice to build out some broken side till it was better than the original structure."(p.116)

Attempting to dismiss this reasoning that leads him to compare himself to Elkins, Dick defends his studying of psychiatry:

> He mocked at his reasoning, calling it specious and "American" –his criteria of uncerebral phrase-making was that it was American. He knew, though, that the price of his intactness was incompleteness.
>
> "The best I can wish you, my child," so said the Fairy Blackstick in Thackeray's The Rose and the Ring [*sic*] "is a little misfortune." (pp.116–117)

In comparing himself to Thackeray's Prince Giglio of Paflagonia, Dick expresses his own understanding of his basic self and his antipathy toward his profession. In "The Rose and the Ring," Giglio is "a thoughtless youth, not much inclined to . . . any kind of learning,"[5] whose achievements are appreciated only by such retainers of the court as the dancing and fencing masters. The Fairy Blackstick is a mysterious person who had given Giglio's mother a present which was to render her charming in the eyes of her husband and to secure his affection as long as he lived. But Giglio's mother, far from appreciating the gift, "became capricious, lazy, ill-humored, absurdly vain" and in addition began to patronize the Fairy Blackstick (p.212). Because her gift had been slighted and misused, the Fairy Blackstick refused at Giglio's birth to provide him with a magic gift. Instead she pronounced: "My poor child, the best thing I can send you is a little misfortune." (p.212)

This misfortune sends Giglio as a young man out into the world, where he retires to a university and studies so steadily that he wins all the medals. At the end of the story Giglio marries his beloved Angelica and hears the Fairy Blackstick proclaim the result of his having suffered misfortune: "*You*, Giglio, had you been bred in prosperity, would scarcely have learned to read or write—you would have been idle and extravagant, and could not have been a good King as you now will be."(p.113) Such, then, is the story of Giglio who because of his misfortune changed from an idle hedonist into a respectable and serious member of society.

Dick realizes that "the price of his intactness" (his desire for *la joie de vivre*) is an "incompleteness" as a psychiatrist. Also he knows that carrying with him this "incompleteness," he will forever be attracted to the Elkins-world and consequently will be incapable of giving himself wholly to the discipline of psychiatry. Yet he is powerless to become what he is not, powerless to alter his basic self and his response to *la joie de vivre*.

Later when he suggests to an intellectual whom he knows that he is fragmented by his two selves, his confidant tells him: "You're not a romantic philosopher—you're a scientist . . . Good sense. That's going to be your trouble—judgment about yourself . . ."(p.117) But the conflict whose existence this intellectual has denied does exist for Dick Diver, and it follows him from Vienna, throughout the war, and finally back to Zurich.

Dick's return to Dohmler's clinic in Zurich is not a return to work and study so much as it is an attempt to escape from a way of life and a side of himself which he does not wish to acknowledge. Fitzgerald explains that the "lavish liquidations taking place under the aegis of American splendor" in the post-war months in France has affected Dick's outlook, and that Dick, realizing "that this was not too good for a serious man," has returned to Zurich.(p.133)

Dick, however, cannot easily dismiss a way of life that he finds attractive:

> Missing something ever since his arrival two days before, Dick perceived that it was the sense he had had in finite French lanes that there was nothing more. In Zurich there was a lot besides Zurich—the roofs upled the eyes to tinkling cow pastures, which in turn modified hilltops further up—so life was a perpendicular starting off to a postcard heaven. The Alpine lands, home of the toy and the funicular, the merry-go-round and the thin chime, were not a being *here* as in France with French vines growing over one's feet on the ground.
>
> In Salzburg once Dick had felt the superimposed quality of a bought and borrowed century of music; once in the laboratories of the university in Zurich, delicately poking at the cervical [*sic*] of a brain, he had felt like a toymaker rather than like the tornado who had hurried through the old red buildings of Hopkins, two years before. . .
>
> Yet he had decided to remain another two years in Zurich, for he did not underestimate the value of toymaking, in infinite precision, of infinite patience. (p.118)

What Dick misses in Zurich is the kind of life he had known in France after the war. The earthly quality of this life—a sense of being (of living life instead of preparing to live life)—is symbolically conveyed in the image that Dick uses to express his nostalgia. He remembers France as "French vines growing over one's feet on the ground." (p.118) In contrast to France, which is finite and whose objective correlative is French vines which bind him to the earth, Zurich suggests to Dick infinity and a "postcard heaven." (p.118) In Zurich Dick feels not the immediacy of life but rather a sense of infinite patience, of life being postponed, which leaves him feeling not like a vital human being but like a toy-maker. Intellectually and as a psychiatrist, Dick may see the value of infinite patience and precision; but emotionally and as a man, he feels that they are antithetical to the kind of life that he desires for himself.

Renewing his earlier friendship in Zurich with Franz and his peasant wife, Dick dines at their home. Again he feels a sense of oppression that has been brought about by his attempt to renounce his hedonistic self:

> He felt vaguely oppressed, not by the atmosphere of modest retrenchment, nor by Frau Gregorovius, who might have been prophesied, but by the sudden contracting of horizons to which Franz seemed so reconciled. [At one time Dick and Franz had planned to establish in New York an up-to-date clinic for "billionaires." Prior to this dinner engagement, Dick had lightly reminded Franz of their plans; Franz had dismissed it: "That was students' talk."] For him the boundaries of asceticism were differently marked—he could see it as a means to an end, even as a carrying on with a glory it would itself supply, but it was hard to think of deliberately cutting life down to the scale of an inherited suit. *The domestic gestures of Franz and his wife as they turned in a cramped space lacked grace and adventure.* (pp.132–133) [Italics mine]

Their lives lack grace and adventure. For the fundamental Dick Diver—the Dick Diver for whom *la joie de vivre* is more important than psychiatry—this is indictment enough. As he enjoys their company, his true thoughts are revealed:

> He made Kaethe Gregorovius feel charming, meanwhile becoming increasingly restless at the all-pervading cauliflower—simultaneously hating himself too for this incipience of he knew not what superficiality.
>
> "God, am I like the rest after all?"—So he used to think starting awake at night—"Am I like the rest?"

> . . . *The truth was that for some months he had been going through that partitioning of the things of youth wherein it is decided whether or not to die for what one no longer believes.* In the dead white hours in Zurich staring into a stranger's pantry across the upshine of a street-lamp, he used to think that he wanted to be good, he wanted to be kind, he wanted to be brave and wise, but it was all pretty difficult. He wanted to be loved, too, if he could fit it in. (p.133) [Italics mine]

What plagues Dick is that his intellect and his respectable ambitions (his better self he might say) compel him toward a way of life (psychiatry) toward which he no longer feels any attraction, while his emotions and desires (his worse self) urge him toward a life which he thinks is ignoble.

It is in Nicole Warren, "the prettiest thing he had ever seen," that Dick discovers a girl whose beauty promises him *la joie de vivre* and apparent escape from psychiatry. Looking at Nicole, Dick sees that "her face, ivory gold against the blurred sunset that strove through the rain, had a promise [he] had never seen before: the high cheekbones, the faintly wan quality, cool rather than feverish, was reminiscent of the frame of a promising colt—a creature whose life did not promise to be only a projection of youth upon a greyer screen, but instead, a true growing; the face would be handsome in old age: the essential structure and the economy were there." (p.141) Nicole's is the gift of eternal youth.

Though Dick is attracted to Nicole, he knows that a doctor-patient marriage would be unwise. Both Franz and Dohmler advise him to forget her and warn him that his problem is a professional one. For this reason, when Nicole parades her accomplishments before Dick, he attempts to dampen her love. The effect, however, of what he says is to make him realize that he cannot treat Nicole only as a patient. Attempting to flee what is so strong in him that he cannot break it off, Dick leaves Zurich but encounters Nicole and her sister, Baby, at a mountain resort. There he begins to lose the battle that he has been waging to stay emotionally detached from Nicole. Appropriately, this capitulation begins as he and Nicole stroll on a horseshoe walk, suggesting symbolically "Lucky Dick," the name given to him when he was a popular figure at New Haven and suggestive of that side of Dick which is hedonistic. As he walks with Nicole, her closeness causes him to forget his rational arguments against marrying her. He thinks: "He was in for it now, possessed by a vast irrationality." (p.154)

In the beginning of Diver's marriage, he has no thought of giving up his practice. So far as Nicole knows, Dick has no doubts about his profession. Unknown to her is the fact that their marriage was prompted not only by his love for her but also by his dissatisfaction with what is to him the sterility of psychiatry and by his desire for a life of "grace and adventure." In the early years of their marriage, however, the seeds are sown which must eventually find their fruition in Dick's falling away from his profession and in his surrendering to his desires for luxury.

Though Nicole had told Baby that "Dick refuses to have anything whatever to do with" her money, at the birth of their first child she demands that he amend this vow: "That seems unreasonable, Dick—we have every reason for taking the bigger apartment. Why should we penalize ourselves just because there's more Warren money than Diver money? Oh, thank you, cameriere, but we've changed our minds." (p.159)

After her breakdown which follows the birth of their second child, Nicole tells Dick, pressing upon him both the appeal of her money and, unknown to her, his still repressed dissatisfaction with his profession: "We must spend my money and have a house. I'm tired of apartments and waiting for you. You're bored with Zurich and you can't find time for writing here and you say that it's a confession of weakness for a scientist not to write . . . We'll live near a warm beach where we can be brown and young together." (p.161)

And in point of time, the next scene in the novel is the Divers' "cliff villa" on the Riviera. Here Dick registers "Mr. and Mrs. Diver" instead of his usual "Doctor and Mrs. Diver." Renouncing what he had originally been drawn to because of an accidental beauty,[6] Dick Diver in so signing the register has signaled the beginning of a new fealty and his own eventual destruction. The reason for his leaving is not altogether the cajoling of Nicole.

Though she expresses her own selfish wishes, Dick's departure is made inevitable by his dissatisfaction with his profession and his own desire for the glamorous life that Nicole represents. Her call to him to be "brown and young" with her finds resonance in that fundamental self that Dick has been seeking to repress since his student days in Vienna.

From the day that Dick decided to marry Nicole his life has been fragmented by his attempt to live in two different worlds. Gradually, however, he has surrendered to his desire for *la joie de vivre*. The poignancy of Dick's situation and one of the reasons for his later collapse, however, is that having studied and devoted himself to a mistress (psychiatry) that was to prove too sterile and demanding, he attempts to escape, and his attempt has been abortive. When Dick meets Rosemary on the Riviera, he has for the past six years been alternately acting as father-doctor and lover-husband to Nicole. Fitzgerald says of Dick: "The dualism in his views of her—that of the husband, that of the psychiatrist—was increasingly paralyzing his faculties."(p.188)

At the age of thirty-four, then, Dick is at an impasse. Instead of being free of psychiatry to enjoy *la joie de vivre*, he is bound by his sense of obligation to the care of Nicole. The result is a fragmented Dick Diver.

It is the strain of Dick's having to lead one life while desiring another (all this after having earlier undergone the turmoil of choosing between psychiatry and Nicole—his better and worse selves) that weakens Dick to the point at which he can be unfaithful to Nicole with Rosemary. Further, it is the passage of the four years between Dick's initial meeting with Rosemary and his later affair in Rome (all this time married to a woman who is his patient, while he yearns for *la joie de vivre*—which he now identifies with Rosemary) that continues to pare away Dick Diver's soul. Finally, it is the failure of his affair in Rome with Rosemary and his realization that he has wasted his youthful years which are the culminating reasons for the increase in his drinking and his later collapse.

When Dick meets Rosemary on the Riviera, he sees "the only girl [he's] seen for a long time that actually did look like something blooming."(p.22) Yet throughout his courtship of Rosemary, Dick is incapable of asserting his aggressiveness; instead he finds himself forced to adopt a paternal attitude by his fear of the effect on Nicole, should she discover him with Rosemary. Dick knows that he must keep "up a perfect front, now and tomorrow, next week and next year."(p.166)

Fitzgerald attempts to make of Dick the protective husband who realizes that more important than his affair with Rosemary is his protecting and staying with Nicole. Though Dick admits his love for Rosemary, he tells her that "Nicole mustn't know—she mustn't suspect even faintly."(p.75) Dick also tells Rosemary that Nicole and he love each other—and then adds "you understand that," in an attempt, I suggest, to convince not Rosemary but himself that he is staying with Nicole not only out of a sense of obligation. But Rosemary questions his love for Nicole and its basis: "She had thought however that it was a rather cooled relation, and actually rather like the love of herself and her mother. When people have so much for outsiders didn't it indicate a lack of inner intensity?" (p.75)

Till his surrender to Rosemary in Paris, Dick had been able to push into the recesses of his mind his growing disappointment in the life he had found with Nicole and in his apathy toward his profession. But Rosemary, answering Dick's need for love and beauty, is the catalyst that excites his hedonistic self which till this time had been held quiescent by Dick's sense of duty. After leaving Rosemary in Paris and returning to the Riviera and Nicole, Dick attempts to purge himself of his reawakened desire for life and to return to his existence with Nicole, thereby fulfilling what he thinks is his duty: "He wanted to be alone so that his thoughts about work and the future would overpower his thoughts of love and to-day."(p.169)

The consequence of his denying his fundamental self and continuing to care for Nicole, however, is a stripping away of his soul until he finds himself, in Fitzgerald's words, "emotionally bankrupt."[7] Four years after his initial meeting with Rosemary and following another of Nicole's relapses, Dick leaves for a three month's rest. At this time he realizes that "he had lost himself—he could not tell the hour when, or the day or the week, the month or the year. Once he had cut through things, solving the most complicated equations as the simplest problems of his simplest patients. Between the time he found Nicole flowering under a stone on the Zurichsee and the moment of his meeting with Rosemary the spear had been blunted."(p.201)

Following his realization that he has lost himself and that only a dutiful life with Nicole awaits him, Dick is "in love with every pretty woman he [sees] . . . their forms at a distance, their shadows on a wall."(p.201) Each of these women, so Dick subconsciously hopes, might be the one to offer him the beauty and the love, the grace and adventure that he has been seeking throughout his life and that he had thought both Nicole and Rosemary were to offer him.

At the end of this rest period, Dick accidentally meets Rosemary in Rome, where their love affair which had begun four years earlier on the Riviera is consummated. The effect of this encounter, however, is to show Dick that neither of them is in love with the other. Returning to Zurich and the clinic which he operates with Franz, Dick is now a broken man. Having been unfaithful to Nicole, he has also failed to find in Rosemary the fulfillment which he has been seeking. The result of Dick's realizing that he has sacrificed his life for a cause in which he did not believe is an increase in his drinking, which ultimately forces Franz to suggest that their partnership be dissolved. Though not prepared for Franz's bold action, Dick "was relieved. Not without desperation he had long felt the ethics of his profession dissolving into a lifeless mass." (p.256)

While Fitzgerald continues to describe Dick's deterioration and Nicole's return to health, he has by this point in the novel firmly established the motivation for Dick's collapse. Having found no emotional attachment in life and prompted by his desire to experience *la joie de vire*, Dick had married Nicole. Forced by his compassion to stay with her even after he realizes that she has failed him, he is gradually drained of his strength as he pretends a role that is alien to him. After six years of marriage and pretence, all the time yearning for the life that he had thought Nicole represented, Dick has reached a point at which his better self can no longer force him to resist the appeal of Rosemary's youthful beauty. In Dick's own words, "the spear had been blunted." (p.201) Dick's subsequent failure to find fulfillment in Rosemary and his realization that only a life in attendance upon Nicole awaits him combine to destroy his desire for life. The result is a Dick Diver dependent upon his drinking and broken by the twelve years he has given to Nicole.

Notes

1. "F. Scott Fitzgerald: The Poet of Borrowed Time," *F. Scott Fitzgerald: The Man and His Work*, ed. Alfred Kazin (Cleveland: World, 1951), p.39.

2. "Scott Fitzgerald–The Authority of Failure," *F. Scott Fitzgerald: The Man and His Work*, p.190.

3. F. Scott Fitzgerald, *Tender Is the Night* (New York: Scribner Library Edition, n.d.), p.201. All quotations are from this text.

4. Weller Embler has, I think, very perceptively touched upon the crux of Fitzgerald's novels: "Among modern writers F. Scott Fitzgerald best illustrates the agonized search for the true inner self. It was in his first book, *This Side of Paradise*, that Fitzgerald began to look for the "fundamental" Amory, and from then on through all his stories and novels the search continues. The essential conflict throughout all his books is that of a man divided against himself. . ." "F. Scott Fitzgerald and the Future," *F. Scott Fitzgerald: The Man and His Work*, p.217.

5. William Makepeace Thackeray, "The Rose and the Ring," *Works*, 24 (New York: Charles Scribner's Sons, 1904), p.313. All quotations are from this edition.

6. In speaking to Franz about the attraction of psychiatry for crippled and broken men, Dick had explained his own reason for becoming a psychiatrist: "I got to be a psychiatrist because there was a girl at St. Hilda's in Oxford that went to the same lectures." (p.138)

7. See *The Crack-Up* for Fitzgerald's explanation of the concept of "emotional bankruptcy."

9. Fitzgerald's Portrait of a Psychiatrist

by A. H. STEINBERG

If F. Scott Fitzgerald's *Tender Is the Night* (1934) is remembered at all, one recalls the Riviera beach, since this backdrop furnishes imagery so eminently suited to the subject matter. The proud hotel cooled by deferential palms mirrors the relations of the flesh-and-blood characters, whose status must be defined with the exactitude of the "thin, hot line" of sea and sky. Between the "nice" people around the Divers and the "not nice" around the McKiscos exists a difference as plain as between good and poor swimmers. The same sharp division between people reappears later in the Swiss inn where the acoustics permit the patrons along the wall to converse easily, unheard by those in the middle. Relentlessly final is the distinction between Dick ascendant and Dick fallen: once he could perform an aquaplane stunt, later he cannot.

Not quite as hard and fast as the distinctions themselves are the criteria underneath. A touch of petulance is directed at those foreigners who fail to uphold American standards of physical cleanliness and at the Italians who violate American canons of

A first draft of this article appeared in the news-letter of the Modern Language Association Conference on *Literature and Psychology* (Feb., 1953), under the title, "Hardness, Light, and Psychiatry in *Tender Is the Night*."

fair play. Such colored people as are here presented are best kept at arm's length and serve only to complicate Dick's life. It is not clear whether the sympathetically drawn Abe North is conceived as Jewish, but the nauseating Von Cohn Morris unmistakably is. Nevertheless the prevailing chauvinistic snobbery is flexible enough to admit the existence of unpleasant Americans and worthwhile Europeans.

Although Fitzgerald has a special reverence for the big money and a special disesteem for penny-pinching, a trait he ascribes to the French, even the possession of wealth does not guarantee automatic acceptance. Women are as a matter of course expected to be beautiful and men brave, but the greatest virtue is hardness: "It was good to be hard, then; all nice people were hard on themselves" (p.72). By hardness is meant self-control and self-discipline (p.24), Rosemary's own virtues which she finds in Dick, virtues well personified in the metallic Nicole.

But even Nicole's hard and lovely face betrays a pitiful aspect. For all the veneration of hardness, the nice people are characterized by a certain tenderness, "a special gentleness"(p.24) apparent in their abandoned, uncontrolled living. As the sharp outlines of the beach begin to dazzle and dance in the intense daylight, so the rigid code which so neatly disposes of people tends to dissolve in the basic aimlessness it is meant to camouflage, so Nicole's set and controlled loveliness aims "straight ahead toward nothing"(p.18). The requirements for acceptability cannot be stated explicitly because they are determined by Dick's whim. His personality binds the wild and delicate spirits around him into a family who remain under his beach umbrella even after the scene shifts to Paris. Outside of his circle the beach appears blank and deserted, apparently devoid of life.

His hardness he reserves for those outside his sway, his tenderness for those within. When he first comes into view, he is "giving a quiet little performance," his every antic calling forth a burst of laughter. Circulating among his intimates with "a bottle and little glasses," he doses his friends with his private brand of excitement, forming around himself "a single assemblage of umbrellas." Such is his typical method of relating (or not relating) to others, to transform them into his enthralled audience and cater to their desires with charming and titillating entertainment, demanding in return an acknowledgment of preeminence.

This unspoken bargain he puts into words in a discussion of acting (pp.371–372) which is really an exposition of his own way of life. The actress, he feelingly declares, should suppress her own desires in order to surprise the audience by acting hard when they expect softness and soft when they expect hardness, tossing them their sop of excitement in return for the chance to redirect their attention to herself. Yet in spite of the intensity of his interest in dramatics, he refuses an offered screen test: "My God, they can't photograph me. I'm an old scientist all wrapped up in his private life"(p.92). His sensitized blindness to the fact that he keeps playing the actor in real life is based on a conscious contempt for actors as empty persons: "The strongest guard is placed at the gateway to nothing . . . because the condition of emptiness is too shameful to be divulged."

For the actor the wishes of his auditors assume precise shape while his inner self remains blank. Dick cannot be photographed because he has no real picture of himself, although as a scientist he is precisely certain about the actions of others. Assuming as the occasion warrants the various roles of doctor, lover, father, or partygoer, Dick is at bottom so unsophisticated about himself that his drinking, brawling, and unproductiveness loom up as so many externally caused events, if he thinks of them at all. In a typically exhibitionistic demonstration at Voisins, he proves that only he has "repose," because unlike everybody else who comes in, he alone does not raise his hand to his face.

Superficial as his self-knowledge is his comprehension of the dynamics of the illnesses in which he is presumably a specialist. That emotional disturbance fills him with distaste is everywhere apparent, although his dislike does not keep him from kissing one of his attractive patients and marrying another. Certain of his charges he takes under his umbrella, others he excludes. His patients can afford to be humored, but they are more the victims of self-indulgence than of disease: "We're a rich person's clinic —we don't use the word nonsense," but nonsense adequately describes those "shell-shocks who merely heard an air raid from a distance"(p.157). The cure, then, is to clamp down hard, like nice people everywhere. Dick's way of bringing Nicole out of a spell is to bark commands at her to control herself. Nicole is intelligent, let her read Freud. If the Spanish homosexual wants to be cured, let him control his sensuality. If Von Cohn Morris were any sort of a man, he would get a grip on himself.

Incurred by a traumatic episode, Nicole's insanity is grudgingly admitted, but the event is taken as something that just happened in an unguarded moment. Nicole's father is distinguished, prominent, magnificently successful; but hard as are these daylight values they do not cover the disgusting, incestuous tenderness of his night mind. To make the connection between the symptomatic event and the person is beyond Dick's power, for he is too ashamed of the paternalistic ingredient in his own behavior to do anything but condemn this kind of softness in others. How his unresolved fears color his expectations is apparent in his reaction to the closing shot of *Daddy's Girl*, a movie showing "Rosemary and her parent united at the last in a father complex so apparent that Dick winced for all psychologists at the vicious sentimentality"(p.91).

Now it is true that Rosemary is all too eager to obey her consummate mother, even requiring her permission to go after Dick. Rosemary's interest is spiced by the knowledge that, like her father, Dick is a doctor, a man "all complete" (p.24) and qualified to replace her all-perfect mother. But this does not absolve Dick, whose implied promise that "he would take care of her" (pp.20,26) gives evidence of his own "paternal interest" (p.36) in Rosemary. Another glimpse of the goings-on inside Dick is disclosed later when, trying to think of Rosemary, a comparison with his own daughter springs to mind (p.271).

With Nicole Dick has set up a similar relationship in the guise of doctor and patient. Playing doctor allows him to maintain a detached, scientific superiority which cloaks the fact that he cannot participate as husband on an equal basis with his wife in the marriage relation. What Dick wants is a love involvement in which he is not involved, and when Nicole first voices her awareness of this truth during their courtship, her "impertinence, the right to invade implied, astounded him" (p.203). To partake of her money is to refute his self-sufficiency, to expose a softness in the armor of this distant god, laying open perhaps his silent and carefully shielded need to clutch at people. And so he reverts to his pose of undesiring desirability, treating Nicole like a patient who might contaminate him, until she finally bursts out: "You're a coward! You've made a failure of your life, and you want to blame it on me"(p.389).

"*L'amour de famille.*" With this sneer Tommy Barban writes off Dick's attachment to Nicole. One wonders about the truth of this allegation, recalling perhaps the joke which temporarily reunited the Divers in uproarious laughter. Dick's pretended threat to divorce his son (p.341)—"Did you know there was a new law in France that you can divorce a child?" If this kind of feeling is in fact the groundwork of the family happiness, progressive deterioration would not be unexpected. The question next arises, and Dick asks it, "If you and Nicole married won't that be 'l'amour de famille'?"

This question Tommy chooses to ignore. Neither does the author supply any answer, and for the best of possible reasons: he does not know one himself. *Tender Is the Night* is Fitzgerald's inadvertent version of Dick's unpublished treatise, *A Psychology for Psychiatrists.* In this system the emphasis on status allows little room for human growth, and the novel similarly exhibits a curiously static quality in spite of the surface motion, a blankness beneath the precision. In accord with the author's tenets, Nicole becomes well as she removes herself from dependency on Dick. In the process she learns that "she hated the beach, resented the places where she had played planet to Dick's sun" (p.373); having grown hard as "Georgia pine, which is the hardest wood known, except lignum vitae" (p.356), she is ultimately able to dethrone her doctor-husband. But we are left wondering whether she is drawn to Barban the man or to Barban harder and more barbarous than Dick, Barban the more efficient parental protector of her soft core of insanity. Who will say whether Nicole is really liberated or simply embarked on another pointless, joyless round of "l'amour de famille?"

For a while it seems that Fitzgerald might, in the Gregoroviuses, depict a love in which the conflicts of childhood have been more successfully overcome, but his heart fails him. Afraid this kind of portrayal would mark him as soft, he is also afraid to hear others espouse any cure less rigorous than his own; in a fit of adolescent bravado he has consequently christened his hero with a name whose slang meaning amply conveys the author's contempt for softness. In this topsy-turvy world it is no wonder that the patient flees such a doctor to regain her health, just as her father breaks out of the hospital to live on in defiance of his doctor's ministrations. In the end Dick Diver leaves the field in defeat to his patients because he is softer than they.

Had Fitzgerald accepted his own psychology at face value, this novel might fairly be dismissed as a faded chronicle of the high jinks of a forgotten café society, a curious footnote to the jazz age. But one must be insensitive indeed to miss the pulse beneath the glittering surface, the shy, sympathetic questions behind the toughness. Behold what has happened to this resplendent creature on the beach: Why? What did Dick do wrong? These wistful searchings prove that the author has managed, despite the constrictions of a limited and distorted point of view, to invest something of himself in honest creation. An effort of this type invariably carries with it an intrinsic dignity, on which must rest the slender but secure claim this novel makes as literature.

10. Dialogue and Theme in *Tender is the Night*

by WILLIAM F. HALL

Fitzgerald's handling of dialogue in *Tender is the Night* has not so far received sufficient critical attention. In this article I intend to examine three quotations to demonstrate that it is, in fact, in the dialogue that the essential theme of the novel is most clearly revealed.

In the early part of the novel we witness the Divers' relationship through the innocent eyes of Rosemary, who "knew the Divers loved each other because it had been her primary assumption."[1] The Divers have a party to which Dick invites Rosemary and her mother. There has been no indication before this point that Dick is interested in Rosemary, though she already loves him, and, to Rosemary, Nicole seems a cool self-possessed woman of the world. At the party Dick makes the following apparently empty remarks to Rosemary and her mother.

> "What a beautiful garden," Mrs. Speers exclaimed.
>
> "Nicole's garden," said Dick. "She won't let it alone. She nags it all the time, worries about its diseases. Any day now I expect to have her come down with Powdery Mildew or Fly Speck or Late Blight." He pointed his forefinger decisively at Rosemary, saying with a lightness seeming to conceal a paternal interest,
>
> "I'm going to save your reason—I'm going to give you a hat to wear on the beach."

From *Modern Language Notes*, LXXVI (November 1961). Reprinted by permission of the author and The Johns Hopkins Press.

> He turned them from the garden to the terrace, where he poured a cocktail. (p.85)

Here, without any pursuit of the Freudian convolutions of the forefinger and the hat, Dick's unconscious preoccupations lie clear under the light, flippant, almost meaningless remarks. He stresses Nicole's ownership of the garden, revealing his own touchiness about the fact that they live on her money. His preoccupation with Nicole's disease is equally apparent and combined with his interest in Rosemary (*seeming* to conceal a paternal interest) expresses almost a wish that Nicole might become totally sick. Then his sudden leap to "I'm going to save your reason" (just as he consciously set out, at the beginning of his relationship with Nicole, to save hers) reveals, as does the reference to paternal affection, that he is already thinking of Rosemary as he did of Nicole at the beginning of the novel. For, as I shall point out in more detail later, an integral part of the theme is that Dick's affair with Rosemary repeats for him every stage of his original feeling for Nicole.

The second quotation is taken from the final section of the book. Consciously, and this part of the novel is seen from Nicole's viewpoint, Nicole still respects Dick. She still regards herself as dependent on him, just as he still consciously maintains that he loves her and consciously ignores the possibility of an affair between her and Tommy Barban. But their true unconscious relationship, unrealised by either of them at this juncture, is clearly revealed to the reader in the exchange that takes place between them the morning after Dick has made a fool of himself on Golding's yacht. Nicole sits between Dick and Tommy, making a sketch of Tommy's head.

> "Hands never idle—distaff flying," Dick said lightly.
>
> How could he talk so trivially with the blood still drained down from his cheeks so that the auburn lather of beard showed red as his eyes? She turned to Tommy saying:
>
> "I can always do something. I used to have a nice active little Polynesian ape and juggle him around for hours till people began to make the most dismal rough jokes—"
>
> She kept her eyes resolutely away from Dick. Presently he excused himself and went inside. (p.296)

Here Dick's suspicions are apparent to the reader in his opening remark, which ironically stresses their relationship as man and wife. But he speaks *lightly*, unaware of his own motive for saying it. And Nicole does not understand the unconscious barb any more than he does. To her he is talking *trivially*. Her own hidden contempt for Dick is even more obvious (though significantly not to either her or Dick or, we assume, Tommy) in her reference to the Polynesian ape after she has just noticed the red growth of beard on Dick's face and the redness of his eyes. Moreover what is further revealed by her remarks here—"I used to have a nice . . . ape and juggle him around"—is that at this point she is unconsciously viewing Dick as her sister has viewed him from the beginning; as bought with the Warren money, to serve the Warren purposes. She does not, as the action continues, persist in this view, but it brushes her mind, recorded only in the dialogue.

The third example occurs towards the end of the novel. At this point Nicole feels herself "so delicately balanced . . . between an old foothold that had always guaranteed her security, and the imminence of a leap from which she must alight changed in the very chemistry of blood and muscle, that she did not dare bring the matter into the true forefront of consciousness" (p.298). Dick feels himself to have "gone into a process of deterioration" (p.304). Rosemary, whom neither have seen for some time, comes to visit them at Antibes.

Just before the passage to be quoted here Rosemary has been surprised at Dick's bitterness about Mary North. She had "thought of him as all-forgiving, all-comprehending" (p.305). Then the following scene takes place:

> . . . She [Nicole] guessed that Dick . . . would grow charming . . . make Rosemary respond to him. Sure enough, in a moment . . . he had said:
>
> "Mary's all right—. . . . But it's hard to go on liking people who don't like you."
>
> Rosemary, falling into line, swayed toward Dick and crooned:
>
> "Oh, you're so nice. I can't imagine anybody not forgiving you anything, no matter what you did to them."

Rosemary then goes on to ask what they have thought of her latest pictures. Nicole says nothing but Dick goes on:

> ". . . Let's suppose that Nicole says to you that Lanier is ill. What do you do in life? What does anyone do? They *act*— . . . the face shows sorrow, the voice shows shock, the words show sympathy." . . .
>
> "But, in the theatre, no . . . all the best comediennes have built up their reputations by burlesquing the correct emotional responses—fear and love and sympathy." . . .
>
> "The danger to an actress is in responding. Again let's suppose that somebody told you, 'Your lover is dead.' In life you'd probably go to pieces. But on the stage you're trying to entertain—the audience can do the 'responding' for themselves. First the actress has lines to follow, then she has to get the audience's attention back on herself. . . . So she must do something unexpected. If the audience thinks the character is hard she goes soft on them—if they think she's soft she goes hard. You go all *out* of character—you understand?" . . .
>
> "You do the unexpected thing until you've manoeuvered the audience back from the objective fact to yourself. *Then* you slide into character again." (pp.305–306)

This is clearly no answer at all to Rosemary's question about her pictures; yet everything Dick says is intensely relevant to his relationship with Rosemary, and with Nicole. That something of crucial importance has clearly been communicated to the two women, though not at the conscious level, is clear from their actions following the conversation. Rosemary turns to the Divers' daughter, Topsy, and asks her "Would you like to be an actress when you grow up?" indicating that a part of herself has understood that Dick has been discussing his own relationship with her and that the relationship has been, at a certain level, that of father and daughter. Nicole, who has, we are told, consciously understood nothing immediately remarks, "in her grandfather's voice," "it's absolutely *out* to put such ideas in the heads of other people's children." She then leaves; and in the scene immediately following she has "a sense of being cured and in a new way. Her ego blooming like a great rich rose" (p.307).

Dick begins by making an unconscious comment on Rosemary's reaction to the appeal of his "It's hard to go on liking people who don't like you." It is, as it were, dawning on him that she is burlesquing. She has "gone soft" to get the audience's (Dick's) attention "back on herself." He is acknowledging the truth about her. She is an actress in life. She does not "respond." Her audience does so. But this truth about Rosemary is a truth also about himself. In Paris Rosemary had "said her most sincere thing to him: 'Oh we're such *actors*—you and I' "(p.167). He had, he is suggesting, in his bitterness about Mary North, been doing the "unexpected thing," to get Rosemary's attention back on himself. He had done the unexpected in being bitter and unpleasant and is now "sliding into character again": the character of the charming, protective, essentially paternal figure. The sense that this is only a *role* and not his true nature is, I think, the main significance of this passage for Dick himself. And his apparently off-hand examples, "Let's suppose Nicole says to you that Lanier is ill," "Suppose that somebody told you, 'Your lover is dead' " indicate that at least a hint about the real truth of his own nature and of his relationship with Nicole is already afloat in his mind. This is a truth Nicole has begun to recognise a little earlier when in response to his wish to show his skill on the aquaplane "she indulged him as she might have indulged Lanier"(p.301).

The passage reveals a dim awareness, then, on Dick's part, that no real relationship has ever existed between himself and Rosemary and that none can exist—because each of them is incapable of "responding." Unconsciously he also senses that the role he has maintained with Nicole is now slipping from him, that he is the child, the dependent and that she is sliding back "into character again." For Nicole the return to "character" is to be a return, as she tells Tommy Barban, to her "true self."

If my interpretation of these three examples is valid, it is clear that Fitzgerald reveals in his dialogue both what his characters consciously know and communicate to each other, and what lies buried beneath the surface of their own and others' consciousness where the truth about themselves and their relationships is to be found. And this buried knowledge is revealed only in the dialogue. Fitzgerald, as author, makes no explicit comment upon it and neither do any of the characters. "Here [in the world of the novel] there is no light" as the quotation from Keats on the title-page suggests there will not be.

Further, this interpretation of the dialogue suggests that Dick Diver's tragedy is internal and not caused by the corrupting influence of Nicole's wealth. This is assuredly a contributing factor, since it affords Dick, as no other condition could, the opportunity to use to the full what is in fact his only talent (despite his own and others' misapprehensions about his brilliance); that is, his charm and great social ability. It is his final realization of the fact that this is all he in fact has, that destroys him. For in realizing this, he realizes also that despite his varied relationships, his apparent adult control of them, and his ability to arouse "a fascinating and uncritical love in others for himself," *he* is unable to love. He is capable not of responding, or of acting, but only of burlesquing.

Nicole's return to "her original self" (p.298) results from a similar realization of the hidden truth about herself. She understands that her dependence on Dick has been in fact her disease: a false dependence on a false reality.

The true nature of their relationship with each other is forced upon them both by Dick's parallel relationship with Rosemary. The discussion of the 1st example on pages 2 and 3 above suggests that with both women, Dick plays the *role* of father.[2] And it is clear that both Nicole and Rosemary attribute this *role* to him. Nicole, who was Rosemary's age when she first met Dick, leans on him for support as she might on an 'ideal' father until her return to health, when she abandons "her dry suckling at his lean chest"(p.297). Her view of him as father is so complete that in her mad spells she sees him as the 'evil' father who seduced her (p.174).

And that this is Rosemary's view of him is made equally clear. He is to her "the beautiful cold image she had created"(p.167), the idealized image of her dead father. Dick's refusal to take Rosemary when she offers herself in Paris confirms this image in her mind. When later Dick does make physical demands the result is to destroy whatever potential she may have had for real love. Her experience with him, in other words, parallels subtly and psychologically the brutal physical disillusion of Nicole as a child with her actual father.

The relationships are complicated by the fact that Dick, like the two women, has assumed that the thin layer of his "attentive seriousness" has concealed a deep fund of adult love and power. Whereas in fact, as the discussion of the third example indicates, he has been an actor burlesquing "the correct emotional responses." Incapable of loving, he has been beneath his role, a child seeking parental love—as he is in his final conversation with Mary North when "His eyes, for a moment clear as a child's, asked her sympathy"(p.332). His "lesion of vitality," then, is rooted, as are Nicole's and Rosemary's, in a past family relationship; and the 'adult' relationships of all three are conditioned by this.

If this interpretation is accepted, it is clear that *Tender is the Night* is not a fumbling attempt to reproduce again what Alfred Kazin describes as Fitzgerald's only theme, "the fitful glaring world of Jay Gatsby's dream and of Jay Gatsby's failure." The novel has its weaknesses, but these result, at least partly, from Fitzgerald's attempt to express a new theme. He is here concerned, as not before, with the hidden roots of adult relationships; and with the waste that results from the characters' misunderstanding of themselves and of each other. Throughout the novel this misunderstanding is the result of their mistaking *persona* for true self, even though in their communication with each other the preoccupations, motives, and desires of that true self are constantly revealed to the attentive reader.

Notes

1. *Tender Is the Night* ed. Malcolm Cowley in *Three Novels of F. Scott Fitzgerald* (New York, 1953), p.137. All subsequent page numbers given immediately in the text refer to this edition.

2. Robert Stanton has drawn attention to this aspect of Dick's relationships in his " 'Daddy's Girl': Symbol and Theme in *Tender Is the Night*," *Modern Fiction Studies*, IV (Summer, 1958), 136–142.

11. Sensuality and Asceticism in *Tender Is the Night*

by MARVIN J. LAHOOD

Scott Fitzgerald's *Tender Is the Night* has suffered from somewhat adverse criticism for over three decades. Because it is less successful than *The Great Gatsby*, critics have felt compelled to account for its relative failure. The most noxious critiques hover over biographical facts as an index: Zelda's progressing illness, Fitzgerald's personal weaknesses. Others feel that he attempted too much, that the novel was written over too long a period of time to be cohesive, that the material is intractable, or even that he was no longer a "serious" writer. Fitzgerald himself was always puzzled by the novel's reception. He never determined what went wrong, but his undying interest and faith in it are evidenced by his attempt to make it more appealing by putting the opening Rosemary section after the narrative of Dick's education and marriage to Nicole. He died while still revising.

His attempt was unnecessary; from the well-chosen epigraph to the remarkable final chapter the novel is, in my opinion, the masterpiece he thought he had written. The painfully poignant last chapter is a nearly perfect rendering of the tone of Keats' "Ode to a Nightingale." And the Rosemary section is precisely where it should be. It is through the eyes of someone as naive and insensitive as Rosemary—who can see the glittering surface but not the dark depths of the Divers' world—that we must first see this world so that the nightmare-become-reality of the latter chapters can have its effect. It is Rosemary's image of Dick as the ideal of sophisticated manhood that makes so meaningful Dick as the alcoholic general practitioner whose involvement with a grocery store clerk means still another move at novel's end.

No other modern American novel chronicles so poignantly and painfully the deterioration of a man of such great talent and promise. *The Great Gatsby* is a bitterly ironic commentary on the American dream; *Tender Is the Night* is an even more damning version. Grandfather Warren is the epitome of the American success story, "a self-made American capitalist," a hard, ruthless robber baron. It is his money and his granddaughter, with her "white crook's eyes," that destroy the selfless Dick Diver, psychologist. Doctor Diver's "night" has not the clear finality of Gatsby's violent death, but it is an even truer insight into the American tragedy Fitzgerald recorded so sensitively.

In *The Great Gatsby* it is the careless world of the rich Buchanans against which the protagonist's idealism shatters; here it is the anarchic world of Tommy Barban and the Warrens. The Buchanans, Barbans, and Warrens are considered the successes of the modern world; idealists Gatsby and Diver come to an even more ignominious end than Quixote. Nick Carraway isn't sure whether Gatsby experiences tragic recognition just before death. If he does, Nick conjectures, "He must have felt that he had lost the old warm world, paid a high price for living too long with a single dream." Dick's enlightenment is surer. He recognizes the forces that are destroying him, but only when it is too late. He gives Nicole to Tommy Barban without a struggle because he realizes their natural affinity. Nicole's ruthless materialism is, like her grandfather's, perfectly complemented by the nihilism of the professional soldier. When Nicole and Barban finally come together in the scene punctuated by the sailors and their whores saying good-bye, Fitzgerald says she welcomes "the anarchy of her lover."

Doctor Diver's blessing of the beach he "created" will not take, although Nicole is on her knees for the blessing. Dick can do nothing to redeem the world of Gausse's Hotel; he has spent himself (Fitzgerald called him *homme épuisé*) on a lost cause. But one of the reasons for the book's greatness is the magnitude of this cause. Hemingway's antidotes to the malaise of the postwar world in *The Sun Also Rises* are the code and the hero, Pedro Romero. But Fitzgerald attempted something much more difficult—he tried to redeem the lost generation by using the old, traditional matter. For Western man the psychologist is one of the possible priest-substitutes of the twentieth century. And Dick is a psychologist (like Eliot's more successful Harcourt-Reilly), not a code hero, for whom Roncesvalles would always be more meaningful than trout fishing in the Irati River.

Dick loses, but not without a heroic struggle. The poor son of a poor minister, he is attacked from without by the debilitating luxury of too much Warren money. From within he is weakened by a never-outgrown, fatally romantic fascination for women. Fitzgerald chronicles this more carefully than any other facet of Dick's character. It is most obvious in his puerile concern over Rosemary's previous love-life, evidenced in the oft-recurring phrase he imagines being said to her, "Do you mind if I pull down the curtain?" For one thing, if he still had his integrity he would not have come close to falling in love with such a fribble. Fitzgerald clearly points out the ludicrousness of the affair: "Finally it was good-by with their hands stretching to touch along the diagonal of the banister and then the fingers slipping apart." We are told at the end of the book what we suspect from the beginning, that she never "grows up." But beyond that it is simply Dick's falling back, as he weakens, to the level of his boyhood when he "worried between five or ten cents for the collection plate, because of the girl who sat in the pew behind." It is the same indication of weakness so much in evidence as his story draws to a close: "He was in love with every pretty woman he saw now, their forms at a distance, their shadows on a wall."

This fatal romanticism is intimately connected with the sensuality he reverts to once he loses control of himself: from the Rosemary affair to the final image of his settling down "with someone to keep house for him." Fitzgerald explains: "A part of Dick's mind was made up of the tawdry souvenirs of his boyhood. Yet in that somewhat littered Five-and-Ten, he had managed to keep alive the low painful fire of intelligence." When the fire goes out, the tawdry takes over: "Dignified in his fine clothes, with their fine accessories, he was yet swayed and driven as an animal."

Related to this is the appearance of the Chilean nobleman's homosexual son. Dick advises the boy: " 'If you want to face the world you'll have to begin by controlling your sensuality—and, first of all, the drinking that provokes it.' " Just before this a patient dies of syphilis at the clinic. "Dick sat exhausted in the chair nearest the door. Three nights he had remained with the scabbed anonymous woman-artist he had come to love, formally to portion out the adrenalin, but really to throw as much wan light as he could into the darkness ahead." Fitzgerald well knew the unending struggle between the artist's efforts to order existence and the chaos resulting from uncurbed natural appetites. In these two cases sensuality pays a very high price in suffering, but they are not isolated. The sensuality motif is everywhere in the novel—from the incestuous basis of Nicole's schizophrenia (Devereux Warren calls himself a "Goddamned degenerate") to the strange coincidence which causes an Italian mob to confuse Dick with a native of Frascati who raped and murdered a five-year-old child. Its antithesis is the ascetic life.

Dick reaches the height of asceticism at Vienna in 1917 when, for lack of coal, he burns medical textbooks to keep warm, but only after having thoroughly digested everything in them. "For him the boundaries of asceticism were . . . marked—he could see it as a means to an end, even as a carrying on with a glory it would itself supply." He is still trying to live ascetically at the beginning of the Rosemary episode, but the Warren money and the old romanticism are weakening him. He finally falls from self-discipline to self-indulgence, his fall carefully presaged by Abe North's decline and death. "He had lost himself, he could not tell the hour when, the day or the week, the month or the year. Once he had cut through things . . . Between the time he found Nicole flowering under a stone on the Zurichsee and the moment of his meeting with Rosemary the spear had been blunted." Dick at the height of his powers can bring order to anything: Nicole's mind, their Riviera beach, his professional life, the lives of many others. When the inner tension of his being is destroyed he cannot control even a conversation with old friend Mary North. The basis of this control is a rigid self-discipline developed through asceticism. When the self-discipline crumbles through loss of self-respect, the control vanishes.

In a way Dick chooses his end. At the moment when Rosemary waits in her hotel room and he, instead of going to her, goes to the Bonbonieri and is subsequently beaten, he turns from a world where love is meaningless, toward death. What he finds is worse than death. "He would be a different person henceforward, and in his raw state he had bizarre feelings of what the new self would be." Gatsby is murdered and his death seems tragic; Dick lives on, and because Fitzgerald was courageous enough to end the novel the way he did, Dick's story is more poignant than tragic. Doctor Diver, with "a big stack of papers on his desk that were known to be an important treatise on some medical subject, almost in process of completion," is not a tragic figure. And I think Fitzgerald meant this too. The final index of the book's greatness is that in it the modern world is seen as one in which the only possibility is not tragedy, but pathos.

12. "Daddy's Girl": Symbol and Theme in *Tender is the Night*

by ROBERT STANTON

Francis Scott Fitzgerald has come a long way from the limbo into which some of his obituaries tried to thrust him in 1941; his return has been marked and encouraged by several important editions of his stories, novels, and articles, an outstanding biography, and a gradually increasing supply of critical articles. Fortunately, although the interest in his writing still stems largely from the excitement of the 1920's and the glamour and pathos of the author's life, his critics have become increasingly willing to view him—as they must, if his reputation is not to decline again—as an artist and craftsman.

The purpose of this article is to examine one of the major artistic devices used in *Tender Is the Night*. It will show that the novel contains a large number of "incest-motifs," which, properly understood, take on symbolic value and contribute to the thematic unity of the novel. The term "incest-motifs" may seem ill-chosen at first, since most of these passages allude, not to consanguineous lovers, but to a mature man's love for an immature girl. I have used the term chiefly because the first of these passages concerns Devereux Warren's incestuous relation with his fifteen-year-old daughter Nicole, so that whenever Fitzgerald

From *Modern Fiction Studies*, IV (Summer 1958).

later associates a mature man with an immature girl, the reader's reaction is strongly conditioned by this earlier event. Devereux's act is the most obvious, and the only literal, example of incest in the novel. It is of basic importance to the plot, since it causes Nicole's schizophrenia and thus necessitates her treatment in Dr. Dohmler's clinic, where she meets Dick Diver. Nicole's love for Dick is in part a "transference" caused by her mental disorder; the character of their marriage is dictated largely by the requirements of her condition.

In spite of the importance of Devereux's act, the use of incest as *motif* is more evident in the fact that Dick, Nicole's husband and psychiatrist, falls in love with a young actress whose most famous film is entitled *Daddy's Girl.* As this coincidence suggests, Fitzgerald deliberately gives an incestuous overtone to the relationship between Dick Diver and Rosemary Hoyt. Like Rosemary's father, Dick is of Irish descent and has been an American army doctor, a captain. At his dinner-party on the Riviera, he speaks to Rosemary "with a lightness seeming to conceal a paternal interest."[1] He calls her "a lovely child" just before kissing her for the first time, and in the Paris hotel he says, again with a "paternal attitude," "When you smile . . . I always think I'll see a gap where you've lost some baby teeth" (124,125). Dick is thirty-four, twice Rosemary's age, and to emphasize this, Fitzgerald continually stresses Rosemary's immaturity. When she first appears in 1925, her cheeks suggest "the thrilling flush of children after their cold baths in the evening" (58–59); "her body hovered delicately on the last edge of childhood–she was almost eighteen, nearly complete, but the dew was still on her" (59). She and her mother are like "prize-winning school-children" (59). Even Nicole pointedly refers to Rosemary as a child (161).

By the time of Abe North's departure, Dick admittedly loves Rosemary; now, "he wanted to . . . remove the whole affair from the nursery footing upon which Rosemary persistently established it"; but he realizes that Rosemary "had her hand on the lever more authoritatively than he" (146,147). Helpless as is, he remains conscious–even over-conscious–of the incongruity of the situation; he tells Rosemary, "When a child can disturb a middle-aged gent—things get difficult" (154). Finally he tells Nicole that Rosemary is "an infant. . . . there's a persistent aroma of the nursery" (179).

After Rosemary leaves the Riviera, Dick begins to exaggerate the immaturity of *other* women as well. He is uneasy when Nicole suggests that he dance with a teen-age girl at St. Moritz, and protests, "I don't like ickle durls. They smell of castile soap and peppermint. When I dance with them, I feel as if I'm pushing a baby carriage" (188). He looks at a pretty woman, and thinks, "Strange children should smile at each other and say, 'Let's play' " (219). Gradually an obscure sense of guilt appears. When Nicole accuses him, falsely and irrationally, of seducing a patient's daughter—"a child," she says, "not more than fifteen"—he feels guilty (206). When he is being taken to court after the taxi-driver fight, a crowd boos him, mistaking him for a man who has raped and slain a five-year-old child; later that day Dick cries, "I want to make a speech. . . . I want to explain to these people how I raped a five-year-old girl. Maybe I did—" (253).

As his decline continues, Dick's attitude toward his own children, Topsy and Lanier, begins to change. In Rome, he decides that Rosemary "was young and magnetic, but so was Topsy" (225). When Nicole realizes that his aquaplaning at the Riviera is inspired by Rosemary's "exciting youth," she remembers that "she had seen him draw the same inspiration from the new bodies of his children . . ." (301). Earlier, Dick has exclaimed, "What do I care whether Topsy 'adores' me or not? I'm not bringing her up to be my wife" (276), apparently assuming that the love of a child does not differ essentially from the love of an adult; he jokes with Lanier about "a new law in France that you can divorce a child" (283). Finally, late in the novel Nicole notices his "almost unnatural interest in the children" (286).

The presence of these incest-motifs may be explained in several ways. First, they may have been suggested, if only slightly and indirectly, by Fitzgerald's own ambivalent attitudes toward his mother and his daughter. He vacillated between being ashamed of his mother and devoted to her;[2] one of the early titles for *Tender Is the Night* was *The Boy Who Killed His Mother*. According to his biographer, with his daughter Scottie, Fitzgerald was alternately "the severe father, the difficult alcoholic, and the man who loved his child intensely."[3] But opposing this explanation is the fact that incest is not mentioned in his other works, and only "Babylon Revisited" and "The Baby Party" concern the love of father for daughter.

In any case, the incest-motifs may be fully accounted for by *Tender Is the Night* itself. Most of them grow logically out of Dick's relationships to Nicole. When Nicole first begins writing to Dick, she still pathologically mistrusts all men; her first letter to him speaks of his "attitude base and criminal and not even faintly what I had been taught to associate with the role of gentleman" (10). Gradually Dick begins to take the place once occupied by her father, as a center of trust and security. As a psychiatrist, Dick realizes the value of this situation; he also realizes that Nicole must eventually build up her *own* world. After her psychotic attack at the Agiri fair, for example, he says, "You can help yourself most," and refuses to accept the father-role into which she tries to force him (207). But this sort of refusal costs him a difficult and not always successful effort of will. First, loving Nicole, "he could not watch her disintegrations without participating in them" (207). Second, he is by nature a "spoiled priest," the father for all of his friends; he creates the moral universe in which they live. His nature and his love oppose his profession. It is therefore plausible, once his character begins to crumble, that he compensates for his long self-denial by falling in love with a girl literally young enough to be his daughter; that after the crowd has booed him for raping a five-year-old girl, he makes a mock-confession; and that when Nicole accuses him of seducing a patient's fifteen-year-old daughter, "He had a sense of guilt, as in one of those nightmares where we are accused of a crime which we recognize as something undeniably experienced, but which upon waking we realize we have not committed" (206).

Ironically, although Dick's fascination with immaturity gives him an opportunity to be both lover and father, it also reveals his own fundamental immaturity. Like Nicole, who responds to Tommy Barban because she sees her own hardness and unscrupulousness reflected in his character, and like Rosemary, who responds to Dick at first because of his "self-control and . . . self-discipline, her own virtues" (75), Dick is attracted to Rosemary's immaturity partly because of a corresponding quality within himself. Behind his facade of self-discipline, this central immaturity appears in the obsessive phrase, "Do you mind if I pull down the curtain?" Rosemary calls him "Youngster" (171,227), "the youngest person in the world" (154), and while he waits for Rosemary outside her studio, he circles the block "with the fatuousness of one of Tarkington's adolescents" (152). When Abe North talks to Nicole in the railroad station, Fitzgerald says, "Often a man can play the helpless child in front of a woman, but he can almost never bring it off when he feels most like a helpless child" (143); similarly, when Dick talks to Mary Minghetti just before leaving the Riviera, "his eyes, for the moment clear as a child's, asked her sympathy . . ." (332).

The significance of the incest-motifs is not limited to Dick's personal disaster. After all, they do not all *issue* from him. It is not of Dick's doing that a patient accuses him of seducing her fifteen-year-old daughter or that a crowd boos him for raping a five-year-old girl. And except for Devereux Warren's act, the most conspicuous incest-motif in the novel is the motion picture for which Rosemary is famous, *Daddy's Girl.* Everyone, we are told, has seen it; and lest we miss the point of the title, we are given Dick's reaction to the final scene of the picture, "a lovely shot of Rosemary and her parent united at the last in a father complex so apparent that Dick winced for all psychologists at the vicious sentimentality" (131). As the universal popularity of *Daddy's Girl* suggests, the incest-motifs symbolize a world-wide situation. In 1934, C. Hartley Grattan wrote of the relation between Nicole and her father, "Fitzgerald has tried to use this situation, this extreme (according to our tabus) example of decadence, to symbolize the rottenness of the society of which Nicole is a part."[4] But the meaning of the repeated motif is both broader and more precise than this.

During the 1920's, the relationship between the prewar and postwar generations was curiously reversed. In Mark Sullivan's words,

> The Twenties, reversing age-old custom, Biblical precept and familiar adage, was a period in which, in many respects, youth was the model, age the imitator. On the dance-floor, in the beauty parlor, on the golf course; in clothes, manners, and many points of view, elders strove earnestly to look and act like their children, in many cases their grand-children.[5]

And Frederick Lewis Allen notes that "the women of this decade worshipped not merely youth, but unripened youth. . . ."[6] That Fitzgerald agreed with this interpretation of the period is evident from a late essay in which he described the Jazz Age as "a children's party taken over by their elders. . . . By 1923 [the] elders, tired of watching the carnival with ill-concealed envy, had discovered that young liquor will take the place of young blood, and with a whoop the orgy began."[7]

Here, on a world-scale, is Dick Diver's fascination with immaturity; and since the younger generation is the child of the elder, here is a situation to which the incest-motifs are relevant. Dick Diver's generation is older than Rosemary's, and he is the product of an older generation still, his minister-father's, with its stress upon " 'good instincts,' honor, courtesy, and courage."[8] Rosemary is the product of Hollywood, with its emphasis upon the future, and we are told that in *Daddy's Girl* she embodies "all the immaturity of the race" (130). In embracing Rosemary, therefore, Dick Diver is a symbol of America and Europe turning from a disciplined and dedicated life to a life of self-indulgence, dissipation, and moral anarchy—a symbol of the parent generation infatuated with its own offspring. Dick's collapse, appropriately, occurs in 1929.

Even aside from Dick's relationship with Rosemary, there are many hints that he is gradually shifting allegiance from the past culture of his father to an unworthy future. In the beginning, he exhibits dignity and self-discipline, unfailing courtesy, and a firm (if unexpressed) moral code; before the novel is over, he has been beaten in a brawl with taxi-drivers, has insulted his friend Mary Minghetti, and, at the very end, has been forced to leave Lockport, New York, because he "became entangled with a girl who worked in a grocery store" (334). To clarify this change, Fitzgerald underlines it in several passages. The most memorable example is Dick's remark at his father's grave, "Good-bye my father—good-bye, all my fathers"; later, as he enters the steamship to return to Europe, he is described as hurrying from the past into the future (222). But this is only his formal farewell to something he has long since left behind. Most of the allusions to the shift occur four years earlier, during the episode in which Dick falls in love with Rosemary. At the battlefield near Amiens, he tells Rosemary that the "whole-souled sentimental equipment" of the past generations was all spent in World War I (118). Next day, he takes her to the Cardinal de Metz's palace: the threshold of the palace connects the past without (the stone facade) to the future within (blue steel and mirrors), and crossing that threshold is an experience "perverted as a breakfast of oatmeal and hashish" (133). Just after leaving the palace, Dick admits for the first time that he loves Rosemary. Next day, his attempt to visit Rosemary at her studio is explicitly labelled "an overthrowing of his past" (152). And on the following day, in the hotel dining room, although Dick sees in the gold-star mothers "all the maturity of an older America," and remembers his father and his "old loyalties and devotions," he turns back to Rosemary and Nicole, the "whole new world in which he believed" (162). It is worth noticing that at both the beginning and end of this episode, Fitzgerald emphasizes Rosemary's significance by placing her beside the memory of World War I.

One reason for the broad applicability of the incest-motif is its inherent complexity: it simultaneously represents a situation and expresses Fitzgerald's judgment of it. First, it suggests how appealing youth can be (whether as person or as quality) to the adult in whom the long-opposed edges of impulse and self-restraint have begun to dull. He longs not only for youth's vitality but for its innocence, which apparently confers moral freedom. In the first flush of love, Dick and Rosemary seem to share

> an extraordinary innocence, as though a series of pure accidents had driven them together, so many accidents that at last they were forced to conclude that they were for each other. They had arrived with clean hands, or so it seemed, after no traffic with the merely curious and clandestine. (136)

Similarly, most of the rebels of the Twenties sought not merely to discard the Victorian morality but to do so without any aftermath of guilt—to recapture the amorality of youth. But the incest-motif also suggests decadence and the violation of a universal taboo—particularly since in *Tender Is the Night* it appears first as the cause of Nicole's insanity—and thus indicates that the unconscious innocence of youth is forever lost to the adult, and that in searching for it he may find disaster: "that madness akin to the love of an aging man for a young girl."[9]

The purpose of this study has been to give a glimpse of Fitzgerald's artistry by examining one of the major patterns in *Tender Is the Night.* The incest-motifs, as we have seen, help to unify the novel on several levels, as well as to show how those levels are interrelated. First, these motifs function literally as one result of Dick's relationship to Nicole; they are symptoms of his psychological disintegration. Second, they both exemplify and symbolize Dick's loss of allegiance to the moral code of his father. Finally, by including such details as *Daddy's Girl* as well as Dick's experience, they symbolize a social situation existing throughout Europe and America during the Twenties. Fitzgerald's ability to employ this sort of device shows clearly that he not only felt his experience intensely, but *understood* it as an artist, so that he could reproduce its central patterns within the forms and symbols of his work. His experience transcends the historical Fitzgerald who felt it and the historical Twenties in which it occurred, and emerges as art.

Notes

1. *Tender Is the Night*, in *Three Novels of F. Scott Fitzgerald*, ed. Malcolm Cowley & Edmund Wilson (N.Y., 1953), p.85.

2. Arthur Mizener, *The Far Side of Paradise: A Biography of F. Scott Fitzgerald* (Cambridge, Mass., 1951), p.8.

3. Mizener, *The Far Side of Paradise*, p.261.

4. *F. Scott Fitzgerald: The Man and His Work*, ed. Alfred Kazin (Cleveland, 1951), p.105.

5. *Our Times: The United States 1900–1925*, Vol. VI: *The Twenties* (N.Y., 1935), pp.385–86.

6. *Only Yesterday* (N.Y., 1931), p.108.

7. "Echoes of the Jazz Age," *The Crack-Up*, ed. Edmund Wilson (N.Y., 1945), p.15.

8. P.221. Arthur Mizener discusses Dick as inheritor of the past in *The Far Side of Paradise*, pp.243–44; for a discussion of the extent to which Fitzgerald's image of Dick's father as the "symbol . . . of an ideal moral order" was based upon his own father, see Henry Dan Piper, "F. Scott Fitzgerald and the Image of His Father," *PULC*, XII (1951), 181–86.

9. *The Last Tycoon*, in *Three Novels*, p.116.

13. *Tender Is the Night* and George Herbert Mead: an "Actor's" Tragedy

by LEE M. WHITEHEAD

Vacationing on a small beach on the French Riviera, a young Hollywood starlet observes an interesting group:

> . . . The man in the jockey cap was giving a quiet little performance for this group; he moved gravely about with a rake, ostensibly removing gravel and meanwhile developing some esoteric burlesque held in suspension by his grave face. Its faintest ramification had become hilarious, until whatever he said released a burst of laughter. Even those who, like herself, were too far away to hear, sent out antennae of attention until the only person on the beach not caught up in it was the young woman with the string of pearls. Perhaps from modesty of possession she responded to each salvo of amusement by bending closer over her list.[1]

The man in the jockey cap is Dick Diver, hero of *Tender Is the Night*; the woman with the string of pearls is his wife Nicole. The starlet observing them is Rosemary Hoyt, recuperating on the Riviera from the rigors of her recent part in *Daddy's Girl.* Rosemary sees Dick here in a characteristic role: he is the center of a group, the focal point of attention, drawing the group together, making it happy by "performing" before it. Nicole is

From *Literature and Psychology*, XV (Summer 1965). Reprinted by permission of the author and *Literature and Psychology*.

the only one not quite integrated into the group; her relationship to Dick, after all, is quite different from that of those others who admire him—she possesses him.

The appearance of warmth and solidarity that intrigues Rosemary and calls out in her an immediate response to Dick and his circle is, however, just that—an appearance. It makes a reality of quite a different nature:

> Naivete responded whole-heartedly to the expensive simplicity of the Divers, unaware of its complexity and its lack of innocence, unaware that . . . the simplicity of behaviour . . . the nursery-like peace and goodwill, the emphasis on the simpler virtues, was part of a desperate bargain with the gods and had been attained through struggles she could not have guessed at. . . . A qualitative change had already set in that was not at all apparent to Rosemary. (20)

Due to Dick's continual vigilance, the Divers are able to maintain a solid front to the world, but in reality Nicole is a mental patient still recuperating from the results of *her* role as Daddy's girl (her schizophrenia stems from her seduction as a teen-age girl by her father), and she is still subject to attacks of dissociation. Dick is a promising young American psychiatrist with a gift for making people like him. He has become both husband and doctor to Nicole. The change that has set in, which Rosemary doesn't notice, is that Dick's role as husband has become absorbed by his role as doctor. Rosemary, as a matter of fact, precipitates this process because she and Dick fall in love, alienating him still further from his role as Nicole's husband.

Rosemary has discovered the Divers on their Riviera beach *in medias res*, at the calm, outwardly ordered center of their relationship, succeeding a troubled beginning and preceding a troubled end. From this point Nicole's personality mends, Dick's disintegrates—a reversal of their original relationship. Nicole learns to face reality independently (becoming, as Dick observes, hard as Georgia pine) and is thus able to release herself from her child-like dependence on Dick. Dick, on his side, has so trimmed his own life to the requirements of Nicole's disease (he has to be the protecting, unbetraying father that she did not have) that when she is able to stand alone he has nothing in himself to fall back upon. His role as her doctor had become the essence of his life, and when she no longer needs him in this role, his life withers into failure and obscurity. The tragedy, however, is perhaps as much Nicole's as it is Dick's, for in her reintegration she has lost the delightful unconventionality that she had had when she first met Dick, and has accepted the superficial, self-seeking value of the international moneyed circle to which she belongs.

It is clear that the movement of the novel follows the integration of Nicole's personality and the corresponding disintegration of Dick's. "Integration" and "disintegration" are psychological terms, but the psychology of this novel about a psychiatrist and his patient-wife has been criticised for its lack of sophistication. Abraham H. Steinberg, for instance, in a 1953 article in this journal,[2] while pointing out some of the depth of Fitzgerald's psychological acuteness, shows the superficiality of Dick Diver's practice of psychiatry (and indicates that this was perhaps partly motivated by Fitzgerald's hostility to depth psychiatry). Depth psychology might indeed shed a good deal of light on this novel, but, I think, one of the most promising ways of approaching it is through the social psychology of George Herbert Mead. To an astonishing extent Fitzgerald thinks about his characters in terms explicitly similar to Mead's. The texture of the book is social; its focal point is not so much Dick Diver as the group of which he is the center. His failure is not so much from an individual inadequacy or some romantic unconventionality as from a social inadequacy, an inability to adapt successfully to a social milieu for which his upbringing has not prepared him. If anything, his failure is the result of a cultural system that has made him define himself too narrowly in terms of his social role. The view of the self as primarily a social phenomenon, as a performance before the eyes of others, structures the novel.

Mead's conception of the self throws a great deal of light upon this structure. Two aspects of his social psychology are especially important and relevant: first, his theory of the way in which the self becomes conscious of itself, and second, his conception of the two aspects of the self, the "I" and the "Me." The first of these structures the relationships between all the people of the novel. The second gives a clue to the nature of Nicole's self realization and Dick's collapse.

The core of Mead's theory of the nature of self-consciousness lies in the following quotation:

> The individual experiences himself as such, not directly, but only indirectly, from the particular standpoints of other individual members of the same social group, or from the generalized standpoint of the social group as a whole to which he belongs. For he enters his own experience as a self or individual, not directly or immediately, not by becoming a subject to himself, but only in so far as he first becomes an object to himself just as other individuals are objects to him . . . and he becomes an object to himself only by taking the attitudes of other individuals toward himself.[3]

Two things are of note in this passage: first, the individual perceives what he is by perceiving what he appears to be in the eyes of others; second, he perceives what he is by assuming the attitudes of others towards himself. Perhaps there is no final distinction between these, but it will be useful to consider each separately in an analysis of the structure of this novel.

That the first point above clearly describes the elemental relationship of individuals to each other in this novel might be seen from the following series of quotations:

> He looked at her and for a moment she lived in the bright blue worlds of his eyes, eagerly and confidently. (Rosemary of Dick, p.10)

> Seeing from their eyes how beautiful she was. . . . (Nicole of the group, p.52)

> He was thankful to have existence at all, if only as a reflection in her wet eyes. (Dick of Nicole, p.154)

> You will feel your own reflection sliding along the eyes of those who look at you. (Nicole of Dick, p.159)

> Later in the garden she was happy; she did not want anything to happen, but only for the situation to remain in suspension as the two men tossed her from one mind to another; she had

> not existed for a long time, even as a ball. (Nicole of Dick and Tommy Barban, pp.273–274)

This sort of shorthand is used very frequently in the novel to indicate the way in which the characters feel themselves to exist, but existence is, of course, much more complex than simply perceiving oneself as the object of another's perception; in order to do this the individual has to internalize the attitudes of others, both in the sense of "becoming the other," assuming his role, and in the sense of becoming that which the other thinks him to be.

Mead suggests that the individual in some sense actually does become the others who form his social group, thus even the normal individual will have a multiple personality.[4] We play a number of different roles, and we are, in some sense, no more than the roles we play. Nicole, whose illness has perhaps given her a good deal of insight into herself, can say for instance: "When I talk I say to myself that I am probably Dick. Already I have even been my son, remembering how wise and slow he is. Sometimes I am Doctor Dohmler and one time I may even be an aspect of you, Tommy Barban" (161).

When these multiple selves are in harmony the self is integrated, when out of harmony, disintegrated–or schizophrenic. The integration in oneself of the attitudes of all others in one's social environment Mead calls the "generalized other,"[5] and it is by achieving this that Nicole is finally cured. But what one ends up as when one is integrated depends upon the nature of the society indentified with, and we will have to return to this later when we examine the nature of Nicole's integration. What happens, however, when society as it presents itself to the individual is fragmentary, or if the key members of it are not themselves complete? "The unity and structure of the complete self," Mead says, "reflects the unity and structure of the social process as a whole; and each of the elementary selves of which it is composed reflects the unity and structure of one of the various aspects of that process in which the individual is implicated."[6] To Nicole, her father had been almost in himself her "generalized other," and when he appeared in the role of lover as well as father, this split caused her own personality to split. She could trust no man, having found the man she trusted the most to be untrustworthy.

Dick, moreover, well on the way towards a split personality of his own, puts this notion in a way that sounds something like Mead's own formulation:

> [He realized] that the totality of life may be different . . . from its segments, and also that life during the forties seemed capable of being observed only in segments. His love for Nicole and Rosemary, his friendship with Abe North, with Tommy Barban . . . in such contacts the personalities had seemed to press up so close to him that he became the personality itself. . . . It was as if for the remainder of his life he was condemned to carry with him the egos of certain people, early met and early loved, and only to be complete as they were complete themselves. (243)

And they, of course, are not complete. Abe North, for instance, drinks himself to death, prefiguring Dick's disintegration. Rosemary becomes so absorbed into the role of actress that whatever was inside the shell withers away. As Dick says, she doesn't grow up. She continually plays roles, but doesn't finally integrate them into one that is her own unique role, or her own individual personality. When Dick discovers this about her in Rome, the first dramatic evidence of the break-up in his own nature occurs. He gets drunk, fights with the Italian police, and is thoroughly humiliated by them.

The full poignancy of Dick's decline, however, is to be seen in the other way in which the individual internalizes the attitudes of others—by becoming what he is thought to be. At every stage in the long process of disintegration, it happens that the view that Dick will shortly come to take of himself is first suggested to him by someone else. It even happens that he sometimes mistakes the other's view and so becomes something that surprises them both. For instance, one of the first steps down for Dick is his engagement to Nicole. Nicole's sister, the multi-millionairess Baby Warren, suggests to him that what Nicole needs, since she will probably be a mental patient all her life, is to marry a psychiatrist. Finding one should be no problem, with Nicole's money. Dick laughs cynically at the notion that Baby wants to buy a permanent and personal caretaker for Nicole and assumes that she has him in mind—an idea that is reinforced when Baby leaves suddenly and Dick is left to take Nicole back to the hospital in Zurich. As a matter of fact, Baby has not had him in mind at all, but, as Fitzgerald says, "her request had the effect that Dick assumed she desired" (156). Her plans help crystallize his feelings for Nicole and he marries her.

This might seem simply a coincidence, were it an isolated incident, but the same pattern occurs again and again. Nicole, for instance, assumes that he has been unfaithful to her with the daughter of a patient of his clinic (she has never admitted the possibility of infidelity before, since it would threaten her image of Dick), and shortly after this Dick is for the first time unfaithful to her with Rosemary. The father of one of his patients removes his son indignantly, accusing Dick of alcoholism; Dick's partner, moreover, comments on his heavy drinking; and what had been a "food" for Dick becomes a major problem. Towards the end, Nicole begins to get some insight into what her part has been in Dick's disintegration: "I've ruined you," she asserts. "So I'm ruined, am I?" Dick inquires pleasantly, not yet thinking of himself in this manner, but seven pages later he recurs to it, now realizing its truth: "You ruined me, did you? Then we're both ruined" (264, 271). Again, instances could be multiplied.

It would be a mistake to think that Dick becomes an alcoholic, a philanderer, or a wreck *because* he is considered so to be. The impulse is there, but unconscious until his perception of the impression he makes upon others fixes it for his own consciousness. Implicit in this is the central defect of Dick's character. When Dick becomes aware that he has "lost himself" in some sense, he tries to remember when it happened, when the turning point might have been. But,

> . . . he could not tell the hour when, or the day or the week, the month or the year. . . . Between the time he found Nicole flowering under a stone in the Zurichsee and the moment of his meeting Rosemary the spear had been blunted.
>
> Watching his father's struggles in poor parishes had wedded a desire for money to an essentially unacquisitive nature. It was not a healthy necessity for security—he had never felt more sure

> of himself, more thoroughly his own man, than at the time of his marriage to Nicole. Yet he had been swallowed up like a gigolo. (201)

The source of his deterioration was not a wrong choice at some crucial juncture of his life, but a basic defect of character that could allow him to be "swallowed up like a gigolo" at just the moment when he was most sure of being his own man.

What would being "swallowed up like a gigolo" indicate about the way in which one conceives of himself? A gigolo is a piece of property, something bought and sold, an object. Dick's basic defect of character is that his awareness of himself is primarily as an object—i.e., the attitude of the "generalized other," which is the point of view of all others in his social context viewing him as an object, predominates in his sense of self. He is perhaps the pure type of what David Riesman has called the "other-directed" personality, or what Mead called the personality in which the sense of "Me" dominates.

The distinction that Mead makes between the "Me" and the "I" as aspects of the self reflects a crucial distinction in this novel between characters such as Dick and Rosemary on the one hand and Nicole and Tommy Barban on the other. The "Me" is "all of the attitudes of others organized and taken over into one's self"[7]—i.e., the sense of one's self as an object; one acts the role that others expect. The "I," however, is "the principle of action and impulse,"[8] the self as the center of action, subject rather than object. Its basis is "the biologic individual"; it is the result of the unique physiological pressures of the individual. This aspect of the self is perceived as a sense of the possible roles that might be taken to fulfill impulse; thus, the "I" is the source of the sense of freedom to create oneself, the "Me" of the sense of being determined. The "I" is the "novel reply to the social situation," while the "Me" is conventional and habitual. The complete self balances these two elements, but in the incomplete self they are in disharmony.

We can illustrate the predominance of the "Me" in Dick's personality by asking what the source of his "other-directedness" might be. We will remember Dick in his characteristic role as the man in the jockey cap making others happy, giving the group a sense of unity. How is this related to the concept of the "Me"? Primarily in that his concern for the happiness of others stems from his need to be loved—i.e., to be an object of affection. This is made quite clear in a number of places, and especially so in the following passage from near the end of the book. Dick is awakened in the middle of the night to go to the rescue ot Mary (North) Minghetti and the terrible Lady Sibley-Biers:

> He got up and, as he absorbed the situation, his self-knowledge assured him that he would undertake to deal with it—the old fatal pleasingness, the old forceful charm, swept back with its cry of "Use me!" He would have to go fix this thing that he didn't care a damn about, because it had early become a habit to be loved. . . . On an almost parallel occasion, back in Dohmler's clinic on the Zurichsee, realizing this power, he had made his choice, chosen Ophelia, chosen the sweet poison and drunk it. Wanting above all to be brave and kind, he had wanted, even more than that, to be loved. (300)

So he is now able to see for himself in what way he had been a gigolo, and to see also what the price had been.

What are the consequences of this distortion of personality? Rosemary has an intuition of what happens to people like Dick: "When people have so much for outsiders didn't it indicate a lack of inner intensity?" (75). Such people are simply acting, their whole life is acted on the stage or screen before others, and thus her comment about Dick is prophetic of what is to happen to herself. Dick, too, had recognized the tragic hollowness of the actor when he was given a chance for a screen test: "The strongest guard is placed at the gateway to nothing. . . . Maybe the condition of emptiness is too shameful to divulge" (69). It is only a day or two later that Rosemary says to him, "Oh, we're *such* actors—you and I."

At the outset of his career Dick had been aware of this hollowness or incompleteness. He felt he was incomplete, paradoxically, because of what he called his intactness (115). He even longed rather wistfully for some small misfortune or a slight neurosis that would make him "complete." His wish was answered with a vengeance, and his real "I"—a rather narrow-minded, aggressive, sardonic "I"—begins to assert itself. It was what he lacked all along for completeness, but it remains unintegrated with his "Me"—his ability to make others love him. The split can be seen in the last scene, where he deliberately turns on his charm for Mary Minghetti: "His glance fell soft and kind upon hers, suggesting an emotion underneath; their glances married suddenly, bedded, strained together. Then as the laughter inside him became so loud that it seemed as if Mary must hear it, Dick switched off the light and they were back in the Riviera sun" (312).

Dick is now the one with the split personality; Nicole's has healed. To understand how this comes about we will have to examine the figure who embodies the opposite principle to Dick's "Me." Nicole leaves Dick for Tommy Barban, symbolizing her change from a passive state, existing as an integrated whole only as a reflection of Dick's constant concern for her, to an independent, integrated state in which she discovers her values for herself.

Tommy Barban is clearly made Dick's opposite. He is described as one who "does not like any man very much nor feel their presence with much intensity" (197). If Dick's role is the passive one of being loved, Tommy's is the active role of lover. His name, Barban, suggests "barbarian," in contrast to the civilized Dick. Dick, moreover, is an American, with the characteristic "other-directedness" of Americans that is emphasized throughout the novel (pp.11–12), while Tommy is half French, with the Frenchman's individualism. Tommy, moreover, is constantly going to wars, while Dick, in contrast, devotes himself to the consolidation of social groups. And Dick, finally, represents what is most modern in modern man (his other-directedness, his scientific work on the frontiers of psychiatry, etc.), while Tommy is a throwback—e.g., to the *code duello*, the soldier of fortune, and the criminal.

In his 1951 edition of *Tender Is the Night*, the editor, Malcolm Cowley, added an appendix containing a section deleted by Fitzgerald in which Tommy takes Nicole to the machine-gun guarded, barbed-wire encircled estate of a friend of his, a Chicago gangster, and seduces her there on the beach.[9] This only emphasizes what is implicit in the novel as it was published. Tommy tells Nicole that she has "white crook's eyes," which offends her until she "internalizes" it and comes to see herself in this way. "I have no mirror here . . . but if my eyes have changed it's because I'm well again. And being well perhaps I've gone back to my true self—I suppose my grandfather was a crook and I'm a crook by heritage, so there we are" (290). "Better a sane crook than a mad puritan," she adds later, and it is significant that she is from Chicago, Dick from New England; that her father was the son of a nineteenth-century American robber baron, Dick's father a Protestant clergyman.

Nicole's sanity, then, lies in her accepting her "I," the freedom of her individual impulsive nature, and harmonizing it with the "generalized other" of her society. But that is a society of crooks and the descendants of crooks—typified by Baby Warren and Tommy Barban. Mead defines the criminal as "the individual who lives in a very small group, and then makes depredations upon the larger community,"[10] which is an accurate description of the international moneyed class to which Nicole belongs.

Dick had gone out of his depth by marrying into this class. His generalized other came from the larger community, and eventually to this smaller group it could only appear as "bluff": "When people are taken out of their depth," Baby Warren remarks of Dick, "they lose their heads, no matter how charming a bluff they put up"(310). Mental stability, in Mead's psychology, is primarily a matter of harmonizing the individual "I" with the generalized other of the social group from which he draws his identity. Dick would perhaps have been safer had he, like his colleague Franz, married within his depth.

A view of the nature of the self very much like George Herbert Mead's structures the characterization, the relationships between characters, and the upward and downward progress of the main characters of this novel. This view would also help to explain other important themes of the novel, such as the American in Europe, the effects of money upon character, Hollywood as the expression of American other-directedness, etc. But analysis in such terms misses the pathos and the tragedy of a man like Dick Diver whom such a psychology would seem to describe. What questions of self-identity would face one who became conscious of the debt of himself that he owes to others? Might he not legitimately wonder what, apart from the roles he plays, he himself really was? If he were one like Dick Diver, who lived only before the eyes of others, "performing" for them as he is expected to perform, he might have to face the fact that aside from the roles he plays he is nothing.

Because Fitzgerald faced up to that fact about himself, we need not suppose, despite extensive similarities, that he was influenced by George Herbert Mead either directly or indirectly. In an article in *Esquire Magazine* for March 1936, "Handle With Care," he said of himself:

> After a long time I came to these conclusions just as I write them here:
>
> (1) That I had done very little thinking save within the problems of my craft. For twenty years a certain man had been my intellectual conscience. That was Edmund Wilson.
>
> (2) That another man represented my sense of the "good life". . . . In difficult situations I have tried to think what *he* would have thought, how *he* would have acted.
>
> (3) That a third contemporary had been an artistic conscience to me . . . .
>
> (4) That a fourth man had come to dictate my relations with other people when these relations were successful: How to do, what to say, how to make people at least momentarily happy . . . .
>
> (5) That my political conscience had scarcely existed for ten years save as an element of irony in my stuff. When I became again concerned with the system I should function under, it was a man much younger than myself who brought it to me with a mixture of passion and fresh air.
>
> So there was not an "I" any more—not a basis on which I could organize my self-respect—save my limitless capacity for toil that it seemed I possessed no more. It was strange to have no self—to be like a little boy left alone in a big house . . . ."[11]

If we were to ask where Fitzgerald discovered the view of the self that structures what is perhaps his most profound novel, I think we would have to agree that he found it where artists usually find their inspiration, in a searching examination of himself. But, as we have seen, the self is a compound of influences and attitudes in the society within which one finds its positive existence. This view was there in the America of his time; Mead—and Dewey, who had similar views—were only theorizing from observed facts. But a novelist's society is in part made up of the books he has read and has been impressed by, and it may well be that this view of the self is another of Fitzgerald's debts to Joseph Conrad, who, in *Under Western Eyes*, had said "a man's real life is that accorded him in the thoughts of other men," and who had Lena say to Heyst in *Victory*, "if you were to stop thinking of me I shouldn't be in the world at all." In *The Rescue*, published in 1920, one of Conrad's characters describes the tragedy of life in terms that would seem to apply to Dick Diver: "Life is a sort of ritual dance, that most of us have agreed to take seriously. . . . Woe to him or her who breaks it. Directly they leave the pageant they get lost . . . and end by hating their very selves." And Conrad's Nostromo is described as a man the very essence of whose life "consisted in its reflection from the admiring eyes of men."[12]

Notes

1. F. Scott Fitzgerald, *Tender Is the Night*, new Bantam edition, 1962, pp.4–5. All later references are to this edition and are indicated by page numbers in parentheses in the text.

2. "Hardness, Light, and Psychiatry in *Tender Is the Night*," *Literature and Psychiatry*, III (1953), 1, 3–8.

3. George Herbert Mead, *Mind, Self and Society*, ed. Charles W. Morris, Chicago, 1934, p.138.

4. Mead, p. 142.

5. Mead, p.142.

6. Mead, p.154.

7. Mead, p.xxiv.

8. Mead, p.xxx.

9. F. Scott Fitzgerald, *Tender Is the Night: A Romance*, with the author's final revisions. Preface by Malcolm Cowley (New York, 1951), pp.345–348.

10. Mead, p.265.

11. Reprinted in *The Crack Up*, edited by Edmund Wilson, New Directions paperback (New York, 1956), pp.78–79.

12. Joseph Conrad, *Under Western Eyes*, Doubleday Anchor Book (Garden City, 1963), p.10; *Victory*, Modern Library edition (New York, n.d.), p.177; *The Rescue*, The Uniform edition (London and Toronto, 1924), p.412; *Nostromo*, Modern Library edition (New York, 1951), p.586.

14. *Tender Is the Night:* Keats and Scott Fitzgerald

by JOHN GRUBE

F. Scott Fitzgerald was deeply influenced by poetry during his entire life. In a letter to his daughter (August 3, 1940) he says:

> *The Grecian Urn* is unbearably beautiful, with every syllable as inevitable as the notes of Beethoven's Ninth Symphony, or it's just something you don't understand. It is what it is because an extraordinary genius paused at that point in history and touched it. I suppose I've read it a hundred times. About the tenth time I began to know what it was about, and caught the chime in it, and the exquisite inner mechanics. Likewise with *The Nightingale*, which I can never read through without tears in my eyes.

In the same letter he says, "For awhile after you quit Keats all other poetry seems to be only whistling or humming." It was from Keats' *Ode to a Nightingale* that he chose the title of his fourth novel, *Tender Is the Night.*

The heroine of *Tender Is the Night* is Nicole Warren, a beautiful young girl from an extremely wealthy Chicago family who has had sexual intercourse with her father and has been placed in a Swiss sanatorium to recover from the shock and consequent mental breakdown. Here she meets the handsome American psychiatrist, Dick Diver, full of enthusiasm and the first flush of youthful contact with the great men of European psychoanalysis. After a series of letters and meetings, they fall in love. Much

From the *Dalhousie Review*, XLIV (Winter 1964–65). Reprinted by permission of the author and the Review Publishing Company, Limited.

against the advice of his European colleagues, Dick marries Nicole. They settle on the Riviera, where she builds a magnificent villa and begins to entertain, gradually collecting about her a glittering circle of friends. But as she gets better, Dick gets "worse." He becomes more and more dependent on her and the protection of her money. Finally they are divorced, she remarries happily, and he disappears into a small and unsuccessful medical practice in upstate New York.

Fitzgerald not only took the title of his novel from Keats' "Ode to a Nightingale," but places a quotation from the poem at the beginning of the book. Let us look for a moment at this section of the poem:

> Already with thee! tender is the night,
> And haply the Queen-Moon is on her throne,
> Cluster'd around by all her starry Fays;
> But here there is no light,
> Save what from heaven is with the breezes blown
> Through verdurous glooms and winding mossy ways.

That is the part of the poem he chose to quote and emphasize. Curiously enough he omits these two lines:

> And haply the Queen-Moon is on her throne,
> Cluster'd around by all her starry Fays;

We shall see that he had a reason for drawing attention to these two lines; he chose to make the moon, in her many aspects—queen, goddess, suggestive of madness—an important symbol in the book.

The novel, too, even in its structure is full of echoes of Keats' famous poem. Enwrapped in Nicole's money and beauty, Dr. Diver leaves the world of science and the intellect for the world of sense (". . . a drowsy numbness pains/My sense"), abandons his medical practice, and even forgets the promising research of his youth (". . . Lethe-wards had sunk"). The poem's word "opiate" has a medical touch, just as the parallel "hemlock," with its overtones of the death of Socrates, suggests the end of his rational life.

At this point Nicole's family buy him a half-interest in a

private mental hospital, partly to restore his professional self-confidence and feelings of manliness. She names the house for incurable male patients The Eglantine (". . . the pastoral eglantine") and the corresponding house for female patients The Beeches: ("In some melodious plot/Of beechen green, and shadows numberless"). The "shadows numberless" of the poem become in the novel "those sunk in eternal darkness."[1]

Dr. Diver often contrasts Nicole's innocence of human suffering with his own experience as a psychiatrist:

> What thou among the leaves hast never known,
> The weariness, the fever, and the fret
> Here, where men sit and hear each other groan

Further, we are shown Dick on his daily medical rounds. There are the hopelessly old and senile ("Where palsy shakes a few, sad, last grey hairs"); the young, usually schizophrenic, who always touch his heart ("Where youth grows pale, and spectre-thin, and dies"); the formidably intelligent whose grief is that they can now think only in circles ("Where but to think is to be full of sorrow"); finally there are those who were once beautiful, twisted by despair until they become objects of profound pity and regret ("Where beauty cannot keep her lustrous eyes").

Soon Dick and Nicole tire of the Swiss mental home and again resume their search for the "hot, sweet south" (p.91) where they had first found so much happiness ("Dance and Provençal song, and sunburnt mirth"). Settling in their villa, they become the glass of fashion and mould of form as Nicole increasingly attracts the admiration and attention of a large coterie. The men respond to her beauty, and in the process somewhat lose their manliness and cue for action ("The Queen-Moon is on her throne/Cluster'd around by all her starry Fays"). At this point in the novel they are at the supposed peak of human happiness, surrounded by friends, good food, and particularly good wine ("With beaded bubbles winking at the brim/And purple-stained mouth"). But the wink turns into a leer as Dick goes on a serious drinking spree in Rome. His personality begins to crack, and he pursues a self-destructive course, sometimes violent as on the Roman holiday where he is seriously beaten up, sometimes simply alienating friends. But the death wish is there ("Darkling I listen; and for many a time/I have been half in love with easeful death"). He is more and more adrift on the "perilous" seas of "fancy", while Nicole is daily growing in health and vitality ("While thou art pouring forth thy soul abroad/In such an ecstasy").

Finally Nicole falls in love with Tommy Barban, a soldier of fortune; Dick and Nicole are divorced, and as Dr. Diver disappears to America at the end of the story, he is left only the haunting memory of her beauty. The corresponding lines of Keats' poem have a similar haunting quality and a theme of separation:

> Adieu! Adieu! the plaintive anthem fades
> Past the near meadows, over the still stream,
> Up the hillside; now 'tis buried deep
>
> In the next valley-glades:
> Was it a vision, or a waking dream?
> Fled is that music:—do I wake or sleep?

Fitzgerald worked for nine years on *Tender Is the Night*, and made many revisions both of the structure and the text. Malcolm Cowley, his most recent editor, speaks of an entry in Fitzgerald's notebook outlining the changed order and dividing the novel into five books instead of three. The entry reads:

> *Analysis of Tender*
> I Case History 151–212 61 pps. (change moon) p.212
> II Rosemary's Angle 3–104 101 pps. P.3
> III Casualties 104–148, 213–224 55 pps. (–2) (120–121)
> IV Escape 225–306 82 pps.
> V The Way Home 306–408 103 pps. (–8) (332–341)

Cowley remarks, "I haven't been able to find the 'moon' that was to be changed in Book 1; perhaps Fitzgerald gave some special meaning to the word, and in any case it doesn't occur on 212."[2] I think Cowley is right, that Fitzgerald did give a special meaning to the word, and that its importance as a symbol in the book is definitely indicated by the fact that Fitzgerald, in this outline prepared for his own use, chose to mention specifically only this one object—the moon.

What, then, is the special meaning? The moon first appears in a context of madness. After a brief meeting, the only contact between Nicole and Dr. Diver is in the form of letters that she sends to him, encouraged by the doctors who feel it would be good for her to develop a healthy interest in the outside world. The letters indicate, of course, a high degree of schizophrenia. For example:

> However you seem quieter than the others, all soft like a big cat. I have only gotten to like boys who are rather sissies. Are you a sissy? There were some somewhere.
>
> Excuse all this, it is the third letter I have written to you and will send immediately or never send. I've thought a lot about moonlight too, and there are many witnesses I could find if only I could be out of here (p.10).

Not only is the moon introduced here as associated with madness, but also another and related theme: Dick's later disintegration as a man. Under the pressure of caring for her, of dealing with her recurrent "lunacy", he cracks up, becomes a "sissy", or becomes, to use Keats' imagery, a "Fay" at the court of the "Queen-Moon".

Shortly afterwards we see the Divers through the eyes of Rosemary Hoyt, a young Hollywood actress who has just made her first film, *Daddy's Girl.* She is very much impressed with Nicole, thinking of the setting in which she met her in terms of: "Gausse's hotel through the darkening banks of trees . . . the moon already hovered over the ruins of the aqueduct" (p.71). The imagery not only gives us historical perspective, taking us back in time to the antique world, but also foreshadows the ruin that is hovering over the Diver household, torn apart as it is soon to be by a recurrence of Nicole's schizophrenia. For it is at a fabulous party on the terrace of the Divers' villa that the book reaches its climax. Nicole has her first relapse; Dick first loses control of the situation; the family secret is out in the open. And the incident leaves a trail of destruction and ruin in its wake. Long-standing friendships break up. Even a duel ensues as a direct result of the mad scene.

But the moon is not only a symbol of lunacy. The name of the Divers' house on the Riviera is the Villa Diana, and in many ways Nicole is depicted as that virginal goddess. Early in the book Dick sees her under this aspect:

> Her hair, drawn back of her ears, brushed her shoulders in such a way that the face seemed to have just emerged from it, as if this were the exact moment when she was coming from a wood into clear moonlight. The unknown yielded her up; Dick wished she had no background, that she was just a girl lost with no address save the night from which she had come (p.25).

To the other women in the book, such as Rosemary, she also appears to have the hard ruthless quality of the huntress: "Her face was hard, lovely, pitiful . . ."(p.61). or: "Her face hard, almost stern . . . save for the soft gleam that looked from her green eyes"(p.82). Many also notice the innocence and beauty that Dick perceived.

But the moon's other and more sinister side is also hinted at by Abe North, the Divers' closest friend, who is both jester and chorus throughout the novel:

> Abe North was talking to her about his moral code: "Of course I've got one", he insisted—"a man can't live without a moral code. Mine is that I'm against the burning of witches. Whenever they burn a witch I get all hot under the collar" (p.90).

It is Abe North, too, who explains to Rosemary Hoyt why the charmed circle of the Divers' friends is breaking up—why a duel is fought over Nicole's honour. He can only say, in his capacity of chorus: " 'Plagued by the nightingale,' Abe suggested, and repeated, 'probably plagued by the nightingale' " (p.100). This enigmatic comment, carrying us back to Keats' Ode, to the title of the book, and to the verses that stand at its head, reminds us that the nightingale traditionally has two aspects. Not only is it a bird whose beautiful notes have been celebrated by poets throughout the entire history of literature, but it also has a long mythological association with blood and violence, as in the story of Philomela. And Nicole creates both beauty and violence wherever she goes. Later in the novel this aspect is underlined when the Divers are staying at a Paris hotel. A murder occurs in the room across the way; Nicole has another seizure, and even her ravings are full of images of blood:

> Nicole knelt beside the tub swaying sidewise and sidewise. "It's you!" she cried,—"it's you come to intrude on the only privacy I have in the world—with your spread with red blood on it" (p.174).

Though Nicole as "Queen-Moon" presides over her court of "starry Fays", we are never allowed to forget entirely the other image borrowed from Keats' poem, the nightingale, or its two-fold character.

There is another incident of great interest in this regard. As a prelude to the famous party on the terrace of the Villa Diana, the Divers have their two children sing "Au Clair de la Lune":

> "Hello, Lanier, how about a song? Will you and Topsy sing me a song?"
> "What shall we sing?" agreed the little boy, with the odd charming accent of American children brought up in France.
> "That song about 'Mon Ami Pierrot'.
> Brother and sister stood side by side without self-consciousness and their voices soared sweet and shrill upon the evening air.
>
> Au clair de la lune,
> Mon ami Pierrot,
> Prête-moi ta plume
> Pour écrire un mot.
> Ma chandelle est morte,
> Je n'ai plus de feu,
> Ouvre-moi ta porte,
> Pour l'amour de Dieu.
>
> The singing ceased and the children, their faces aglow with the late sunshine, stood smiling calmly at their success (p.85).

Not only is this incident a treble variation, so to speak, on the darker variations of the lunar theme that run throughout the book. It also recapitulates the story. Diver gradually turns into Pierrot, actor, clown, and finally puppet. "Prête-moi ta plume/ Pour écrire un mot" recalls the touching letters Nicole wrote from the asylum when her "chandelle" was truly "morte", when the light of her mind was eclipsed. Finally the last two lines of the stanza, "Ouvre-moi ta porte/Pour l'amour de Dieu", suggest her desperate appeals to Dr. Diver to open to her the gates of sanity, the door of the asylum, and there is a religious aspect to the work Diver did for mental patients and for his friends—he makes a papal cross as he retires from the beach at the end of the book.

There are four stanzas to this charming song, which is both known to every schoolchild and also deeply imbued with the wit and grace of *la vieille France*. It is the story of Pierrot, traditionally "habillé en blanc . . . c'est la candeur, la naïveté, l'enthousiasme, la jeunesse." What better description of the young Dr. Diver could there be? His opponent is Harlequin, who traditionally "porte le masque noir et le costume bigarré; et représente la malice, l'adresse, l'insouciance".[3] The character who comes to fill this latter role in the novel is Tommy Barban. In fact the last part of the book is a contest between Dick Diver and Tommy Barban for the love of Nicole, a contest between Pierrot and Harlequin. But Nicole has changed during the course of the book until she is completely freed of psychosis. She is no longer praying for help; she is ready for the spontaneity of love. There is the same ironic twist in "Au Clair de la Lune". The lines in the first stanza,

> Ouvre-moi ta porte,
> Pour l'amour de Dieu,

become at the end of stanza three

> Ouvrez votre porte,
> Pour le dieu d'amour

and to this approach of Harlequin, in his guise of Tommy Barban, she responds.

Fitzgerald often reinforces his main story-line with subplots or incidents that echo the main plot. For example, the striking opening chord of the novel—Nicole's seduction by her father—is repeated when Rosemary Hoyt, the Hollywood actress, shows her friends, including Nicole, her latest film *Daddy's Girl*. The Shirley Temple aspect of the story contains a similar though unrealized emotional situation, sugared over though it is by the sentimental clichés of the film. Given this method of Fitzgerald, I think the introduction of "Au Clair de la Lune", the selection of this particular piece of music, deserves the close attention given it above in analysing the essential structure of the novel.

But there is another aspect to the incident. Just as the showing of *Daddy's Girl* gives Fitzgerald the opportunity to denounce the arrested emotional states that are induced in young Americans by Hollywood, and the subsequent difficulties they experience while maturing emotionally, I think that the Pierrot scene is meant to indicate the large gap that separates the expatriate American from the country he "escapes" to—in Fitzgerald's time almost always France. The expatriate never succeeds in establishing real contact with the people. They remain, whether Marseilles dockhands or duchesses, picturesque, literary. How little, after all, do the Divers and their friends understand "Au Clair de la Lune", which is a witty and urbane poem, a poem they have reduced to a child's recitative? They can only see by reflected light—*au clair de la lune*. The last stanza, for example is typically French in feeling:

> Au clair de la lune,
>   On n'y voit que peu.
> On chercha la plume,
>   On chercha le feu.
> Cherchant de la sorte
>   Ne sais ce qu'on trouva,
> Mais je sais qu'la porte
> Sur eux se ferma.

It illustrates, perhaps, the light touch that a Frenchman can lend to his affairs of the heart, as opposed to the gloom and complexity that an Anglo-Saxon introduces into his—at least in novels.

Fitzgerald spent the nine years prescribed by Horace revising this book before sending it out into the world. It received a cool reception. Since then it has been both attacked and defended, slowly attaining a wider circulation and popularity. Part of the difficulty readers experience with the book is due, I think, to a failure to realize its essential *genre*. It is in part an allegory, structurally close in many ways to such allegorical works of the past as, say, Edmund Spenser's *The Faerie Queene*.

It is well known that Spenser used the fictional characters of his poem to represent his ideas about religious questions, morality, contemporary politics, and the relation of England to her past. In like manner *Tender Is the Night* appears to be a tragic love story, but the characters are used by Fitzgerald quite frequently to convey his own ideas. For example, he uses Nicole as a peg on which to hang his poetic version of *The Communist Manifesto*:

> Nicole was the product of much ingenuity and toil. For her sake trains began their run at Chicago and traversed the round belly of the continent to California; chicle factories fumed and link belts grew link by link in factories; men mixed toothpaste in vats and drew mouthwash out of copper hogsheads; girls canned tomatoes quickly in August or worked rudely at the Five-and-Tens on Christmas Eve; half-breed Indians toiled on Brazilian coffee plantations and dreamers were muscled out of patent rights in new tractors—these were some of the people who gave a tithe to Nicole and, as the whole system swayed and thundered onward, it lent a feverish bloom to such processes of hers as wholesale buying, like the flush of a fireman's face holding his post before a spreading blaze. She illustrated very simple principles, containing in herself her own doom, but illustrated them so accurately that there was grace in the procedure . . . (p.113).

In this passage he is using Nicole much in the way Spenser uses Duessa, or, to take a modern example, the way Sinclair Lewis uses Babbitt. As Fitzgerald says, "She illustrated certain principles, containing in herself her own doom". But *Tender Is the Night* is not just a *roman à thèse* like *Babbitt*, any more than it is a simple love story, or even a "psychological novel". It is all of these and more. Fitzgerald had a deep moral and religious "concern"; he also had a profound interest in the relation of the American past to the modern United States (General Grant is a key figure in the novel from this point of view, as is the girl in the American military cemetery in France, unable to find the grave of her brother); he intended further to present in a wide panorama the life of his times.

It is with this in mind that we should approach the novel, its characters, and its symbolic structure, not looking for exact and mathematical equivalences, for the symbols take on different meanings at different times during the story. We have seen the cluster of imagery that surrounds the figure of Nicole, based in part on the nightingale and the moon, shift in meaning or emphasis. *Tender Is the Night* is an enchanting and disturbing work of art, but it can be fully understood and enjoyed only by those who approach it with the same respect as that with which they approach the court of Gloriana, as did Keats, through whom Fitzgerald caught a fleeting glimpse of "the Queen-Moon", her kingdom, and its strange and confusing landscape.

Notes

1. F. Scott Fitzgerald, *Tender Is the Night*, ed. Malcolm Cowley (New York: Scribners, 1956), p.91. All references are to this edition of the novel.

2. Ibid., p.xii, Introduction.

3. R. P. Jameson et A. E. Heacox, eds. *Chants de France* (Boston: D. C. Heath & Co., 1922), p.46.

15. *Tender Is the Night* and The "Ode to a Nightingale"

by WILLIAM E. DOHERTY

Critics often express a feeling that there is something mysterious about Fitzgerald's *Tender Is the Night*, that there is something unsatisfying in the analyses we have had—a discomfort one does not feel with the more elaborately structured *The Great Gatsby*, or with the intriguing, unfinished *The Last Tycoon*. Searching the critical opinion on *Tender Is the Night*—this "magnificent failure"—one is likely to feel that something *is* missing; one seems to have, as Maxwell Geismar says, "the curious impression at times that the novel is really about something else altogether."[1]

It seems strange that the relationship between the novel and Keats's "Ode to a Nightingale," which supplied Fitzgerald with both title and epigraph, should have received no more than passing attention from the critics. The epigraph reads:

> Already with thee! tender is the night,
>
> . . .
>
> But here there is no light,
> Save what from heaven is with the breezes blown
> Through verdurous glooms and winding mossy ways.

We know that Fitzgerald had a lifelong and deep response to Keats: "for awhile after you quit Keats all other poetry seems to be only whistling or humming." The "Ode to a Nightingale" was especially important to him; he found it unbearably beautiful, confessed he read it always with tears in his eyes.[2]

I

It is true that the title *Tender Is the Night* was chosen late in the extended course of the book's writing; but it seems clear that Fitzgerald was conscious of the "Ode" not merely in the last stages of composition. The title is appropriate, though no one has said why. Yet, a moment's reflection will show that there is a good deal of Keatsian suggestiveness in *Tender Is the Night* in both decor and atmosphere—the Provençal summers of sunburnt mirth, the nights perfumed and promising, the dark gardens of an illusory world. But I suggest that there are parallels more significant than those of color and mood. The correspondences I offer in this case, when taken individually, might seem no more than coincidental; but considered in their cumulative weight, they indicate a calculated pattern of allusion beneath the literal surface of the novel which deepens the psychoanalytic rationale and adds context to the cultural analysis the book offers. In addition, the "Ode" appears to provide us with a sort of thematic overlay which clarifies unsuspected symbolic structures, essential to the understanding of the book.

I will begin with an admission that weakens my case. Fitzgerald dropped a reference to the nightingale from his second and subsequent version of the published novel. In the *Scribner's Magazine* version he wrote of "roses and the nightingales" that had become an essential part of the beauty of that "proud gay land," Provence.[3] Why that observation was dropped, I cannot say; but its appearance, however brief, suggests that like Keats, Fitzgerald associated the south of France with the romantic bird. There is a second and more interesting reference which remained. It too connects the bird and the south of France. To understand its significance, one must consider it in context.

The Riviera, Mediterranean France, came to be, as Maxwell Geismar has pointed out, that apogee of ease and grace, that "psychological Eden" in which Fitzgerald and his heroes took refuge.[4] None of his characters responds more fully to this environment than does Rosemary, coming as she does from the "salacious improvisations of the frontier." At the party at the Villa Diana, no guest is more enchanted by the life that seems promised there; she feels a sense of homecoming, feels drawn as if by magnetic lights. The spell of the party is still on her as she lies awake in her room "suspended in the moonshine, . . . cloaked by the erotic darkness." She is disturbed by secret noises in the night: an "insistent bird" sings in the tree outside. She is not sure what bird it is, but the singing and the Divers seem to merge in her mind: "Beyond the inky sea and far up that high, black shadow of a hill lived the Divers. She thought of them both together, heard them still singing faintly a song like rising smoke, like a hymn, very remote in time and far away."[5] But Rosemary is confused by it all; she cannot think as yet except through her mother's mind. Abe North identifies the bird for her:

> "What are *you* doing up?" he demanded.
> "I just got up." She started to laugh. . . .
> "Probably plagued by the nightingale," Abe suggested and repeated, "probably plagued by the nightingale"(42).

The entire chapter, heavy with night imagery, seems to lead up to this identification. Rosemary has been brought up with the idea of work. Now she is on a summer's holiday, an emotionally lush interval between two winters of reality; and what she discovers is a world remote, romantic, something southern, a mysterious dark lure of life to which she responds—symbolized by the night bird. It is unreal; a duel will be fought; "up north the true world thundered by."

What I suggest is that the novel deals with characters who are plagued by the nightingale, those enamoured of the romantic illusion. Nicole seems to be the Nightingale.

Consider the scene in which Nicole sings to Dick. As she waits for Dick at the sanatorium, singing surrounds Nicole, summer songs of ardent skies and wild shade. The night, the woods, gardens, flowers are associated with Nicole throughout the novel. Here, the unknown seems to yield her up, "as if this were the exact moment when she was coming from a wood into the clear moonlight"(135). Dick responds to that illusion, wishes that she had no other background, "no address save the night from which she had come." She leads him to a secret copse. In this melodious plot she has hidden a phonograph. She plays for him "thin tunes, holding lost times and future liaison." Through song the two of them are transported out of the copse into another world. The journey is chronicled in ironic song titles. Finally Nicole herself sings to Dick. She supposes he has heard all these songs before. " 'Honestly, you don't understand—I haven't heard a thing.' Nor known, nor smelt, nor tasted, he might have added"(136). Now here was this girl bringing him the essence of a continent, "making him a profound promise of herself for so little. . . . Minute by minute the sweetness drained down into her out of the willow trees, out of the dark world"(136). But there is danger in the promise of this "waif of disaster," in the song of this "young bird with wings crushed."

The brief transport from the world which the "Ode" details, the emotional adventure of climax and decline is suggested in this and in a number of other scenes in *Tender Is the Night.* Indeed, the pattern describes the very rhythm of the novel. The party at the Villa Diana, as Malcolm Cowley suggests, appears to be the high point in the story. The scene marks a change of mood; thereafter, the light romantic atmosphere is dispelled.[6] We see there the Divers at their point of greatest charm—a "vision of ease and grace," commanding all the delicacies of existence. It is a high point for another reason. It is in this scene that the principals of the story make an escape from the prosaic and temporal world. In the rarified atmosphere of the party a moment is caught in which a delicate triumph over time is achieved.

The party is given out of doors in the garden, Nicole's garden. To Rosemary the setting seems to be the center of the world: "On such a stage some memorable thing was sure to happen"(29). The guests arrive under a spell, bringing with them the excitement of the night. Dick now seems to serve Nicole as prop man, arranging the set, dressing the trees with lamps. The guests are seated at Nicole's table:

> There were fireflies riding on the dark air and a dog baying on some far-away ledge of the cliff. The table seemed to have risen

> a little toward the sky like a mechanical dancing platform, giving the people around it a sense of being alone with each other in the dark universe, nourished by its only food, warmed by its only lights. And, as if a curious hushed laugh from Mrs. McKisco were a signal that such a detachment from the world had been attained, the two Divers began suddenly to warm and glow and expand, as if to make up to their guests, already so subtly assured of their importance, so flattered with politeness, for anything they might still miss from that country well left behind. Just for a moment they seemed to speak to everyone at the table, singly and together, assuring them of their friendliness, their affection. And for a moment the faces turned up toward them were like the faces of poor children at a Christmas tree. Then abruptly the table broke up—the moment when the guests had been daringly lifted above conviviality into the rarer atmosphere of sentiment, was over before it could be irreverently breathed, before they had half realized it was there.
>
> But the diffused magic of the hot sweet South had withdrawn into them—the soft-pawed night and the ghostly wash of the Mediterranean far below—the magic left these things and melted into the two Divers and became part of them (34–35).

When we consider the care with which Fitzgerald dresses this scene, we sense an emphasis beyond what the mere events of the party would demand. This garden, the fireflies riding on the dark air, the summer evening, the wine-colored lanterns hung in the trees—the Romantic decor is there, and the Keatsian atmosphere: "the diffused magic of the hot sweet South . . . the soft-pawed night and the ghostly wash of the Mediterranean far below." There is no need to insist that these images have their antecedents in the "Ode"—in its "murmurous haunt of flies on summer eves," or its "warm south," its "tender night," its "charmed magic casements opening on perilous seas"; for the clearest parallel to the poem lies in the brief achievement of the precious atmosphere, achieved through the familiar Romantic formula of escape at the moment of emotional pitch—here ironically, a moment of social ecstasy, but suggesting inevitably the dynamics of the sexual event. The imagery itself reiterates the pattern: the fragile loveliness of Nicole's garden increases "until, as if the scherzo of color could reach no further intensity, it broke off suddenly in mid-air, and moist steps went down to a level five feet below"(26).

It seems unlikely that the material of the "Ode" was so immediate in Fitzgerald's mind that it would come to add to the novel a dimension of allusion of which he was unaware. We are willing to concede unlimited conscious subtlety to his contemporaries in the novel; but Fitzgerald, despite the evidence of his deliberate workmanship, is too often pictured by critics as a somewhat fatuous tool of the muse, whose mind was inferior to his talent. The intricacies of *Tender Is the Night* would suggest otherwise. Not only is the pattern of the momentary climax a repeated one in the novel; there occurs, too, the *recall to reality* that marks the ending of the "Ode." In the novel it is not the sound of a bell that signals the descent from bliss—or the word "forlorn" striking like a bell, tolling the poet back to his sole self; it is another sound heard three times in the book: when Dick falls in love with Nicole, when Abe leaves on the train from Paris, and when Tommy becomes Nicole's lover. Each time a shot is heard, a loud report that breaks the illusion, signifies the end of happiness and the escape from self.

After Nicole leaves the sanatorium, Dick tries to avoid her; but she fills his dreams. Their chance meeting in the Alps ends in Dick's complete surrender of self: "he was thankful to have an existence at all, if only as a reflection in her wet eyes"(155). As in all her love situations, Nicole is triumphant, self-controlled, cool: "I've got him, he's mine" (155). The scene remains tender; it is raining, the appropriate weather for love in Fitzgerald's novels. But, "suddenly there was a booming from the wine slopes across the lake; like cannons were shooting at hail-bearing clouds in order to break them. The lights of the promenade went off, went on again. Then the storm came swiftly . . . with it came a dark, frightening sky and savage filaments of lightning and world-splitting thunder, while ragged, destroying clouds fled along past the hotel. Mountains and lakes disappeared—the hotel crouched amid tumult, chaos and darkness"(155–56).

This is not the storm of passion. Dick has come suddenly to his senses: "For Doctor Diver to marry a mental patient? How did it happen? Where did it begin?" The moment of passion and illusion is over. He laughs derisively. "*Big* chance—oh, yes. My God!—they decided to buy a doctor? Well, they better stick to whoever they've got in Chicago" (156). But Dick has committed himself to Nicole. His clear sight comes too late, and when the storm is over her beauty enters his room "rustling ghostlike through the curtains."

A loud shot sounds the ominous recall another time, in the Paris railway station. Here is departure and farewell; a gunshot cracks the air. Abe, on the train, waves good-by, unaware of what has happened. The shots do not mark the end of his happiness, for he has long been in misery, though they do forebode his violent death. It is the brief summer happiness of Dick—won in a desperate bargain with the gods—that is ending. It marks the end of a summer mirth for the Divers' group, the beginning of misfortune for Dick. Dick and his friends move out of the station into the street as if nothing had happened. "However, everything had happened—Abe's departure and Mary's impending departure for Salzburg this afternoon had ended the time in Paris. Or perhaps the shots, the concussions that had finished God knew what dark matter, had terminated it. The shots had entered into all their lives . . ." (85).

The third of these recalls to reality occurs just after Tommy possesses Nicole. The entire account from the arrival of Tommy at the Villa Diana to the departure from the hotel presents a curious parallel to the ending of the "Ode." Tommy comes to Nicole like a worshipper before a mystery. His happiness intensifies: "And, my God, I have never been so happy as I am this minute" (294). But the time of joy is brief; the point of greatest happiness is a moment outside of self, a taste of oblivion. The ecstasy passes; disappointment and foreboding follow: "the nameless fear which precedes all emotions, joyous or sorrowful, inevitable as a hum of thunder precedes a storm." After the act, things begin to look tawdry to Tommy. He is edgy and apprehensive. Outside there are disturbing noises: "There's that noise again. My God, has there been a murder?" The final recall is heard. As they leave the room "a sound split the air outside: Cr-ACK-Boom-M-m-m!

It was the battleship sounding a recall. Now, down below their window, it was pandemonium indeed . . ."(296–97). There is a rush to depart. Cries and tears are heard as the women shout farewells to the departing launch. The last ludicrous moments of the scene, the girls shouting their tearful good-byes from the balcony of Tommy's room, waving their underwear like flags, appear to be Fitzgerald's ironic counterpart to the adieu of the final stanza of the poem. The fading anthem of the "Ode" becomes the American National Anthem: "Oh, say can you see the tender color of remembered flesh?—while at the stern of the battleship arose in rivalry the Star-Spangled Banner"(297).

II

The title of the novel and the epigraph Fitzgerald offers illuminate the significance of "night" and "darkness" in the story. An enquiry reveals a complicated and careful symbolic structure in *Tender Is the Night* involving a contrast between the night and the day, darkness and light. The title of the novel declares that the night is tender. There is in it an implicit corollary about the day.

Early in the story, the sun is established as something harsh and painful, even maddening. The sun troubles the Divers and their group. They seek shelter from it under their umbrellas which "filter" its rays. At the beach the sea yields up its colors to the "brutal sunshine." Rosemary retreats from the "hot light" on the sand. Dick promises her a hat to protect her from the sun and to "save her reason." In the scene in which Nicole lapses into madness at the Agiri Fair "a high sun with a face traced on it beat fierce on the straw hats of the children." The day scenes are those of pain and fear: "the April sun shone pink upon the saintly face of Augustine, the cook, and blue on the butcher's knife she waved in her drunken hand"(265).

On the other hand, darkness and the night are addressed in fond, in honorific terms: "the lovely night," the "soft rolling night," the "soft-pawed night," the "erotic darkness." Fitzgerald's description of Amiens reveals something of the character and virtue of the night: "In the daytime one is deflated by such towns . . . and the very weather seems to have a quality of the past, faded weather like that of old photographs. But after dark all that is most satisfactory in French life swims back into the picture—the sprightly tarts, the men arguing with a hundred Voilà's in the cafes, the couples drifting, head to head, toward the satisfactory inexpensiveness of nowhere"(59). Part of the meaning is here, but the symbolism of the night is not merely opposite in meaning to that of the day; it is more complicated and more intricately woven into the story. The night is the time of enchantment, masking the ugliness of reality that the day exposes. The night, as in the "Ode," is the time of beauty and the time of illusion. Dick and his friends prefer the night: "All of them began to laugh spontaneously because they knew it was still last night while the people in the streets had the delusion that it was bright hot morning"(79). But the night is not entirely superior to the day. The desirable night is the all allowing darkness. It is a dimness preferred, perhaps, by those ineffective in dealing with the practical day-lit reality. If the day is harsh, it has vigor; the night is the time of ease and also weakness. Some hint of these sinister implications may be detected in the scene in which Baby Warren makes her frustrated effort to aid Dick after he has been beaten and thrown into the Roman jail. She cannot function in the real world: "She began to race against the day; sometimes on the broad avenues she gained but whenever the thing that was pushing up paused for a moment, gusts of wind blew here and there impatiently and the slow creep of light began once more" (227). She cringes at the unstable balance between night and day. The strange creature she encounters in the embassy, wrapped and bandaged for sleep, "vivid but dead," appears an unwholesome figure of the night, incongruous with the day.

It would appear that Fitzgerald has divided his world into two parts—the night and the day. The day is reality, hard, harsh, and vigorous; the night is illusion, tender, joyful, but devitalizing.

The most significant illusion that the night fosters is the illusion of happiness. To the Romantic, happiness consists in preserving the high moment of joy. He has a dread of endings.

Tender Is the Night is a book of endings: "Things are over down here," says Dick. "I want it to die violently instead of fading out sentimentally"(37–38). Paradoxically, the Romantic dream is that the moment of joy can be embalmed forever in the final night; death then appears to be a welcome extenuation of the night, ending all endings. Both the poem and the novel deal with these lovely illusions; but what they teach is that the fancy cannot cheat so well, that disillusionment is the coefficient of time.

There is a difference in tone between the two works which is due to the fact that Keats emphasizes the swelling dimension of the ecstatic experience, while Fitzgerald deals more with its deflation. Where Keats conveys a sense of disappointment, fond regret, Fitzgerald expresses a Romantic's anti-Romantic argument; for in tracing the grim disenchantment Fitzgerald underscores the sense of deception, trickery, the sense of victimage in the martyring of the dreamer. The "immortal bird" of the "Ode" becomes the "perverse phoenix" Nicole; the deceiving elf becomes the "crooked" Nicole, one of a long line of deceivers, pretending to have a mystery: "I've gone back to my true self," she tells Tommy; ". . . I'm a crook by heritage"(292). We suspect complicity in her father's sin; he tells the doctor, "She used to sing to me"(129).

There are other victims of the Romantic deception—the inmates of the sanatorium where Dick labors without accomplishment. "I am here as a symbol of something"(185), the American woman artist tells Dick. She and the others are there because "life is too tough a game" for them. Unlike the thick-ankled peasants who can take the punishment of the world on every inch of flesh and spirit, these are the fine-spun people suffering private illusions, their "compasses depolarized." They are "sunk in eternal darkness," people of the night, spirits sensitive and weak, now caught in Nicole's garden. For it is Nicole who has designed the means of holding these inmates fast. With floral concealment and deceptive ornament she has created those camouflaged strong points in which they are kept. Outwardly these houses are attractive, even cheerful, screened by little copses;

but "even the flowers lay in iron fingers." Perhaps the "Ode" suggested the names: the "Beeches" and the "Eglantine."

III

These inmates are, many of them, the "victims of drug and drink." There is in *Tender Is the Night* what might be called a potion motif, involving liquor, drugs, and poison. As in the "Ode" these are associated with the illusory adventure. Dr. Diver is as much an addict as his patients. In the early parts of the novel wine is associated with the delicacy of living the Divers maintain and with the sensual qualities of their lives. The enjoyable swim in the ocean is like the pleasure of "chilled white wine." The wine-colored lamps at the Villa Diana give a lively flush to Nicole's face. Nicole is gay-spirited after the "rosy wine at lunch." There is a faint spray of champagne on Rosemary's breath when Dick kisses her for the first time. But wine quickly loses its pleasant character. As Dick's esteemed control begins to slip and he acts for the first time without his customary "repose," he stares at the shelf of bottles, "the humbler poisons of France—bottles of Otard, Rhum St. James, Marie Brizard. . . ." Dick's Roman debauch recalls Abe's disastrous drunks. At home Dick drinks brandy from a three-foot bottle. He comes to regard liquor as food, descending to the level of the rich ruins he treats. Late in the novel we see that the sinister qualities of these draughts, potions, beakersful are associated with Nicole: in falling in love with her, in marrying her, Dick "had chosen the sweet poison and drunk it." Again Nicole is characterized as the attractive evil, the sinister allurement.

The draught of vintage from the deep delved earth, the dull opiate, the hemlock of Keats's poem may not be the direct sources of Fitzgerald's images; yet the associations of drug, drink, and poison with the Romantic appetencies are interesting and suggest that Keats and Fitzgerald were dealing with a similar psychological syndrome—the urge to "fade away, dissolve and quite forget. . . ."

This urge, as Albert Guerard, Jr., points out in his essay, "Prometheus and the Aeolian Lyre," is really the urge toward loss of self, the impulse toward self-immolation, to the drowning of consciousness—one of the hallmarks of the Romantic temperament—which accepts the myth of a vital correspondence between man and nature, a correspondence demanding the submersion of our rational, coherent selves. In the "Ode to a Nightingale," Mr. Guerard argues, Keats has written a poem about the actual submersion of consciousness, dramatizing the process itself, and presenting in the poem a symbolic evasion of the actual world:

> In one sense this ode is a dramatized contrasting of actuality and the world of the imagination, but the desire to attain this fretless imaginative world becomes at last a desire for reason's utter dissolution: a longing not for art but for free reverie of any kind. . . . This sole self from which Keats escapes at the beginning of the poem, and to which he returns at its close, is not merely the conscious intellect aware of life's weariness, fever, and fret, but truly the sole self: the self locked in drowsy numbness, the self conscious of its isolation. . . .[7]

Mr. Guerard's analysis may be modified, perhaps, to this degree: the "Ode" seems not so much a product of the Romantic myth of a prevailing correspondence between man and nature as it is an acknowledgment that the correspondence does not prevail. This thesis is reiterated in *Tender Is the Night.* What the nightingale symbolizes and promises in the "Ode," Nicole symbolizes and promises too. The ecstatic union with the bird is a taste of oblivion in loss of self.

Dick manifests the symptoms that Mr. Guerard indicates. There is the obsessive awareness of isolation that characterizes Dick even in his student days. He feels separated from his "fathers." He has the feeling that he is different from the rest, the isolation of the scientist and the artist—"good material for those who do most of the world's work"; but it is a loneliness he cannot endure. He wanted to be good, to be kind; he wanted to be brave and wise; but, as we learn toward the end, "he had wanted, even more than that, to be loved"(302). He gives a strange answer to Franz's criticism of his scholarship: "I am alone today. . . . But I may not be alone to-morrow"(138). One by one he burns his books to keep warm. In marrying Nicole he abandons his work in "effortless immobility." The critics have frequently noted the self-sacrificial aspect of Dick's behavior; but too frequently that self-sacrifice has been taken as the very theme of the novel because Dick gives himself so completely in serving others that he is left with nothing in the end. Rather, this self-sacrifice should be understood as one of the paradoxical impulses which constitute the desire to submerge the self. Self-immolation seems to contradict the longing for freedom from burdens and cares, yet both urges are aspects of the desire to abandon individuality. Abe, like Dick, has a strong desire for loss of self, and forgetfulness. Abe wants oblivion and seeks it in drink; he longs for death. Tommy too has inclinations toward the moribund, following death and violence all over the world. Baby Warren "relished the foretaste of death, prefigured by the catastrophes of friends"(172). Dick looks fondly at death in his decline. At the railing of Golding's yacht he comes close to suicide and to taking Nicole with him. The isolation Dick feels as a young man is never relieved. The entire age is alien to him. Dick mourns on the battlefields of World War I: "All my beautiful lovely safe world blew itself up here with a great gust of high explosive love"(57). Coming home to bury his father, he feels the final tie has been broken; there is no identity with his own land; he feels only a kinship with the dead: "Good-by, my father–good-by, all my fathers"(205).

IV

Finally, what does the correspondence between the novel and the "Ode" reveal about the social and cultural analysis Fitzgerald offers in *Tender Is the Night*? The distinction between the night and the day that Fitzgerald establishes symbolically has its significance in the "class struggle" he presents; the social antagonisms seem to be aspects of the antipathy which arises between the Romantic and the anti-Romantic disposition.

Fitzgerald, as we have seen, divides things into opposing pairs in *Tender Is the Night*. When Rosemary arrives at the Riviera beach she finds two groups. The McKisco party is made up of McKisco, the *arriviste* who has not yet arrived, his silly ambitious wife, two effeminates, and the shabby-eyed Mrs. Abrams. They are pale, gauche people, unattractive beside the Divers' group. The Divers are rich, cultured, talented, leisured. We get a fuller understanding of what these groups may represent in the scene in which Dick and Rosemary visit the house on the Rue Monsieur. It is a place of incongruities and contrasts. Clearly there is a clash between the past and the present, suggesting, it seems, the evolving future of the Western world: "It was a house hewn from the frame of Cardinal de Retz's palace in the Rue Monsieur, but once inside the door there was nothing of the past, nor of any present that Rosemary knew. The outer shell, the masonry, seemed rather to enclose the future so that it was an electric-like shock, a definite nervous experience, perverted as a breakfast of oatmeal and hashish, to cross that threshold . . ."(71). The people within are an odd mixture. They fit awkwardly into the environment. They lack the command over life that earlier ages managed to exert. Rosemary has a detached "false and exalted feeling" of being on a movie set. No one knew what the room meant because it was evolving into something else. It is important to recognize who these people in the room are:

> These were of two sorts. There were the Americans and English who had been dissipating all spring and summer, so that now everything they did had a purely nervous inspiration. They were very quiet and lethargic at certain hours and then they exploded into sudden quarrels and breakdowns and seductions. The other class, who might be called the exploiters, was formed by the sponges, who were sober, serious people by comparison, with a purpose in life and no time for fooling. These kept their balance best in that environment, and what tone there was, beyond the apartment's novel organization of light values, came from them (72).

The room apparently holds the society of the West. We find in it the McKisco group, the sponges, the hard practical people; and there are the Divers' type, the dissipated old "quality" class, the rundown Romantics who are doomed. The sober and serious exploiters set the tone for the future, and in it they will succeed. Rosemary stands between the two groups. Her youth and success separate her from the Divers' crowd, but she inclines toward them by temperament and training. She is a product of her mother's rearing, tutored in the values of the old society. "I'm a romantic too," Rosemary tells Dick. Yet, she is coldly practical, "economically . . . a boy not a girl." The first day on the beach Rosemary does not know which group is hers. She is attracted by the Divers' party; but, "between the dark people and the light, Rosemary found room and spread out her peignoir on the sand" (5–6).

The people of the McKisco type are not the victims of Nicole; they are immune to the Romantic illusion. The "tough minded and perennially suspicious" cannot be charmed. McKisco is the only one at the party at the Villa Diana who remains unassimilated, unaffected by the emotional excursion. In the house on the Rue Monsieur there are others who are likewise immune. The "cobra women" discuss the Divers:

> "Oh, they give a good show," said one of them in a deep rich voice. "Practically the best show in Paris—I'd be the last one to deny that. But after all—" She sighed. "Those phrases he uses over and over and over—'Oldest inhabitant gnawed by rodents.' You laugh once."
>
> "I prefer people whose lives have more corrugated surfaces," said the second, "and I don't like her."
>
> "I've never really been able to get very excited about them, or their entourage either. Why, for example, the entirely liquid Mr. North?" (72–73).

The incapacity for illusion gives these people an advantage in the world. McKisco, for whom the sensual world does not exist, ends successful and honored; his novels are pastiches of the work of the best people of his time. "He was no fool about his capacities—he realized that he possessed more vitality than many men of superior talent, and he was resolved to enjoy the success he had earned" (205). McKisco's duel with Tommy symbolizes the clash between the two groups and underscores the anachronism of the soldier and hero. Tommy is a product of the older civilization, educated in forgotten values. Ironically it is McKisco who is "satisfied" in the duel. He builds a new self-respect from his inglorious performance. Tommy, Abe, and Dick are Romantic remnants, the children of another century, fettered by its illusions—"the illusions of eternal strength and health, and of the essential goodness of people; illusions of a nation, the lies of generations of frontier mothers who had to croon falsely, that there were no wolves outside the cabin door"(117).

They are the salt of the earth—charming, gifted people, but overmatched in the struggle against the cold, shrewd frauds who are inheriting the earth. *Tender Is the Night* deals with the passing of the old order, with the passing of an attitude toward life, or rather with the last remnants of that life, "the oldest inhabitants gnawed by rodents." The specific content of the illusions which fetter them is less important than how Fitzgerald deals with the attraction to the irrational dream which marks the romantic temperament, a dream which may promise the world, the sustained ecstasy of love or the satisfactions of oblivion—symbolized by the beautiful mad woman, Nicole. She is the dream without real referent. She has no existence outside the mind of the dreamer: "When I talk I say to myself that I am probably Dick. Already I have even been my son, remembering how wise and slow he is. Sometimes I am Doctor Dohmler and one time I may even be an aspect of you, Tommy Barban. Tommy is in love with me . . ."(162).

In the end it is Doctor Diver who is "cured" when he releases her from his mind; he returns to the terrible emptiness of the "sole self." Late in the novel Nicole sings to him again in her "harsh sweet contralto." But this time Dick will not listen: "I don't like that one" (290).

The dream and the dreamer are, of course, Fitzgerald's subject matter in fiction; and in treating them he invariably delivers up the dreamer as victim of his own Romantic infatuations. And yet for all his insight, his self-lacerating satire, Fitzgerald leaves the dream and the dreamer somehow inviolable at the end. Gatsby, the most extravagant Romantic, leaking sawdust at every pore, is still intact at the end and dies with his dream intact. "No—Gatsby turned out all right at the end; it was what preyed on Gatsby, what foul dust floated in the wake of his dreams" that defeated him.

The best of the Romantic writers are not vulnerable to their own myths. The "Ode to a Nightingale" declares exquisitely the abandonment of faith in the imagination. It is not until *Tender Is the Night* that Fitzgerald abandons that last comfort of the Romantic, the notion that the botching, the disappointment of the imagination's most cherished ambitions may be blamed on the unworthy environment of the dreamer. *Tender Is the Night* is a harder, harsher book than *Gatsby*; and it tells us that the super dream is an internal corruption, a damaging, self-begotten beauty. Dick's final return to his sole self in upstate New York—"almost certainly in that section of the country, in one town or another"—is an utterly unsentimental fade-out; the hero is gone from the stage before we can cover him with our fond sympathy, before we can murmur, "Alas."

Notes

1. Maxwell Geismar, *The Last of the Provincials* (Cambridge, Mass., 1947), 333.

2. F. Scott Fitzgerald, *The Crack-Up* (New York, 1956), 298.

3. F. Scott Fitzgerald, "Tender Is the Night, A Romance," *Scribner's* Magazine, XCV (January–June, 1934), 7.

4. Geismar, *The Last of the Provincials*, 290–91.

5. F. Scott Fitzgerald, *Tender Is the Night* (New York, 1962), 40. Quotations in the text are from this edition unless otherwise indicated.

6. Malcolm Cowley, "Introduction," *Tender Is the Night* (New York, 1956), xvii.

7. Albert Guerard, Jr., "Prometheus and the Aeolian Lyre," *Yale Review*, XXXIII (March, 1944), 495.

Selected Bibliography

Bruccoli, Matthew J. *The Composition of "Tender Is the Night": A Study of the Manuscripts*. Pittsburgh, Pa.: University of Pittsburgh Press, 1963.

———. *F. Scott Fitzgerald: Collector's Handlist*. Columbus, Ohio: Fitzgerald Newsletter, 1964.

Bryer, Jackson R. *The Critical Reputation of F. Scott Fitzgerald: A Bibliographical Study*. Hamden, Conn.: Archon Books, 1967.

Cross, K. G. W. *F. Scott Fitzgerald*. New York: Grove Press, 1964.

Eble, Kenneth. *F. Scott Fitzgerald*. New York: Twayne, 1963.

Goldhurst, William. *F. Scott Fitzgerald and His Contemporaries*. Cleveland: World, 1963.

Hoffman, Frederick J., ed. *"The Great Gatsby": A Study*. New York: Scribner's, 1962.

Kazin, Alfred, ed. *F. Scott Fitzgerald: The Man and His Work*. Cleveland and New York: World, 1951.

Kuehl, John, ed. *The Apprentice Fiction of F. Scott Fitzgerald, 1909–1917*. New Brunswick, N.J.: Rutgers University Press, 1965.

Lehan, Richard D. *F. Scott Fitzgerald and the Craft of Fiction*. Carbondale: Southern Illinois University Press, 1965.

Miller, James E., Jr. *F. Scott Fitzgerald, His Art and His Technique*. New York: New York University Press, 1964.

———. *The Fictional Technique of Scott Fitzgerald*. The Hague: Martinus Nijhoff, 1957.

Mizener, Arthur, ed. *F. Scott Fitzgerald: A Collection of Critical Essays*. Englewood Cliffs, N.J.: Prentice-Hall, 1963.

———. *The Far Side of Paradise: A Biography of F. Scott Fitzgerald*. Boston: Houghton Mifflin, 1965. (2nd ed. rev.)

Perosa, Sergio. *The Art of F. Scott Fitzgerald*. Ann Arbor: University of Michigan Press, 1965.

Piper, Henry Dan. *F. Scott Fitzgerald, A Critical Portrait*. New York: Holt, Rinehart and Winston, 1965.

Shain, Charles E. *F. Scott Fitzgerald*. University of Minnesota Pamphlets on American Writers, No. 15. Minneapolis: University of Minnesota Press, 1961.

Selected Bibliography

Turnbull, Andrew. *Scott Fitzgerald*. New York: Scribner's, 1962.

———, ed. *Scott Fitzgerald: Letters to His Daughter*. New York: Scribner's, 1965.

———, ed. *The Letters of F. Scott Fitzgerald*. New York: Scribner's, 1963.

A selected list of MIDLAND BOOKS

MB-1	OVID'S METAMORPHOSES *tr. Humphries* (cl. $4.95s)	$1.95
MB-2	OVID'S THE ART OF LOVE *tr. Humphries*	$1.85
MB-6	THE DIPLOMACY OF THE AMERICAN REVOLUTION *Bemis*	$1.95
MB-7	THE LITERARY SYMBOL *Tindall*	$1.95
MB-8	GEOFFREY CHAUCER *Lowes*	$1.95
MB-12	THE DOUBLE *by Dostoevsky; tr. Bird*	$1.75
MB-13	PAUL GAUGUIN'S INTIMATE JOURNALS *tr. Brooks* (illus.)	$1.95
MB-14	AFRICAN NOTEBOOK *Schweitzer* (illus.)	$1.60
MB-15	THE MORAL DECISION: RIGHT AND WRONG IN THE LIGHT OF AMERICAN LAW *Cahn*	$2.25
MB-16	FORMS OF MODERN FICTION *O'Connor*	$1.75
MB-19	THE ESTHETIC BASIS OF GREEK ART *Carpenter* (illus.)	$1.75
MB-20	THE SATIRES OF JUVENAL *tr. Humphries* (cl. $3.75s)	$1.65
MB-24	AGE OF SURREALISM *Fowlie* (illus.)	$1.75
MB-25	COLERIDGE ON IMAGINATION *Richards*	$1.95
MB-26	JAMES JOYCE AND THE MAKING OF ULYSSES *Budgen* (illus.)	$2.25
MB-36	THE GOLDEN ASS *Apuleius; tr. Lindsay*	$1.85
MB-38	DANTE'S LA VITA NUOVA *tr. Musa*	$1.65
MB-40	THE DISCOVERY OF LANGUAGE: LINGUISTIC SCIENCE IN THE NINETEENTH CENTURY *Pedersen* (illus.) (cl. $6.50s)	$2.95
MB-42	AN INTRODUCTION TO THE GREEK THEATRE *Arnott* (illus.)	$2.45
MB-45	VERGIL'S AENEID *tr. Lind* (cl. $5.75s)	$1.95
MB-46	ESSAYS ON THE ODYSSEY: SELECTED MODERN CRITICISM *ed. Taylor* (cl. $6.00s)	$1.95
MB-47	THE LIVING THOUGHTS OF KIERKEGAARD *Auden*	$1.95
MB-51	ARIOSTO'S ORLANDO FURIOSO: SELECTIONS FROM SIR JOHN HARINGTON'S TRANSLATION *ed. Gottfried* (illus.)	$2.95
MB-58	THE CHALLENGE OF EXISTENTIALISM *Wild*	$1.95
MB-59	THE JOURNALS OF JEAN COCTEAU *ed. and tr. Fowlie* (illus.)	$1.95
MB-63	PERSPECTIVES BY INCONGRUITY *by Burke; ed. Hyman*	$2.45
MB-64	TERMS FOR ORDER *by Burke; ed. Hyman* (MB-63, 64 combined, cl. $6.95)	$2.45
MB-65	EARLY MEDIEVAL ART *Kitzinger* (48 plates)	$1.95
MB-67	A STYLE MANUAL FOR STUDENTS *Seeber* (rev. ed.)	$1.00
MB-69	ESSAYS ON DANTE *ed. Musa*	$2.45
MB-71	RATIONAL MAN: A MODERN INTERPRETATION OF ARISTOTELIAN ETHICS *Veatch* (cl. $5.00s)	$1.95
MB-73	BEOWULF *tr. Pearson; ed. Collins* (cl. $5.00s)	$1.65
MB-75	THE POPULATION CRISIS: IMPLICATIONS AND PLANS FOR ACTION *ed. Ng and Mudd*	$2.95
MB-76	A STYLE MANUAL FOR AUTHORS *Seeber*	$1.25
MB-77	THE WELL-TEMPERED CRITIC *Frye* (cl. $4.50s)	$1.75
MB-82	ESSAYS ON THE EIGHTEENTH-CENTURY NOVEL *ed. Spector*	$2.45
MB-83	MYTH: A SYMPOSIUM *ed. Sebeok*	$2.45
MB-84	THE GOOD CITY *by Haworth; pref. Heckscher*	$1.75
MB-85	KANT AND THE PROBLEM OF METAPHYSICS *Heidegger*	$2.45
MB-86	THE LANGUAGE OF TRAGEDY *Prior*	$2.95
MB-87	SHAKESPEARE'S WORLD OF IMAGES: THE DEVELOPMENT OF HIS MORAL IDEAS *Stauffer*	$2.95

(continued on next page)